OXFORD COGNITIVE SCIE

CONCEPTS

OXFORD COGNITIVE SCIENCE SERIES

General Editors
MARTIN DAVIES, JAMES HIGGINBOTHAM, JOHN O'KEEFE,
CHRISTOPHER PEACOCKE, KIM PLUNKETT

Forthcoming in the series

CONCEPTS

Where Cognitive Science Went Wrong

JERRY A. FODOR

CLARENDON PRESS · OXFORD
1998

Oxford University Press, Great Clarendon Street, Oxford OX2 6DP

Oxford New York

Athens Auckland Bangkok Bogota Bombay
Buenos Aires Calcutta Cape Town Dar es Salaam
Delhi Florence Hong Kong Istanbul Karachi
Kuala Lumpur Madras Madrid Melbourne
Mexico City Nairobi Paris Singapore
Taipei Tokyo Toronto Warsaw

and associated companies in
Berlin Ibadan

Oxford is a trade mark of Oxford University Press

Published in the United States by
Oxford University Press Inc., New York

British Library Cataloguing in Publication Data
Data available

Library of Congress Cataloging in Publication Data
Data available
ISBN 0–19–823637–9
ISBN 0–19–823636–0 (pbk.)

1 3 5 7 9 10 8 6 4 2

Typeset by Invisible Ink
Printed in Great Britain
on acid-free paper by
Biddles Ltd, Guildford and King's Lynn

for Janet, KP and Anthony; nuclear family

Chorus: Zuruck!
Tamino: . . . Zuruck?
    Da seh ich noch ein Tur,
    Vielleicht find ich den Eingang hier.

               —*The Magic Flute*

PREFACE

ACTUALLY, I'm a little worried about the subtitle. There is already a big revisionist literature about what's wrong with cognitive science, devoted to throwing out, along with the baby: the bath, the bath towel, the bathtub, the bathroom, many innocent bystanders, and large sections of Lower Manhattan. The diagnoses that these books offer differ quite a lot among themselves, and there's a real worry that the patient may die of over-prescription. What's wrong with cognitive science is that, strictly speaking, there aren't any mental states at all. Or, strictly speaking, there aren't any mental states except the conscious ones. Or, strictly speaking, intentionality is in the eye of the beholder. Or of the interpreter. Or of the translator. Or it's just a stance. Or it's a coarse grid over a neural network. Or whatever.

I find those sorts of views simply not credible, and I have no desire to add to their ranks. On the very large issues, this book is entirely committed to the traditional cognitive science program: higher organisms act out of the content of their mental states. These mental states are representational; indeed, they are relations to mental representations. The scientific goal in psychology is therefore to understand what mental representations are and to make explicit the causal laws and processes that subsume them. Nothing about this has changed much, really, since Descartes.

So this is an internal critique; it's what Auntie likes to call 'constructive' criticism. On the other hand, given the traditional broad consensus about the goals and architecture of theories of cognition, I do think something has gone badly wrong about how the program has been carried out. For reasons I'll try to make clear, the heart of a cognitive science is its theory of concepts. And I think that the theory of concepts that cognitive science has classically assumed is in a certain way seriously mistaken. Unlike practically everybody else who works or has worked in this tradition, I think that the theory of concepts ought to be atomistic. It's a little lonely, being out here all by oneself; but it does give room to manoeuvre. This book is about why the theory of concepts ought to be atomistic. And about how its not having been atomistic has made trouble all over cognitive science. And about what the psychology, the ontology, and the semantics of an atomistic theory of concepts might be like.

The discussion is grouped into three sections. Chapters 1 and 2 are largely expository; they're devoted to sketching what I take to be the general structure of Classical cognitive science theories, and to locating the issues about concepts within this framework. I want, in particular, to set out some constraints on an acceptable theory of concepts that ought, I'll argue, to be conceded by anybody who wants to run a representational theory of mind. Chapters 3–5 then discuss, in light of these constraints, the major theories of concepts that are currently in play in linguistics, philosophy, and cognitive psychology. These are all, so I claim, variants on the 'inferential role' account of conceptual content. I'll argue that this inferential role view of the *content* of concepts and the anti-atomist view of the *structure* of concepts have for too long made their living by taking in one another's wash; and that both will have to go. With them go all the currently standard theories about what concepts are: that they are definitions, that they are stereotypes, that they are prototypes, that they are abstractions from belief systems, and so forth. I hope this critical material will be of interest to empirical toilers in the cognitive science vineyards. I hope the attacks on the standard theories of concepts will keep them awake at night, even if they don't approve my proposals for an atomistic alternative. I do think that most of what contemporary cognitive science believes about concepts is radically, and practically *demonstrably*, untrue; and that something pretty drastic needs to be done about it.

Chapters 6 and 7 explore the atomist alternative. It turns out, not very surprisingly, that atomism about the structure of concepts has deep implications for psychological questions about how concepts are acquired, for metaphysical questions about how concepts are individuated, and for ontological questions about what the kinds and properties are that concepts express. Before we're finished, we'll have much that's revisionist to say about innateness, about information, and about doorknobs. Though the motivations for all this arise within cognitive science, shifting to conceptual atomism requires something very like a change of world view. If so, so be it.

I have had a lot of trouble about tone of voice. Some of the arguments I have on offer are patently philosophical; some turn on experimental and linguistic data; many are methodological; and some are just appeals to common sense. That there is no way of talking that is comfortable for all these sorts of dialectic is part of what makes doing cognitive science so hard. In the long run, I gave up; I've simply written as the topics at hand seemed to warrant. If it doesn't sound exactly like philosophy, I don't mind; as long as it doesn't sound exactly like psychology, linguistics, or AI either.

A condensed version of this material was presented as the 1996 John Locke Lectures at Oxford University. I am, more than I can say, grateful to friends and colleagues at Oxford for providing the occasion to set out this stuff, for sitting through it, and for their criticism, discussion, and unfailing hospitality. I'm especially obliged, in all these respects, to Martin Davies, Chris Peacocke, and Galen Strawson; and to All Souls College for providing me with an office, lodgings, and an e-mail account.

Other intellectual obligations (the list is certainly incomplete): to Kent Bach and Ken Taylor for detailed and very useful comments on an earlier draft. To Paul Boghossian for philosophical lunches. To Ned Block, Paul Bloom, Noam Chomsky, Jim Higginbotham, Ray Jackendoff, Ernie Lepore, Joe Levine, Steven Pinker, Zenon Pylyshyn, Georges Rey, Stephen Schiffer, Gabe Segal, Barry Smith, Neil Smith. And to many, many others.

The Philosophy Department at Rutgers University gave me time off to make the Oxford trip. That was kind, and civilized, and I'm glad to have this chance to extend my thanks.

So here's the book. It's been fun putting it together, I hope it's fun to read. I hope you like it. I hope some of it is true.

New York, 1997   Jerry A. Fodor

CONTENTS

ABBREVIATIONS AND
TYPOGRAPHICAL CONVENTIONS

THE following conventions are adopted throughout:

Concepts are construed as mental particulars. Names of concepts are written in capitals. Thus, 'RED' names the concept that expresses *redness* or *the property of being red*. Formulas in capitals are not, in general, structural descriptions of the concepts they denote. See Chapter 3, n. 1.

Names of English expressions appear in single quotes. Thus ''red'' is the name of the homophonic English word.

Names of semantic values of words and concepts are written in italics. Thus 'RED expresses the property of *being red*' and ''Red' expresses the property of *being red*' are both true.

The following abbreviations are used frequently (especially in Chapters 6 and 7).

RTM: The representational theory of the mind
IRS: Informational role semantics
MOP: Mode of presentation
MR: Mental representation
IA: Informational atomism
SA: The standard argument (for radical concept innateness)
SIA: Supplemented informational atomism (= IA plus a locking theory of concept possession)
d/D problem: The doorknob/DOORKNOB problem.

1

Philosophical Introduction: The Background Theory

Needless to say, this rather baroque belief system gave rise to incredibly complicated explanations by the tribal elders . . .

—Will Self

My topic is what concepts are. Since I'm interested in that question primarily as it arises in the context of 'representational' theories of mind (RTMs), a natural way to get started would be for me to tell you about RTMs and about how they raise the question what concepts are. I could then set out my answer, and you could tell me, by return, what you think is wrong with it. The ensuing discussion would be abstract and theory laden, no doubt; but, with any luck, philosophically innocent.

That is, in fact, pretty much the course that I propose to follow. But, for better or for worse, in the present climate of philosophical opinion it's perhaps not possible just to plunge in and do so. RTMs have all sorts of problems, both of substance and of form. Many of you may suppose the whole project of trying to construct one is hopelessly wrong-headed; if it is, then who cares what RTMs say about concepts? So I guess I owe you some sort of general argument that the project isn't hopelessly wrong-headed.

But I seem to have grown old writing books defending RTMs; it occurs to me that if I were to stop writing books defending RTMs, perhaps I would stop growing old. So I think I'll tell you a joke instead. It's an *old* joke, as befits my telling it.

Old joke: Once upon a time a disciple went to his guru and said: 'Guru, what is life?' To which the Guru replies, after much thinking, 'My Son, life is like a fountain.' The disciple is outraged. 'Is that the best that you can do? Is that what you call wisdom?' 'All right,' says the guru; 'don't get excited. So maybe it's not like a fountain.'

That's the end of the joke, but it's not the end of the story. The guru noticed that taking this line was losing him clients, and gurus have to eat.

So the next time a disciple asked him: 'Guru, what is life?' his answer was: 'My Son, I cannot tell you.' 'Why can't you?' the disciple wanted to know. 'Because,' the guru said, 'the question "What is *having* a life?" is logically prior.' 'Gee,' said the disciple, 'that's pretty interesting'; and he signed on for the whole term.

I'm not going to launch a full-dress defence of RTM; but I do want to start with a little methodological stuff about whether having a concept is logically prior to being a concept, and what difference, if any, that makes to theorizing about mental representation.

It's a general truth that if you know *what an X is*, then you also know *what it is to have an X*. And ditto the other way around. This applies to concepts in particular: the question what they are and the question what it is to have them are logically linked; if you commit yourself on one, you are *thereby* committed, willy nilly, on the other. Suppose, for example, that your theory is that concepts are pumpkins. Very well then, it will have to be a part of your theory that having a concept is having a pumpkin. And, conversely: if your theory is that having a concept is having a pumpkin, then it will have to be a part of your theory that pumpkins are what concepts are. I suppose this all to be truistic.

Now, until quite recently (until this century, anyhow) practically everybody took it practically for granted that the explanation of concept *possession* should be parasitic on the explanation of concept *individuation*. First you say what it is for something *to be* the concept *X*—you give the concept's 'identity conditions'—and then *having* the concept *X* is just *having whatever the concept X turns out to be*. But the philosophical fashions have changed. Almost without exception, current theories about concepts reverse the classical direction of analysis. Their substance lies in what they say about the conditions for *having* concept *X*, and it's the story about *being* concept *X* that they treat as derivative. Concept *X* is just: *whatever it is that having the concept X consists in having*. Moreover, the new consensus is that you really must take things in that order; the sanctions incurred if you go the other way round are said to be terrific. (Similarly, *mutatis mutandis* for *being the meaning of a word* vs. *knowing the meaning of a word*. Here and elsewhere, I propose to move back and forth pretty freely between concepts and word meanings; however it may turn out in the long run, for purposes of the present investigation word meanings just are concepts.)

You might reasonably wonder how there possibly could be this stark methodological asymmetry. We've just been seeing that the link between 'is an *X*' and 'has an *X*' is conceptual; fix one and you thereby fix the other. How, then, could there be an issue of principle about which you should start with? The answer is that when philosophers take a strong line on a methodological issue there's almost sure to be a metaphysical subtext. The present case is not an exception.

On the one side, people who start in the traditional way by asking 'What are concepts?' generally hold to a traditional metaphysics according to which a concept is a kind of mental particular. I hope that this idea will get clearer and clearer as we go along. Suffice it, for now, that the thesis that concepts are mental particulars is intended to imply that *having* a concept is constituted by having a mental particular, and hence to exclude the thesis that having a concept is, in any interesting sense, constituted by having mental traits or capacities.[1] You may say, if you like, that having concept X is having the ability to think about Xs (or better, that having the concept X is being able to think about Xs 'as such'). But, though that's true enough, it doesn't alter the metaphysical situation as traditionally conceived. For thinking about Xs consists in having thoughts about Xs, and thoughts are supposed to be mental particulars too.

On the other side, people who start with 'What is concept *possession*?' generally have some sort of Pragmatism in mind as the answer. Having a concept is a matter of what you are able to *do*, it's some kind of epistemic 'know how'. Maybe having the concept X comes to something like *being reliably able to recognize Xs and/or being reliably able to draw sound inferences about Xness*.[2] In any case, an account that renders having concepts as having capacities is intended to preclude an account that renders concepts as species of mental particulars: capacities aren't kinds of *things*; a fortiori, they aren't kinds of *mental* things.

So, to repeat, the methodological doctrine that concept possession is logically prior to concept individuation frequently manifests a preference

---

[1] I want explicitly to note what I've come to think of as a cardinal source of confusion in this area. If concept tokens are mental particulars, then having a concept is being in a relation to a mental particular. This truism about the *possession conditions* for concepts continues to hold whatever doctrine you may embrace about how concepts *tokens* get assigned to concept *types*. Suppose Jones's TIGER-concept is a mental token that plays a certain (e.g. causal) role in his mental life. That is quite compatible with supposing that what makes it a token of the type TIGER-concept (rather than a token of the type MOUSE-concept; or not a token of a concept type at all) is something dispositional; viz. the dispositional properties *of the token* (as opposed, say, to its weight or colour or electric charge).

The discussion currently running in the text concerns the relation between theories about the ontological status of concepts and theories about what it is to have a concept. Later, and at length, we'll consider the quite different question how concept tokens are typed.

[2] Earlier, less sophisticated versions of the view that the metaphysics of concepts is parasitic on the metaphysics of concept possession were generally not merely pragmatist but also behaviourist: they contemplated reducing concept possession to a capacity for responding selectively. The cognitive revolutions in psychology and the philosophy of mind gagged on behaviourism, but never doubted that concepts are some sort of capacities or other. A classic case of getting off lightly by pleading to the lesser charge.

for an ontology of mental dispositions rather than an ontology of mental particulars. This sort of situation will be familiar to old hands; proposing dispositional analyses in aid of ontological reductions is the method of critical philosophy that Empiricism taught us. If you are down on cats, reduce them to permanent possibilities of sensation. If you are down on electrons and protons, reduce them to permanent possibilities of experimental outcomes. And so on. There is, however, a salient difference between reductionism about cats and reductionism about concepts: perhaps some people think that they *ought* to think that cats are constructs out of possible experiences, but surely nobody actually does think so; one tolerates a little *mauvaise foi* in metaphysics. Apparently, however, lots of people do think that concepts are constructs out of mental (specifically epistemic) capacities. In consequence, and this is a consideration that I take quite seriously, whereas nobody builds biological theories on the assumption that cats are sensations, much of our current cognitive science, and practically all of our current philosophy of mind, is built on the assumption that concepts are capacities. If that assumption is wrong, very radical revisions are going to be called for. So, at least, I'll argue.

To sum up so far: it's entirely plausible that a theory of what concepts are must likewise answer the question 'What is it to have a concept?' and, *mutatis mutandis*, that a theory of meaning must answer the question 'What is it to understand a language?' We've been seeing, however, that this untendentious methodological demand often comports with a substantive metaphysical agenda: viz. the reduction of concepts and meanings to epistemic capacities.

Thus Michael Dummett (1993*a*: 4), for one illustrious example, says that "any theory of meaning which was not, or did not immediately yield, a theory of understanding, would not satisfy the purpose for which, philosophically, we require a theory of meaning". There is, as previously remarked, a reading on which this is true but harmless since *whatever* ontological construal of *the meaning of an expression* we settle on will automatically provide a corresponding construal of *understanding the expression* as *grasping* its meaning. It is not, however, this truism that Dummett is commending. Rather, he has it in mind that an acceptable semantics must explicate linguistic content just by reference to the "practical" capacities that users of a language have qua users of that language. (Correspondingly, a theory that explicates the notion of conceptual content would do so just by reference to the practical capacities that having the concept bestows.) Moreover, if I read him right, Dummett intends to impose this condition in a very strong form: the capacities upon which linguistic meaning supervenes must be such as can be severally and determinately manifested in behaviour. "An axiom earns its place in the theory [of meaning] . . . only to the extent that it is required for the derivation of theorems the ascription of an implicit knowledge of which to a speaker *is explained in terms of specific abilities which manifest that knowledge*" (1993*b*: 38; my emphasis).

I don't know for sure why Dummett believes that, but I darkly suspect that he's the victim of atavistic sceptical anxieties about communication. Passages like the following recur in his writings:

What . . . constitutes a subject's understanding the sentences of a language . . .? [I]s it his having internalized a certain theory of meaning for that language? . . . then indeed his behaviour when he takes part in linguistic interchange can at best be strong but fallible evidence for the internalized theory. In that case, however, the hearer's presumption that he has understood the speaker can never be definitively refuted or confirmed. (1993*c*: 180; notice how much work the word 'definitively' is doing here.)

So, apparently, the idea is that theories about linguistic content should reduce to theories about language use; and theories about language use should reduce to theories about the speaker's linguistic capacities; and theories about the speaker's linguistic capacities are constrained by the requirement that any capacity that is constitutive of the knowledge of a language is one that the speaker's use of the language can overtly and specifically manifest. All this must be in aid of devising a bullet-proof anti-scepticism about communication, since it would seem that for purposes *other* than refuting sceptics, all the theory of communication requires is that a speaker's utterances reliably cause certain 'inner processes' in the hearer; specifically, mental processes which eventuate in the hearer having the thought that the speaker intended him to have.

If, however, scepticism really is the skeleton in Dummett's closet, the worry seems to me to be doubly misplaced: first because the questions with which theories of meaning are primarily concerned are metaphysical rather than epistemic. This is as it should be; understanding what a thing is, is invariably prior to understanding how we know what it is. And, secondly, because there is no obvious reason why behaviourally grounded inferences to attributions of concepts, meanings, mental processes, communicative intentions, and the like should be freer from normal inductive risk than, as it might be, perceptually grounded attributions of tails to cats. The best we get in either case is "strong but fallible evidence". Contingent truths are like that as, indeed, Hume taught us some while back. This is, no doubt, the very attitude that Dummett means to reject as inadequate to the purposes for which we "philosophically" require a theory of meaning. So much the worse, perhaps, for the likelihood that philosophers will get from a theory of meaning what Dummett says that they require. I, for one, would not expect a good account of what concepts are to refute scepticism about other minds any more than I'd expect a good account of what cats are to refute scepticism about other bodies. In both cases, I am quite prepared to settle for theories that are merely *true*.

Methodological inhibitions flung to the wind, then, here is how I propose to organize our trip. Very roughly, concepts are constituents of mental states. Thus, for example, believing that *cats are animals* is a paradigmatic mental state, and the concept ANIMAL is a constituent of the belief that *cats are animals* (and of the belief that *animals sometimes bite*; etc. I'm leaving it open whether the concept ANIMAL is likewise a constituent of the belief that *some cats bite*; we'll raise that question presently). So the natural home of a theory of concepts is as part of a theory of mental states. I shall suppose throughout this book that RTM is the right theory of (cognitive) mental states. So, I'm going to start with an exposition of RTM: which is to say, with an exposition of a theory about what mental states and processes are. It will turn out that mental states and processes are typically species of relations to mental representations, of which latter concepts are typically the parts.

To follow this course is, in effect, to assume that it's OK for theorizing about the nature of concepts to precede theorizing about concept possession. As we've been seeing, barring a metaphysical subtext, that assumption should be harmless; individuation theories and possession theories are trivially intertranslatable. Once we've got RTM in place, however, I'm going to argue for a very strong version of psychological atomism; one according to which what concepts you have is conceptually and metaphysically independent of what epistemic capacities you have. If this is so, then patently concepts couldn't *be* epistemic capacities.

I hope not to beg any questions by proceeding in this way; or at least not to get caught begging any. But I do agree that if there is a knock-down, a priori argument that concepts are logical constructs out of capacities, then my view about their ontology can't be right and I shall have to give up my kind of cognitive science. Oh, well. If there's a knock-down, a priori argument that cats are logical constructs out of sensations, then my views about *their* ontology can't be right either, and I shall have to give up my kind of biology. Neither possibility actually worries me a lot.

So, then, to begin at last:

RTM

RTM is really a loose confederation of theses; it lacks, to put it mildly, a canonical formulation. For present purposes, let it be the conjunction of the following:

First Thesis: *Psychological explanation is typically nomic and is intentional through and through.* The laws that psychological explanations invoke typically express causal relations among *mental states that are specified under intentional description*; viz. among mental states that are picked out by reference to their contents. Laws about causal relations among beliefs, desires, and actions are the paradigms.

I'm aware there are those (mostly in Southern California, of course) who think that intentional explanation is all at best pro tem, and that theories of mind will (or anyhow should) eventually be couched in the putatively purely extensional idiom of neuroscience. But there isn't any reason in the world to take that idea seriously and, in what follows, I don't.

There are also those who, though they are enthusiasts for intentional explanation, deny the metaphysical possibility of laws about intentional states. I don't propose to take that seriously in what follows either. For one thing, I find the arguments that are said to show that there can't be intentional laws very hard to follow. For another thing, if there are no intentional laws, then you can't make science out of intentional explanations; in which case, I don't understand how intentional explanation *could* be better than merely pro tem. Over the years, a number of philosophers have kindly undertaken to explain to me what non-nomic intentional explanations would be good for. Apparently it has to do with the intentional realm (or perhaps it's the rational realm) being autonomous. But I'm afraid I find all that realm talk very hard to follow too. What *is* the matter with me, I wonder?[3]

Second Thesis: *'Mental representations' are the primitive bearers of intentional content.*

Both ontologically and in order of explanation, the intentionality of the propositional attitudes is prior to the intentionality of natural languages; and, both ontologically and in order of explanation, the intentionality of mental representations is prior to the intentionality of propositional attitudes.

Just for purposes of building intuitions, think of mental representations on the model of what Empiricist philosophers sometimes called 'Ideas'. That is, think of them as mental particulars endowed with causal powers and susceptible of semantic evaluation. So, there's the Idea DOG. It's satisfied by all and only dogs, and it has associative-cum-causal relations to, for example, the Idea CAT. So DOG has conditions of semantic evaluation and it has causal powers, as Ideas are required to do.

---

[3] The trouble may well have to do with my being a Hairy Realist. See Fodor 1995*b*.

Since a lot of what I want to say about mental representations includes what Empiricists did say about Ideas, it might be practical and pious to speak of Ideas rather than mental representations throughout. But I don't propose to do so. The Idea idea is historically intertwined with the idea that Ideas are images, and I don't want to take on that commitment. To a first approximation, then, the idea that there are mental representations is the idea that there are Ideas *minus* the idea that Ideas are images.

RTM claims that mental representations are related to propositional attitudes as follows: for each event that consists of a creature's having a propositional attitude with the content *P* (each such event as Jones's believing at time *t* that *P*) there is a corresponding event that consists of the creature's being related, in a characteristic way, to a token mental representation that has the content *P*. Please note the meretricious scrupulousness with which metaphysical neutrality is maintained. I did *not* say (albeit I'm much inclined to believe) that having a propositional attitude *consists in* being related (in one or other of the aforementioned 'characteristic ways') to a mental representation.

I'm also neutral on what the 'characteristic ways' of being related to mental representations are. I'll adopt a useful dodge that Stephen Schiffer invented: I assume that everyone who has beliefs has a belief box in his head. Then:

> For each episode of believing that P, there is a corresponding episode of having, 'in one's belief box', a mental representation which means that P.

Likewise, *mutatis mutandis*, for the other attitudes. Like Schiffer, I don't really suppose that belief boxes are literally boxes, or even that they literally have insides. I assume that the essential conditions for belief-boxhood are functional. Notice, in passing, that this is *not* tantamount to assuming that "believe" has a 'functional definition'. I doubt that "believe" has *any* definition. That most—indeed, overwhelmingly most—words don't have will be a main theme in the third chapter. But denying, as a point of semantics, that "believe" has a functional definition is compatible with asserting, as a point of metaphysics, that belief has a functional essence. Which I think that it probably does. Ditto, *mutatis mutandis*, "capitalism", "carburettor", and the like. (Compare Devitt 1996; Carruthers 1996, both of whom run arguments that depend on not observing this distinction.)

RTM says that there is no believing-that-*P* episode without a corresponding tokening-of-a-mental-representation episode, and it contemplates no locus of original intentionality except the contents of mental representations. In consequence, so far as RTMs are concerned, to explain what it is for a mental representation to mean what it does *is* to explain what it is for a propositional attitude to have the content that it does. I suppose that RTM leaves open the metaphysical possibility that there could be mental states whose content does not, in this sense, derive from the meaning of corresponding mental representations. But it takes such cases not to be *nomologically* possible, and it provides no hint of an alternative source of propositional objects for the attitudes.

Finally, English inherits its semantics from the contents of the beliefs, desires, intentions, and so forth that it's used to express, as per Grice and his followers. Or, if you prefer (as I think, on balance, I do), English *has no semantics*. Learning English isn't learning a theory about what its sentences mean, it's learning how to associate its sentences with the corresponding thoughts. To know English is to know, for example, that the form of words 'there are cats' is standardly used to express the thought that there are cats; and that the form of words 'it's raining' is standardly used to express the thought that it's raining; and that the form of words 'it's not raining' is standardly used to express the thought that it's not raining; and so on for in(de)finitely many other such cases.

Since, according to RTM, the content of linguistic expressions depends on the content of propositional attitudes, and the content of propositional attitudes depends on the content of mental representations, and since the intended sense of 'depends on' is asymmetric, RTM tolerates the metaphysical possibility of thought without language; for that matter, it tolerates the metaphysical possibility of mental representation without thought. I expect that many of you won't like that. I'm aware that there is rumoured to be an argument, vaguely Viennese in provenance, that proves that 'original', underived intentionality must inhere, *not* in mental representations *nor* in thoughts, but precisely in the formulas of public languages. I would be very pleased if such an argument actually turned up, since then pretty nearly everything I believe about language and mind would have been refuted, and I could stop worrying about RTM, and about what concepts are, and take off and go sailing, a pastime that I vastly prefer. Unfortunately, however, either nobody can remember how the argument goes, or it's a secret that they're unprepared to share with me. So I'll forge on.

Third Thesis: *Thinking is computation.*

A theory of mind needs a story about mental *processes*, not just a story about mental states. Here, as elsewhere, RTM is closer in spirit to Hume than it is to Wittgenstein or Ryle. Hume taught that *mental states are relations to mental representations*, and so too does RTM (the main difference being, as we've seen, that RTM admits, indeed demands, mental representations that aren't images). Hume also taught that *mental processes* (including, paradigmatically, thinking) *are causal relations among mental representations*.[4] So too does RTM. In contrast to Hume, and to RTM, the logical behaviourism of Wittgenstein and Ryle had, as far as I can tell, no theory of thinking at all (except, maybe, the silly theory that thinking is talking to oneself). I do find that shocking. How *could* they have expected to get it right about belief and the like without getting it right about belief fixation and the like?

Alan Turing's idea that thinking is a kind of computation is now, I suppose, part of everybody's intellectual equipment; not that everybody likes it, of course, but at least everybody's heard of it. That being so, I shall pretty much take it as read for the purposes at hand. In a nutshell: token mental representations are symbols. Tokens of symbols are physical objects with semantic properties. To a first approximation, computations are those causal relations among symbols which reliably respect semantic properties of the relata. Association, for example, is a bona fide computational relation within the meaning of the act. Though whether Ideas get associated is supposed to depend on their frequency, contiguity, etc., and not on what they're Ideas *of*, association is none the less supposed reliably to preserve semantic domains: *Jack*-thoughts cause *Jill*-thoughts, *salt*-thoughts cause *pepper*-thoughts, *red*-thoughts cause *green*-thoughts, and so forth.[5] So, Hume's theory of mental processes is itself a species of RTM, an upshot that pleases me.

Notoriously, however, it's an inadequate species. The essential problem in this area is to explain how thinking manages reliably to preserve *truth*; and Associationism, as Kant rightly pointed out to Hume, hasn't the resources to do so. The problem isn't that association is a causal relation, or that it's a causal relation among symbols, or even that it's a causal relation among mental symbols; it's just that their satisfaction conditions aren't among the semantic properties that associates generally share. To the contrary, being Jack precludes being Jill, being salt precludes being pepper, being red precludes being green, and so forth. By contrast, Turing's account of thought-as-computation showed us how to specify causal relations among mental symbols that are reliably truth-preserving. It thereby saved RTM from drowning when the Associationists went under.

I propose to swallow the Turing story whole and proceed. First, however, there's an addendum I need and an aside I can't resist.

---

[4] And/or among states of entertaining them. I'll worry about this sort of ontological nicety only where it seems to matter.

[5] Why relations that depend on merely mechanical properties like frequency and contiguity *should* preserve intentional properties like semantic domain was what Associationists never could explain. That was one of the rocks they foundered on.

Addendum: if computation is just causation that preserves semantic values, then the thesis that thought is computation requires of mental representations only that they have semantic values and causal powers that preserve them. I now add a further constraint: many mental representations have *constituent* (*part/whole*) *structure*, and many mental processes are sensitive to the constituent structure of the mental representations they apply to. So, for example, the mental representation that typically gets tokened when you think . . . *brown cow* . . . has, among its constituent parts, the mental representation that typically gets tokened when you think . . . *brown* . . .; and the computations that RTM says get performed in processes like inferring from . . . *brown cow* . . . to . . . *brown* . . . exploit such part/whole relations. Notice that this *is* an addendum (though it's one that Turing's account of computation was designed to satisfy). It's untendentious that RTM tolerates the possibility of conceptual content *without* constituent structure since everybody who thinks that there are mental representations at all thinks that at least some of them are primitive.[6]

The aside I can't resist is this: following Turing, I've introduced the notion of computation by reference to such semantic notions as content and representation; a computation is some kind of content-respecting causal relation among symbols. However, this order of explication is OK *only if the notion of a symbol doesn't itself presuppose the notion of a computation.* In particular, it's OK only if you don't need the notion of a computation to explain what it is for something to have semantic properties. We'll see, almost immediately, that the account of the *semantics* of mental representations that my version of RTM endorses, unlike the account of *thinking* that it endorses, is indeed non-computational.

Suppose, however, it's your metaphysical view that the semantic properties of a mental representation depend, wholly or in part, upon the computational relations that it enters into; hence that the notion of a computation is *prior* to the notion of a symbol. You will then need some *other* way of saying what it is for a causal relation among mental representations to *be* a computation; *some way that does not presuppose such notions as symbol and content.*[7] It may be possible to find such a notion of computation, but I don't know where. (Certainly not in Turing,

---

[6] Connectionists are committed, willy-nilly, to *all* mental representations being primitive; hence their well-known problems with systematicity, productivity, and the like. More on this in Chapter 5.

[7] Not, of course, that there is anything wrong with just allowing 'symbol' and 'computation' to be interdefined. But that option is not available to anyone who takes the theory that thought is computation to be part of a *naturalistic* psychology; viz. part of a programme of metaphysical reduction. As Turing certainly did; and as do I.

who simply takes it for granted that the expressions that computing machines crunch are *symbols*; e.g. that they denote numbers, functions, and the like.) The attempts I've seen invariably end up suggesting (or proclaiming) that *every* causal process is a kind of computation, thereby trivializing Turing's nice idea that *thought* is.

So much for mental processes.

Fourth Thesis: *Meaning is information (more or less)*.

There actually are, in the land I come from, philosophers who would agree with the gist of RTM as I've set it forth so far. Thesis Four, however, is viewed as divisive even in that company. I'm going to assume that what bestows content on mental representations is something about their causal-cum-nomological relations to the things that fall under them: for example, what bestows upon a mental representation the content *dog* is something about its tokenings being caused by dogs.

I don't want to pursue, beyond this zero-order approximation, the question just which causal-cum-nomological relations are content-making. Those of you who have followed the literature on the metaphysics of meaning that Fred Dretske's book *Knowledge and the Flow of Information* (1981) inspired will be aware that that question is (ahem!) mootish. But I do want to emphasize one aspect of the identification of meaning with information that is pretty widely agreed on and that impacts directly on any proposal to amalgamate an informational semantics with RTM: if meaning is information, then coreferential representations must be synonyms.

Just how this works depends, of course, on what sort of causal-cum-nomological covariation content is and what sort of things you think concepts represent (properties, actual objects, possible objects, or whatever). Suppose, for example, that you run the kind of informational semantics that says:

> *A representation* R *expresses the property* P *in virtue of its being a law that things that are* P *cause tokenings of* R *(in, say, some still-to-be-specified circumstances* C*)*.

And suppose, for the sake of the argument, that *being water* and *being H_2O* are (not merely coextensive but) the same property. It then follows that if it's a law that WATER tokens covary with water (in C) it's also a law that WATER tokens covary with H_2O (in C). So a theory that says that WATER means *water* in virtue of there being the first law is also required to say that WATER means H_2O in virtue of there being the second. Parallel reasoning shows that H_2O means *water*, hence that WATER and H_2O mean the same.

You may wonder why I want to burden my up to now relatively uncontroversial version of RTM by adding a theory of meaning that has this uninviting consequence; and how I could reasonably suppose that you'll be prepared to share the burden by granting me the addition. Both questions are fair.

As to the first, suppose that coextension is *not* sufficient for synonymy after all. Then there must be something else to having a concept with a certain content than having a mental representation with the kind of world-to-symbol causal connections that informational semantics talks about. The question arises: *what is this extra ingredient?* There is, as everybody knows, a standard answer; viz. that *what concepts one has is determined*, at least in part, *by what inferences one is prepared to draw* or to accept. If it is possible to have the concept WATER and not have the concept H_2O, that's because it's constitutive of having the latter, but not constitutive of having the former, that you accept such inferences as *contains H_2O → contains H*. It is, in short, received wisdom that content may be constituted in part by informational relations, but that unless coreference is sufficient for synonymy, it must also be constituted by inferential relations. I'll call any theory that says this sort of thing an Inferential Role Semantics (IRS).

I don't want content to be constituted, even in part, by inferential relations. For one thing, as we just saw, I like Turing's story that inference (qua mental process) reduces to computation; i.e. to *operations on symbols*. For fear of circularity, I can't *both* tell a computational story about what inference is *and* tell an inferential story about what content is. Prima facie, at least, if I buy into Inferential Role Semantics, I undermine my theory of thinking.

For a second thing, I am inclined to believe that an inferential role semantics has holistic implications that are both unavoidable and intolerable. A main reason I love RTM so much is that the computational story about mental *processes* fits so nicely with the story that psychological *explanation* is subsumption under intentional laws; viz. under laws that apply to a mental state in virtue of its content. Since computation is presumed to respect content, RTM can maybe provide the mechanism whereby satisfying the antecedent of an intentional law necessitates the satisfaction of its consequent (see Fodor 1994: ch. 1). But I think it's pretty clear that psychological explanation can't be subsumption under intentional laws if the metaphysics of intentionality is holistic. (See Fodor and Lepore 1992.)

For a third thing, as previously noted, the main point of this book will be to argue for an *atomistic* theory of concepts. I'm going to claim, to put it very roughly, that satisfying the metaphysically necessary conditions for having one concept *never* requires satisfying the metaphysically necessary conditions for having any other concept. (Well, *hardly* ever. See below.) Now, the status of conceptual atomism depends, rather directly, on whether coreference implies synonymy. For, if it doesn't, and if it is inferential role that makes the difference between content and reference, then every concept must *have* an inferential role. But it's also common ground that you need more than one concept to draw an inference, so if IRS is true, conceptual atomism isn't. No doubt this line of thought could use a little polishing, but it's surely basically sound.

So, then, if I'm going to push for an atomistic theory of concepts, I *must not* hold that one's inferential dispositions determine, wholly or in part, the content of one's concepts. Pure informational semantics allows me not to hold that one's inferential dispositions determine the content of one's concepts because it says that content is constituted, exhaustively, by symbol–world relations.

It's worth keeping clear on how the relation between concept possession and concept individuation plays out on an informational view: the content of, for example, BACHELOR is constituted by certain (actual and/or counterfactual) causal-cum-nomic relations between BACHELOR-tokenings and tokenings of instantiated *bachelorhood*. Presumably *bachelorhood* is itself individuated, *inter alia*, by the necessity of its relation to *being unmarried*. So, 'bachelors are unmarried' is conceptually necessary in the sense that it's guaranteed by the content of BACHELOR together with the metaphysics of the relevant property relations. It follows, trivially, that *having* BACHELOR is having a concept which can apply only to unmarried things; this is the truism that the interdefinability of concept individuation and concept possession guarantees. But *nothing at all* about the epistemic condition of BACHELOR owners (e.g. about their inferential or perceptual dispositions or capacities) follows from the necessity of 'bachelors are unmarried'; *it doesn't even follow that you can't own BACHELOR unless you own UNMARRIED*. Informational semantics permits atomism about concept possession even if (even though) there are conceptually necessary truths.[8] This is a sort of point that will recur repeatedly as we go along.

So much for why I want an informational semantics as part of my RTM. Since it is, of course, moot whether I can have one, the best I can hope for is that this book will convince you that conceptual atomism is OK unless there is a decisive, independent argument against the reduction of meaning to information. I'm quite prepared to settle for this since I'm

---

[8] What it doesn't do is guarantee the connection between what's conceptually necessary and what's a priori. But perhaps that's a virtue.

pretty sure that there's no such argument. In fact, I think the dialectic is going to have to go the other way around: what settles the metaphysical issue between informational theories of meaning and inferential role theories of meaning is that the former, but not the latter, are compatible with an atomistic account of concepts. And, as I'll argue at length, there are persuasive independent grounds for thinking that atomism about concepts must be true.

In fact, I'm going to be more concessive still. Given my view that content is information, I can't, as we've just seen, afford to agree that the content of the concept H_2O is different from the content of the concept WATER. *But I am entirely prepared to agree that they are different concepts*. In effect, I'm assuming that coreferential representations are *ipso facto* synonyms and conceding that, since they are, *content* individuation can't be all that there is to *concept* individuation.

It may help make clear how I'm proposing to draw the boundaries to contrast the present view with what I take to be a typical Fregean position; one according to which concepts are distinguished along two (possibly orthogonal) parameters; viz. reference and *Mode of Presentation*. (So, for example, the concept WATER is distinct from the concept DOG along *both* parameters, but it's distinct from the concept H_2O only in respect of the second.) I've diverged from this sort of scheme only in that some Fregeans (e.g. Frege) identify modes of presentation with *senses*. By contrast, I've left it open what modes of presentation are, so long as they are what distinguish distinct but coreferential concepts. So far, then, I'm less extensively committed than a Fregean, but I don't think that I'm committed to anything that a Fregean is required to deny.

Alas, ecumenicism has to stop somewhere. The fifth (and final thesis) of my version of RTM does depart from the standard Frege architecture.

> Fifth Thesis: *Whatever distinguishes coextensive concepts is* ipso facto *'in the head'*. This means, something like that it's available to be a proximal cause (/effect) of mental processes.[9]

As I understand it, the Fregean story makes the following three claims about modes of presentation:

5.1 MOPs are senses; for an expression to mean what it does is for the expression to have the MOP that it does.

---

[9] I take it that one of the things that distinguishes Fregeans *sans phrase* from *neo-*Fregeans (like e.g. Peacocke 1992) is that the latter are *not* committed to Fege's anti-mentalism and are therefore free to agree with Thesis Five if they're so inclined. Accordingly, for the *neo-* sort of Fregean, the sermon that follows will seem to be preached to the converted.

5.2 Since MOPs can distinguish concepts, they explain how it is possible to entertain one, but not the other, of two coreferential concepts; e.g. how it is possible have the concept WATER but not the concept H_2O, hence how it is possible to have (de dicto) beliefs about water but no (de dicto) beliefs about H_2O.

5.3 MOPs are abstract objects; hence they are non-mental.

In effect, I've signed on for 5.2; it's the claim about MOPs that everybody must accept who has any sympathy at all for the Frege programme. But I think there are good reasons to believe that 5.2 excludes both 5.1 and 5.3. In which case, I take it that 5.1 and 5.3 will have to go.

—*What's wrong with 5.1*: 5.1 makes trouble for 5.2: it's unclear that you can hold onto 5.2 if you insist, as Frege does, that MOPs be identified with senses. One thing (maybe the only one) that we know for sure about senses is that synonyms share them. So if MOPs are senses and distinct but coextensive concepts are distinguished (solely) by their MOPs, then synonymous concepts must be identical, and it must not be possible to think either without thinking the other. (This is the so-called 'substitution test' for distinguishing modes of presentation.) But (here I follow Mates 1962), it is possible for Fred to wonder *whether John understands that bachelors are unmarried men* even though Fred does not wonder *whether John understands that unmarried men are unmarried men*. The moral seems to be that if 5.2 is right, so that MOPs *just are* whatever it is that the substitution test tests for, then it's unlikely that MOPs are senses.

Here's a similar argument to much the same conclusion. Suppose I tell you that Jackson was a painter and that Pollock was a painter, and I tell you nothing else about Jackson or Pollock. Suppose, also, that you believe what I tell you. It looks like that fixes the senses of the names 'Jackson' and 'Pollock' if anything could; and it looks like it fixes them as both having the *same* sense: viz. *a painter*. (*Mutatis mutandis*, it looks as though I have fixed the same inferential role for both.) Yet, in the circumstances imagined, it's perfectly OK—perfectly conceptually coherent—for you to wonder whether Jackson and Pollock were the *same* painter. (Contrast the peculiarity of your wondering, in such a case, whether Jackson was Jackson or whether Pollock was Pollock.) So, then, by Frege's own test, JACKSON and POLLOCK count as different MOPs. But if concepts with the same sense can be different MOPs then, patently, MOPs can't be senses. This isn't particularly about names, by the way. If I tell you that a flang is a sort of machine part and a glanf is a sort of machine part, it's perfectly OK for you to wonder whether a glanf is a flang.[10]

---

[10] You can't, of course, do this trick with definite descriptions since they presuppose

Oh well, maybe my telling you that Jackson was a painter and Pollock was a painter didn't fix the same senses for both names after all. I won't pursue that because, when it comes to senses, who can prove what fixes what? But it hardly matters since, on reflection, what's going on doesn't seem to have to do with *meaning*. Rather, the governing principle is a piece of logical syntax: If '*a*' and '*b*' are different names, then the inference from '*Fa*' to '*Fb*' is never conceptually necessary.[11] (It's even OK to wonder whether Jackson is Jackson, if the two 'Jacksons' are supposed to be tokens of different but homonymous name types.) It looks like the moral of this story about Jackson and Pollock is the same as the moral of Mates's story about bachelors and unmarried men. *Frege's substitution test doesn't identify senses.* Correspondingly, if it is stipulated that MOPs are whatever substitution *salve veritate* turns on, then MOPs have to be sliced a good bit *thinner* than senses. Individuating MOPs is more like individuating forms of words than it is like individuating meanings.

I take these sorts of considerations *very* seriously. They will return full strength at the end of Chapter 2.

—*What's wrong with 5.3*: This takes a little longer to say, but here is the short form. Your having *n* MOPs for water explains why you have *n* ways of thinking about water *only on the assumption that there is exactly one way to grasp each MOP.*[12] The question thus arises what, if anything, is supposed to legitimize this assumption. As far as I can tell, unless you're prepared to give up 5.3, the only answer a Fregean theory allows you is: sheer stipulation.

Terminological digression (I'm sorry to have to ask you to split these hairs, but this is a part of the wood where it is *very* easy to get lost): I use 'entertaining' and 'grasping' a MOP (/concept) interchangeably. Entertaining/grasping a MOP doesn't, of course, mean *thinking about* the MOP;

---

uniqueness of reference. If you mean by "Jackson" *the horse that bit John*, and you mean by "Pollock" *the horse that bit John*, you can't coherently wonder whether Jackson is the same horse as Pollock.

By the way, I have the damnedest sense of *déjà vu* about the argument in the text; I simply can't remember whether I read it somewhere or made it up. If it was you I snitched it from, Dear Reader, please do let me know.

[11] More precisely: it's never conceptually necessary unless either the inference from *Fa* to *a* = *b* or the inference from *Fb* to *a* = *b* is itself conceptually necessary. (For example, let *Fa* be: '*a* has the property of being identical to *b*'.)

[12] Or, if there is more than one way to grasp a MOP, then all of the different ways of doing so must correspond to the *same* way of thinking its referent. I won't pursue this option in the text; suffice it that doing so wouldn't help with the problem that I'm raising. Suppose that there is more than one way to grasp a MOP; and suppose that a certain MOP is a mode of presentation of Moe. Then if, as Frege requires, there is a MOP corresponding to each way of thinking a referent, all the ways of grasping the Moe-MOP must be the *same* way of thinking of Moe. I claim that, precisely because 5.3 is in force, Frege's theory has no way to ensure that this is so.

there are as many ways of thinking about a MOP as there are of thinking about a rock or a number. That is, innumerably many; one for each mode of presentation of the MOP. Rather, MOPs are supposed to be the *vehicles* of thought, and entertaining a MOP means using it to present to thought whatever the MOP is a mode of presentation of; it's thinking *with* the MOP, not thinking *about* it. End digression. My point is that if there is more than one way to grasp a MOP, then 'grasping a water-MOP is a way of thinking about water' and 'Smith has only one water-MOP' does *not* entail that Smith has only one way of thinking about water.

So, then, what ensures that there is only one way to grasp a MOP? Since Frege thinks that MOPs are senses and that sense determines reference (concepts with the same sense must be coextensive) he holds, in effect, that MOP identity and concept identity come to the same thing. So my question can be put just in terms of the latter: that one has as many ways of thinking of a referent as one has concepts of the referent depends on there being just one way to entertain each concept. What, beside stipulation, guarantees this?

Perhaps the following analogy (actually quite close, I think) will help to make the situation clear. There are lots of cases where things other, and less problematic, than Fregean senses might reasonably be described as 'modes of presentation'; viz. as being used to present the object of a thought to the thought that it's the object of. Consider, for example, using a diagram of a triangle in geometrical reasoning about triangles. It seems natural, harmless, maybe even illuminating, to say that one sometimes reasons about triangles *via* such a diagram; and that the course of the reasoning may well be affected (e.g. facilitated) by choosing to do so. In a pretty untendentious sense, the diagram functions to present triangles (or triangularity) to thought; OK so far.

But notice a crucial difference between a diagram that functions as a mode of presentation and a Fregean sense that does: in the former case, there's more—lots more—than one kind of object that the diagram can be used to present. The very same diagram can represent now triangles, now equilateral triangles, now closed figures at large, now three-sided figures at large . . . etc. depending on *what intentional relation the reasoner bears to it*; depending, if you like, on how the reasoner entertains it. In this sort of case, then, *lots* of concepts correspond to the same mode of presentation. Or, putting it the other way round, what corresponds to the reasoner's concept is not the mode of presentation per se, but the mode of presentation *together with how it is entertained*.

A diagram can be used in all sorts of ways to present things to thought, but a Fregean sense can't be *on pain of senses failing to individuate concepts*; which is, after all, what they were invoked for in the first place. So, question: what stops senses from behaving like diagrams? What guarantees that each sense can serve in only one way to present an object to a thought? I think that, on the Frege architecture with 5.3 in force, nothing prevents this except brute stipulation.

As far as I know, the standard discussions have pretty generally failed to recognize that Frege's architecture has this problem, so let me try once more to make clear just what the problem is. It's because there is more than one way to think about a *referent* that Frege needs to invoke MOPs to individuate concepts; *referents* can't individuate concepts because lots of different concepts can have the same referent. Fine. But Frege holds that MOPs *can* individuate concepts; that's what MOPs are *for*. So he mustn't allow that different MOPs can correspond to the same concept, *nor may he allow that a MOP can correspond to a concept in more than one way*. If he did, then each way of entertaining the MOP would (presumably) correspond to a different way of thinking the referent, and hence (presumably) to a different concept of the referent. Whereas MOPs are supposed to correspond to concepts one-to-one.

So, the question that I'm wanting to commend to you is: what, if anything, supports the prohibition against proliferating ways of grasping MOPs? Frege's story can't be: 'There is only one way of thinking a referent corresponding to each mode of presentation of the referent because there is only one way of entertaining each mode of presentation of a referent; and there is only one way of entertaining each mode of presentation of a referent because I say that's all there is.' Frege needs something that can *both* present referents to thought *and individuate thoughts*; in effect, he needs a kind of MOP that is *guaranteed* to have only one handle. He can't, however, get one just by wanting it; he has to explain *how there could be such things*. And 5.3 is in his way.

I think that if MOPs can individuate concepts and referents can't, that must be because MOPs *are mental objects* and referents aren't. Mental objects are *ipso facto* available to be proximal causes of mental processes; and it's plausible that at least some mental objects are distinguished by the kinds of mental processes that they cause; i.e. they are functionally distinguished.[13] Suppose that MOPs are in fact so distinguished. Then it's hardly surprising that there is only one way a mind can entertain each MOP: since, on this ontological assumption, functionally equivalent MOPs are *ipso facto* identical, the question 'Which MOP are you

---

[13] This doesn't, please notice, commit me to holding that the individuation of thought *content* is functional. Roughly, that depends on whether Frege is right that whatever can distinguish coextensive concepts is *ipso facto* the *sense* of the concepts; i.e. it depends on assuming 5.1. Which, however, I don't; see above.

entertaining?' and the question 'Which functional state is your mind in when you entertain it?' are required to get the same answer.

Frege's structural problem is that, though he wants to be an *externalist* about MOPs, the architecture of his theory won't let him.[14] Frege's reason for wanting to be an externalist about MOPs is that he thinks, quite wrongly, that if MOPs are mental then concepts won't turn out to be public. But if MOPs *aren't* mental, what kind of thing *could* they be such that *necessarily* for each MOP there is only one way in which a mind can entertain it? (And/or: what kind of mental state could entertaining a MOP be such that *necessarily* there is only one way to entertain each MOP?) As far as I can tell, Frege's story offers nothing at all to scratch this itch with.

If, however, MOPS are in the head,[15] then they can be proximal mental causes and are, to that extent, apt for functional individuation. If MOPs are both in the head and functionally individuated, *then a MOP's identity can be constituted by what happens when you entertain it.*[16] And if the identity of a MOP is *constituted* by what happens when you entertain it, then *of course* there is only one way to entertain each MOP. In point of metaphysical necessity, the alleged 'different ways of entertaining a MOP' would really be ways of entertaining different MOPs.

The moral, to repeat, is that even Frege can't have 5.3 if he holds onto 5.1. Even Frege should have been a mentalist about MOPs if he wished to remain in other respects a Fregean. On the other hand (perhaps this goes without saying), to claim that MOPs must be *mental* objects is quite compatible with also claiming that they are *abstract* objects, and that abstract objects are *not* mental. The apparent tension is reconciled by taking MOPS-qua-things-in-the-head to be the tokens of which MOPS-qua-abstract-objects are the types. It seems that Frege thought that if meanings can be shared it somehow follows that they can't also be

[14] In this usage, an 'externalist' is somebody who says that 'entertaining' relates a creature to something mind-independent, so Frege's externalism is entailed by his Platonism. Contrast the prima facie quite different Putnam/Kripke notion, in which an externalist is somebody who says that what you are thinking depends on what world you're in. (Cf. Preti 1992, where the distinction between these notions of externalism is sorted out, and some of the relations between them are explored.)

[15] This way of talking is, of course, entirely compatible with the current fashions in Individualism, Twins, and the like. Twins are supposed to show that referents can distinguish concepts whose causal roles are the same. For the demonstration to work, however, you've got to assume that Twins *ipso facto* have the causal roles of their concepts in common; viz. that whatever *contents* may supervene on, what *causal roles* supervene on is *inside* the head. That's precisely what I'm supposing in the text.

[16] Notice that this is not to say that *concepts* are individuated by the mental processes they cause, since a concept is a MOP together with a content; and I've taken an informational view of the individuation of contents. It's thus open to my version of RTM that 'Twin-Earth' cases involve concepts with different contents but the same MOPs.

particulars. But it beats me why he thought so. You might as well argue from '*being a vertebrate* is a universal' to 'spines aren't things'.

We're almost through with this, but I do want to tell you about an illuminating remark that Ernie Sosa once made to me. I had mentioned to Ernie that I was worried about why, though there are lots of ways to grasp a referent, there's only one way to grasp a MOP. He proceeded to pooh-pooh my worry along the following lines. "Look," he said, "it's pretty clear that there is only one way to instantiate a property, viz. by having it. It couldn't be, for example, that the property *red* is instantiated sometimes by a thing's being red and sometimes by a thing's being green. I don't suppose that worries you much?" (I agreed that it hadn't been losing me sleep.) "Well," he continued, with a subtle smile, "*if you aren't worried about there being only one way to instantiate a property, why are you worried about there being only one way to grasp a mode of presentation?*"

I think that's very clever, but I don't think it will do. The difference is this: It is surely plausible on the face of it that 'instantiating property *P*' is just *being P*; being red is all that there is to instantiating *redness*. But MOP is a technical notion in want of a metaphysics. If, as seems likely, the identity of a mental state turns on its causal role, then if MOPs are to individuate mental states they will have to be the sorts of things that the causal role of a mental state can turn on. But it's a mystery how a MOP *could* be that sort of thing if MOPs aren't in the head. If (to put the point a little differently) their non-mental *objects* can't distinguish thoughts, how can MOPS distinguish thoughts if they are non-mental too? It's as though the *arithmetic* difference between 3 and 4 could somehow explain the *psychological* difference between thinking about 3 and thinking about 4.

That red things are what instantiate redness is a truism, so you can have it for free. But Frege can't have it for free that, although same denotation doesn't mean same mental state, *same MOP* does. That must depend on some pretty deep difference between the *object* of thought and its *vehicle*. Offhand, the only difference I can think of that would do the job is ontological; it requires MOPs to be individuated by their roles as causes and effects of mental states, and hence to themselves be mental. So I think we should worry about why there's only one way to grasp a MOP even though I quite agree that we shouldn't worry about why there's only one way to instantiate a property.

Well, then, that's pretty much it for the background theory. All that remains is to add that in for a penny, in for a pound; having gone as far as we have, we might as well explicitly assume that MOPs are mental representations. That, surely, is the natural thing to say if you're supposing, on the one hand, that MOPs are among the proximal determinants of mental processes (as per Thesis Five) and that mental processes are computations on structured mental representations (as per Thesis Two). It's really the basic idea of RTM that Turing's story about the nature of mental processes provides the very candidates for MOP-hood that Frege's story about the individuation of mental states independently requires. If that's true, it's about the nicest thing that ever happened to cognitive science.

So I shall assume that it is true. From here on, I'll take for granted that wherever mental states with the same satisfaction conditions have different intentional objects (like, for example, wanting to swallow the Morning Star and wanting to swallow the Evening Star) there must be corresponding differences among the mental representations that get tokened in the course of having them.

Now, finally, we're ready to get down to work. I'm interested in such questions as: 'What is the structure of the concept DOG?' Given RTM as the background theory, this is equivalent to the question: 'What is the MOP in virtue of entertaining which thoughts have dogs as their intentional objects?' And this is in turn equivalent to the question: 'What is the structure of the mental representation DOG?'

And my answer will be that, on the evidence available, it's reasonable to suppose that such mental representations *have no structure*; it's reasonable to suppose that they are atoms.

2

Unphilosophical Introduction: What Concepts Have To Be

THIS is a book about concepts. Two of its main theses are:

—that if you are going to run a representational/computational theory of mind (that is, any version of RTM; see Chapter 1) you will need a theory of concepts.

And:

—that none of the theories of concepts that are currently taken at all seriously either in cognitive science or in philosophy can conceivably fill the bill.

To argue this, I shall first need to say what bill it is that needs to be filled. That's the burden of this chapter. I want to set out five conditions that an acceptable theory of concepts would have to meet. Several chapters following this one will be devoted to making clear by how much, and for what reasons, current theories of concepts fail to meet them.

A word about the epistemic status of the conditions I'm about to endorse: I regard them as fallible but not negotiable. Not negotiable, that is, short of giving up on RTM itself; and RTM remains the only game in town, even after all these years. In effect, I'm claiming that these constraints on concepts follow just from the architecture of RTMs together with some assumptions about cognitive processes and capacities which, though certainly contingent, are none the less hardly possible to doubt. (I mean, of course, hardly possible to doubt really, not hardly possible to doubt philosophically.) If this is indeed the status of these constraints, then I think we had better do what we can to construct a theory of concepts that satisfies them.

So, then, here are my five not-negotiable conditions on a theory of concepts.

1. Concepts are mental particulars; specifically, they satisfy whatever ontological conditions have to be met by things that function as mental causes and effects.

Since this is entailed by RTM (see Chapter 1), and hence is common to all the theories of concepts I'll consider, I won't go on about it here. If, however, you think that intentional causation explains behaviour only in the way that the solubility of sugar explains its dissolving (see Ryle 1949), or if you think that intentional explanations aren't causal at all (see e.g. Collins 1987), then nothing in the following discussion will be of much use to you, and I fear we've reached a parting of the ways. At least one of us is wasting his time; I do hope it's you.

2. Concepts are categories and are routinely employed as such.

To say that concepts are categories is to say that they apply to things in the world; things in the world 'fall under them'. So, for example, Greycat the cat, but not Dumbo the elephant, falls under the concept CAT. Which, for present purposes, is equivalent to saying that Greycat is in the extension of CAT, that 'Greycat is a cat' is true, and that 'is a cat' is true of Greycat. I shall sometimes refer to this galaxy of considerations by saying that applications of concepts are susceptible of '*semantic evaluation*': claims, or thoughts, that a certain concept applies to a certain thing are always susceptible of evaluation in such semantical terms as satisfied/unsatisfied, true/false, correct/incorrect, and the like. There are, to be sure, issues about these various aspects of semantic evaluability, and about the relations among them, that a scrupulous philosopher might well wish to attend to. But in this chapter, I propose to keep the philosophy to a bare minimum.[1]

Much of the life of the mind consists in applying concepts to things. If I think *Greycat is a cat* (de dicto, as it were), I thereby apply the concept CAT to Greycat (correctly, as it happens). If, looking at Greycat, I take him to be a cat, then too I apply the concept CAT to Greycat. (If looking at Greycat I take him to be a meatloaf, I thereby apply the concept MEATLOAF to Greycat; incorrectly, as it happens.) Or if, in reasoning about Greycat, I infer that since he's a cat he must be an animal, I thereby proceed from applying one concept to Greycat to the licensed application of another concept; the license consisting, I suppose, in things I know about how the extensions of the concepts CAT and ANIMAL are related.

In fact, RTM being once assumed, most of cognitive psychology, including the psychology of memory, perception, and reasoning, is about how we apply concepts. And most of the rest is about how we acquire the concepts that we thus apply. Correspondingly, the empirical data to which cognitive psychologists are responsible consist largely of measures of subject performance in concept application tasks. The long and short is: whatever else a theory of concepts says about them, it had better exhibit

---

[1] Or, at least, to confine it to footnotes.

concepts as the sorts of things that get applied in the course of mental processes. I take it that consensus about this is pretty general in the cognitive sciences, so I won't labour it further here.

Caveat: it's simply untendentious that concepts have their satisfaction conditions essentially. Nothing in any mental life could be the concept CAT unless it is satisfied by cats. It couldn't be that there are some mental lives in which the concept CAT applies to CATS and others in which it doesn't. If you haven't got a concept that applies to cats, that *entails* that you haven't got the CAT concept. But though the *satisfaction* conditions of a concept are patently among its essential properties, it does not follow that the *confirmation* conditions of a concept are among its essential properties. Confirmation is an epistemic relation, not a semantic relation, and it is generally theory mediated, hence holistic. On the one hand, given the right background theory, the merest ripple in cat infested waters might serve to confirm an ascription of cathood; and, on the other hand, no cat-containing layout is so well lit, or so utterly uncluttered, or so self-certifying that your failure to ascribe cathood therein would *entail* that you lack the concept. In short, it is OK to be an atomist about the metaphysical conditions for a concept's *having* satisfaction conditions (which I am and will try to convince you to be too), and yet be a holist about the confirmation of claims that a certain concept is satisfied in a certain situation. Shorter still: just as Quine and Duhem and those guys taught us, *there aren't any criteria*. So at least I shall assume throughout what follows.

   3. Compositionality: concepts are the constituents of thoughts and, in indefinitely many cases, of one another. Mental representations inherit their contents from the contents of their constituents.

Some terminology: I'll use 'thoughts' as my cover term for the mental representations which, according to RTMs, express the propositions that are the objects of propositional attitudes. Thus, a belief that it will rain and a hope that it will rain share a thought as well as a proposition which that thought expresses. For present purposes, it will do to think of thoughts as mental representations analogous to closed sentences, and concepts as mental representations analogous to the corresponding open ones. It may strike you that mental representation is a lot like language, according to my version of RTM. Quite so; how could language express thought if that were not the case?

Qua constituents of thoughts, and of each other, concepts play a certain role in explaining why the propositional attitudes are productive and systematic. The outlines of this story are well known, though by no means untendentious:

Beliefs are *productive* in that there are infinitely many distinct ones that a person can entertain (given, of course, the usual abstraction from 'performance limitations'). Beliefs are *systematic* in that the ability to entertain any one of them implies the ability to entertain many others that are related to it in content. It appears, for example, to be conceptually possible that there should be a mind that is able to grasp the proposition that Mary loves John but not able to grasp the proposition that John loves Mary. But, in point of empirical fact, it appears that there are no such minds. This sort of symmetry of cognitive capacities is a ubiquitous feature of mental life.[2] It implies a corresponding symmetry of representational capacities since RTM says, 'no cognition without representation'. That is, RTM says that you can't grasp a proposition without entertaining a thought.

So, the question presents itself: what must mental representation be like if it is to explain the productivity and systematicity of beliefs? This question is loaded, to be sure: that the systematicity of the attitudes requires the systematicity of mental representation doesn't itself require that the systematicity of mental representation is what explains the systematicity of the attitudes. Perhaps both are the effects of a common cause. Maybe, for example, 'the world' somehow teaches the mind to be systematic, and the systematicity of mental representation is the by-product of its doing so.

The stumbling-block for this sort of suggestion is that the mind is much more systematic than the world: that John loves Mary doesn't make it true, or even very likely, that Mary reciprocates. Sad for John, of course, but where would The Western Canon be if things were otherwise? In fact, the only thing in the world that is as systematic as thought is language. Accordingly, some philosophers (Dan Dennett 1993 in particular) have suggested that it's *learning language* that makes a mind systematic.

But we aren't told how an initially unsystematic mind *could* learn a systematic language, given that the latter is *ipso facto* able to express propositions that the former is unable to entertain. How, for example, does a mind that can think that *John loves Mary* but not that *Mary loves John* learn a language that is able to say both? Nor is it clear what could make *language itself* systematic if not the systematicity of the thoughts that it is used to express; so the idea that the mind learns systematicity from language just sweeps the problem from under the hall rug to under the rug in the parlour. On balance, I think we had better take it for granted,

---

[2] It bears emphasis that systematicity concerns symmetries of cognitive *capacities*, not of actual mental states. It is, for example, patently not the case that whoever thinks that Mary loves John also thinks that John loves Mary. Compare van Gelder and Nicklasson 1994.

and as part of what is not negotiable, that systematicity and productivity are grounded in the 'architecture' of mental representation and not in the vagaries of experience. If a serious alternative proposal should surface, I guess I'm prepared to reconsider what's negotiable. But the prospect hasn't been losing me sleep.

So, to repeat the question, what is it about mental representation that explains the systematicity and productivity of belief? Classical versions of RTM offer a by now familiar answer: there are infinitely many beliefs because there are infinitely many thoughts to express their objects. There are infinitely many thoughts because, though each mental representation is constructed by the application of a finite number of operations to a finite basis of primitive concepts, there is no upper bound to how many times such operations may apply in the course of a construction. Correspondingly, thought is systematic because the same primitive concepts and operations that suffice to assemble thoughts like JOHN LOVES MARY also suffice to assemble thoughts like MARY LOVES JOHN; the representational capacity that is exploited to frame one thought implies the representational capacity to frame the other. Since a mental representation is individuated by its form and content (see Chapter 1), both of these are assumed to be determined by specifying the inventory of primitive concepts that the representation contains, together with the operations by which it is assembled from them. (In the case of the primitive concepts themselves, this assumption is trivially true.) As a shorthand for all this, I'll say that what explains the productivity and systematicity of the propositional attitudes is the *compositionality* of concepts and thoughts.

The requirement that the theory of mental representation should exhibit thoughts and concepts as compositional turns out, in fact, to be quite a powerful analytic engine. If the content of a mental representation is inherited from the contents of its conceptual constituents then, presumably, the content of a constituent concept is just whatever it can contribute to the content of its hosts. We'll see, especially in Chapter 5, that this condition is not at all easy for a theory of concepts to meet.

4. Quite a lot of concepts must turn out to be learned.

I want to put this very roughly since I'm going to return to it at length in Chapter 6. Suffice it for now that all versions of RTM hold that if a concept belongs to the primitive basis from which complex mental representations are constructed, it must *ipso facto* be *un*learned. (To be sure, some versions of RTM are rather less up front in holding this than others.) Prima facie, then, where a theory of concepts draws the distinction between what's primitive and what's not is also where it draws the

distinction between what's innate and what's not. Clearly, everybody is
going to put this line somewhere. For example, nobody is likely to think
that the concept BROWN COW is primitive since, on the face of it,
BROWN COW has BROWN and COW as constituents. Correspondingly,
nobody is likely to think that the concept BROWN COW is innate since,
on the face of it, it could be learned by being assembled from the
previously mastered concepts BROWN and COW.

A lot of people have Very Strong Feelings about what concepts are
allowed to be innate,[3] hence about how big a primitive conceptual basis an
acceptable version of RTM can recognize. Almost everybody is prepared
to allow RED in, and many of the liberal-minded will also let in CAUSE
or AGENT. (See, for example, Miller and Johnson-Laird 1978). But there
is, at present, a strong consensus against, as it might be, DOORKNOB or
CARBURETTOR. I have no desire to join in this game of pick and
choose since, as far as I can tell, it hasn't any rules. Suffice it that it would
be nice if a theory of concepts were to provide a principled account of
what's in the primitive conceptual basis, and it would be nice if the
principles it appealed to were to draw the distinction at some
independently plausible place. (Whatever, if anything, that means.)
Chapter 6 will constitute an extended reconsideration of this whole issue,
including the question just how the relation between a concept's being
primitive and its being innate plays out. I hope there to placate such
scruples about DOORKNOB and CARBURETTOR as some of you may
feel, and to do so within the framework of an atomistic RTM.

5. Concepts are *public*; they're the sorts of things that lots of people
   can, and do, *share*.

Since, according to RTM, concepts are symbols, they are presumed to
satisfy a type/token relation; to say that two people share a concept (i.e.
that they have literally the same concept) is thus to say that they have
tokens of literally the same concept type. The present requirement is that
the conditions for typing concept tokens must not be so stringent as to
assign practically every concept token to a different type from practically
any other.

---

[3] I put it this way advisedly. I was once told, in the course of a public discussion with
an otherwise perfectly rational and civilized cognitive scientist, that he "could not permit"
the concept HORSE to be innate in humans (though I guess it's OK for it to be innate in
horses). I forgot to ask him whether he was likewise unprepared to permit neutrinos to lack
mass.

Just why feelings run so strongly on these matters is unclear to me. Whereas the ethology
of all other species is widely agreed to be thoroughly empirical and largely morally neutral,
a priorizing and moralizing about the ethology of our species appears to be the order of the
day. Very odd.

It seems pretty clear that all sorts of concepts (for example, DOG, FATHER, TRIANGLE, HOUSE, TREE, AND, RED, and, surely, lots of others) are ones that all sorts of people, under all sorts of circumstances, have had and continue to have. A theory of concepts should set the conditions for concept possession in such a way as not to violate this intuition. Barring very pressing considerations to the contrary, it should turn out that people who live in very different cultures and/or at very different times (me and Aristotle, for example) both have the concept FOOD; and that people who are possessed of very different amounts of mathematical sophistication (me and Einstein, for example) both have the concept TRIANGLE; and that people who have had very different kinds of learning experiences (me and Helen Keller, for example) both have the concept TREE; and that people with very different amounts of knowledge (me and a four-year-old, for example) both have the concept HOUSE. And so forth. Accordingly, if a theory or an experimental procedure distinguishes between my concept DOG and Aristotle's, or between my concept TRIANGLE and Einstein's, or between my concept TREE and Helen Keller's, etc. that is a very strong prima facie reason to doubt that the theory has got it right about concept individuation or that the experimental procedure is really a measure of concept possession.

I am thus setting my face against a variety of kinds of conceptual relativism, and it may be supposed that my doing so is itself merely dogmatic. But I think there are good grounds for taking a firm line on this issue. Certainly RTM is required to. I remarked in Chapter 1 that RTM takes for granted the centrality of intentional explanation in any viable cognitive psychology. In the cases of interest, what makes such explanations intentional is that they appeal to covering generalizations about people who believe that such-and-such, or people who desire that so-and-so, or people who intend that this and that, and so on. In consequence, the extent to which an RTM can achieve generality in the explanations it proposes depends on the extent to which mental contents are supposed to be shared. If everybody else's concept WATER is different from mine, then it is literally true that only I have ever wanted a drink of water, and that the intentional generalization 'Thirsty people seek water' applies only to me. (And, of course, only I can state that generalization; words express concepts, so if your WATER concept is different from mine, 'Thirsty people seek water' means something different when you say it and when I do.) Prima facie, it would appear that any very thoroughgoing conceptual relativism would preclude intentional generalizations with any very serious explanatory power. This holds in spades if, as seems likely, a coherent conceptual relativist has to claim that conceptual identity can't be maintained even across time slices of the same individual.

There is, however, a widespread consensus (and not only among conceptual relativists) that intentional explanation can, after all, be preserved without supposing that belief contents are often—or even ever—literally public. The idea is that a robust notion of content *similarity* would do just as well as a robust notion of content *identity* for the cognitive scientist's purposes. Here, to choose a specimen practically at random, is a recent passage in which Gil Harman enunciates this faith:

Sameness of meaning from one symbol system to another is a similarity relation rather than an identity relation in the respect that sameness of meaning is not transitive . . . I am inclined to extend the point to concepts, thoughts, and beliefs . . . The account of sameness of content appeals to the best way of translating between two systems, where goodness in translation has to do with preserving certain aspects of usage, with no appeal to any more 'robust' notion of content or meaning identity . . . [There's no reason why] the resulting notion of sameness of content should fail to satisfy the purposes of intentional explanation. (1993: 169–79)[4]

It's important whether such a view can be sustained since, as we'll see, meeting the requirement that intentional contents be literally public is non-trivial; like compositionality, publicity imposes a substantial constraint upon one's theory of concepts and hence, derivatively, upon one's theory of language. In fact, however, the idea that content similarity is the basic notion in intentional explanation is affirmed a lot more widely than it's explained; and it's quite unclear, on reflection, how the notion of similarity that such a semantics would require might be unquestion-beggingly developed. On one hand, such a notion must be robust in the sense that it preserves intentional explanations pretty generally; on the other hand, it must do so *without itself presupposing a robust notion of content identity*. To the best of my knowledge, it's true *without exception* that all the construals of concept similarity that have thus far been put on offer egregiously fail the second condition.

Harman, for example, doesn't say much more about content-similarity-cum-goodness-of-translation than that it isn't transitive and that it "preserves certain aspects of usage". That's not a lot to go on. Certainly it leaves wide open whether Harman is right in denying that his account of content similarity presupposes a "'robust' notion of content or meaning identity". For whether it does depends on how the relevant "aspects of

[4] See also Smith, Medin, and Rips: "what accounts for categorization cannot account for stability [publicity] . . . [a]s long as *stability of concepts* is equated with *sameness of concepts* . . . But there is another sense of stability, which can be equated with *similarity of mental contents* . . . and for this sense, what accounts for categorization may at least partially account for 'stability' "(1984: 268). Similar passages are simply ubiquitous in the cognitive science literature; I'm grateful to Ron Mallon for having called this example to my attention.

usage" are themselves supposed to be individuated, and about this we're told nothing at all.

Harman is, of course, too smart to be a behaviourist; 'usage', as he uses it, is itself an intentional-cum-semantic term. Suppose, what surely seems plausible, that one of the 'aspects of usage' that a good translation of 'dog' has to preserve is that it be a term that implies *animal*, or a term that doesn't apply to ice cubes, or, for matter, a term that means *dog*. If so, then we're back where we started; Harman needs notions like *same* implication, *same* application, and *same* meaning in order to explicate his notion of content similarity. All that's changed is which shell the pea is under.

At one point, Harman asks rhetorically, "What aspects of use determine meaning?" Reply: "It is certainly relevant what terms are applied to and the reasons that might be offered for this application . . . it is also relevant how some terms are used in relation to other terms" (ibid.: 166). But I can't make any sense of this unless some notion of 'same application', 'same reason', and 'same relation of terms' is being taken for granted in characterizing what good translations *ipso facto* have in common. NB on pain of circularity: *same* application (etc.), not *similar* application (etc.). Remember that *similarity of semantic properties* is the notion that Harman is trying to explain, so his explanation mustn't *presuppose* that notion.

I don't particularly mean to pick on Harman; if his story begs the question it was supposed to answer, that is quite typical of the literature on concept similarity. Though it's often hidden in a cloud of technical apparatus (for a detailed case study, see Fodor and Lepore 1992: ch. 7), the basic problem is easy enough to see. Suppose that we want the following to be a prototypical case where you and I have different but similar concepts of George Washington: though we agree about his having been the first American President, and the Father of His Country, and his having cut down a cherry tree, and so on, you think that he wore false teeth and I think that he didn't. The similarity of our GW concepts is thus some (presumably weighted) function of the number of propositions about him that we both believe, and the dissimilarity of our GW concepts is correspondingly a function of the number of such propositions that we disagree about. So far, so good.

But the question now arises: what about the shared beliefs themselves; are they or aren't they *literally* shared? This poses a dilemma for the similarity theorist that is, as far as I can see, unavoidable. If he says that our agreed upon beliefs about GW are literally shared, then he hasn't managed to do what he promised; viz. introduce a notion of similarity of content that dispenses with a robust notion of publicity. But if he says that the agreed beliefs aren't literally shared (viz. that they are only required to be similar), then his account of content similarity begs the very question it was supposed to answer: his way of saying what it is for concepts to have similar but not identical contents presupposes a prior notion of beliefs with similar but not identical contents.

The trouble, in a nutshell, is that all the obvious construals of *similarity of beliefs* (in fact, all the construals that I've heard of) take it to involve *partial overlap* of beliefs.[5] But this treatment breaks down if the beliefs that are in the overlap are themselves construed as similar but not identical. It looks as though a robust notion of content similarity *can't but* presuppose a correspondingly robust notion of content identity. Notice that this situation is not symmetrical; the notion of content identity doesn't require a prior notion of content similarity. Leibniz's Law tells us what it is for the contents of concepts to be identical; Leibniz's Law tells us what it is for *anythings* to be identical.

As I remarked above, different theorists find different rugs to sweep this problem under; but, as far as I can tell, none of them manages to avoid it. I propose to harp on this a bit because confusion about it is rife, not just in philosophy but in the cognitive science community at large. Not getting it straight is one of the main things that obscures how very hard it is to construct a theory of concepts that works, and how very much cognitive science has thus far failed to do so.

Suppose, for example, it's assumed that your concept PRESIDENT is similar to my concept PRESIDENT in so far as we assign similar subjective probabilities to propositions that contain the concept. There are plenty of reasons for rejecting this sort of model; we'll discuss its main problems in Chapter 5. Our present concern is only whether constructing a probabilistic account of concept similarity would be a way to avoid having to postulate a robust notion of content identity.

Perhaps, in a typical case, you and I agree that p is very high for 'FDR is/was President' and for 'The President is the Commander-in-Chief of the Armed Forces' and for 'Presidents have to be of voting age', etc.; but, whereas you rate 'Millard Fillmore is/was President' as having a probability close to 1, I, being less well informed, take it to be around $p = 0.07$ (*Millard Fillmore???*). This gives us an (arguably) workable construal of the idea that we have similar but not identical PRESIDENT concepts. But it does so only by helping itself to a prior notion of belief identity, and to the assumption that there are lots of thoughts of which

---

[5] 'Why not take content similarity as primitive and *stop trying* to construe it?' Sure; but then why not take content *identity* as primitive and stop trying to construe *it*? In which case, what is semantics *for*?

our respective PRESIDENTs are constituents that we literally share. Thus, you and I are, by assumption, both belief-related to the thoughts that Millard Fillmore was President, that Presidents are Commanders-in-Chief, etc. The difference between us is in the *strengths* of our beliefs, not in their contents.[6] And, as usual, it really does seem to be *identity* of belief content that's needed here. If our respective beliefs about Presidents having to be of voting age were supposed to be merely *similar*, circularity would ensue: since content similarity is the notion we are trying to explicate, it mustn't be among the notions that the explication presupposes. (I think I may have mentioned that before.)

The same sort of point holds, though even more obviously, for other standard ways of construing conceptual similarity. For example, if concepts are sets of features, similarity of concepts will presumably be measured by some function that is sensitive to the amount of overlap of the sets. But then, the atomic feature assignments must themselves be construed as literal. If the similarity between your concept CAT and mine depends (*inter alia*) on our agreement that '+ has a tail' is in both of our feature bundles, then the assignment of that feature to these bundles must express a literal consensus; it must literally be the property of *having a tail* that we both literally think that cats literally have. (As usual, nothing relevant changes if feature assignments are assumed to be probabilistic or weighted; or if the feature assigned are supposed to be "subsemantic", though these red herrings are familiar from the Connectionist literature.)

Or, suppose that concepts are thought of as positions in a "multi-dimensional vector space" (see e.g. Churchland 1995) so that the similarity between your concepts and mine is expressed by the similarity of their positions in our respective spaces. Suppose, in particular, that it is constitutive of the difference between our NIXON concepts that you think Nixon was even more of a crook than I do. Once again, a robust notion of content identity is presupposed since each of our spaces is required to have a dimension that expresses crookedness; a fortiori, both are required

---

[6] Alternatively, a similarity theory might suppose that what we share when our PRESIDENT concepts are similar are similar beliefs about the probabilities of certain propositions: you believe that p(presidents are CICs) = 0.98; I believe that p(presidents are CICs) = 0.95; Bill believes that p(Presidents are CICs) = 0.7; so, all else equal, your PRESIDENT concept is more like mine than Bill's is.

But this construal does nothing to discharge the basic dependence of the notion of content similarity on the notion of content identity since what it says makes our beliefs similar is that they make similar estimates of the probability *of the very same proposition*; e.g. of the proposition that presidents are CICs. If, by contrast, the propositions to which our various probability estimates relate us are themselves supposed to be merely similar, then it does *not* follow from these premises that *ceteris paribus* your PRESIDENT concept is more like mine than like Bill's.

to have dimensions which express degrees of *the very same property*. That should seem entirely unsurprising. Vector space models identify the dimensions of a vector space *semantically* (viz. by stipulating what the location of a concept along that dimension is to *mean*), and it's just a truism that the positions along dimension *D* can represent degrees of *D*-ness only in a mind that possesses the concept of being *D*. You and I can argue about whether Nixon was merely crooked or very crooked only if the concept of *being crooked* is one that we have in common.

It may seem to you that I am going on about such truisms longer than necessity demands. It often seems that to me, too. There are, however, at least a zillion places in the cognitive science literature, and at least half a zillion in the philosophy literature, where the reader is assured that some or all of his semantical troubles will vanish quite away if only he will abandon the rigid and reactionary notion of content identity in favour of the liberal and laid-back notion of content similarity. But in none of these places is one ever told how to do so. That's because nobody has the slightest idea how. In fact, it's all just loose talk, and it causes me to grind my teeth.

Please note that none of this is intended to claim that notions like belief similarity, content similarity, concept similarity, etc. play less than a central role in the psychology of cognition. On the contrary, for all I know (certainly for all I am prepared non-negotiably to assume) it may be that every powerful intentional generalization is of the form "If *x* has a belief similar to *P*, then . . ." rather than the form "If *x* believes *P*, then . . .". If that is so, then so be it. My point is just that assuming that it is so doesn't exempt one's theory of concepts from the Publicity constraint. To repeat one last time: all the theories of content that offer a robust construal of conceptual similarity do so by presupposing a correspondingly robust notion of concept identity. As far as I can see, this is unavoidable. If I'm right that it is, then the Publicity constraint is *ipso facto* non-negotiable.

OK, so those are my five untendentious constraints on theories of concepts. In succeeding chapters, I'll consider three stories about what concepts are; viz. that they are definitions; that they are prototypes/ stereotypes; and (briefly) something called the 'theory theory' which says, as far as I can make out, that concepts are abstractions from belief systems. I'll argue that each of these theories violates at least one of the non-negotiable constraints; and that it does so, so to speak, not a little bit around the edges but egregiously and down the middle. We will then have to consider what, if any, options remain for developing a theory of concepts suitable to the purposes of an RTM.

Before we settle down to this, however, there are a last couple of preliminary points that I want to put in place.

Here is the first: although I'm distinguishing three theories of concepts for purposes of exposition and attack, and though supporters of each of these theories have traditionally wanted to distance themselves as much as possible from supporters of the others, still all three theories are really versions of one and the same idea about content. I want to stress this since I'm going to argue that it is primarily because of what they agree about that all three fail.

The theories of concepts we'll be considering all assume a metaphysical thesis which, as I remarked in Chapter 1, I propose to reject: namely, that primitive concepts, and (hence) their possession conditions, are at least partly constituted by their inferential relations. (That complex concepts—BROWN COW, etc.—and their possession conditions are exhaustively constituted by their inferential relations to their constituent concepts is not in dispute; to the contrary, compositionality requires it, and compositionality isn't negotiable.) The current near-universal acceptance of Inferential Role Semantics in cognitive science marks a radical break with the preceding tradition in theories about mind and language: pre-modern theories typically supposed that primitive concepts are individuated by their (e.g. iconic or causal) relations to things in the world. The history of the conversion of cognitive scientists to IR semantics would make a book by itself; a comedy, I think, though thus far without a happy ending:

—In philosophy, the idea was pretty explicitly to extend the Logicist treatment of logical terms into the non-logical vocabulary; if IF and SOME can be identified with their inferential roles, why not TABLE and TREE as well?

—In linguistics, the idea was to extend to semantics the Structuralist notion that a level of grammatical description is a 'system of differences': if their relations of equivalence and contrast are what bestow phonological values on speech sounds, why shouldn't their relations of implication and exclusion be what bestow semantic values on forms of words?

—In AI, the principle avatar of IRS was 'procedural semantics', a deeply misguided attempt to extend the principle of 'methodological solipsism' from the theory of mental processes to the theory of meaning: if a mental process (thinking, perceiving, remembering, and the like) can be 'purely computational' why can't conceptual content be purely computational too? If computers qua devices that perform inferences can *think*, why can't computers qua devices that perform inferences *mean*?

—I don't know how psychology caught IRS; perhaps it was from philosophy, linguistics, and AI. (I know one eminent developmental psychologist who certainly caught it from Thomas Kuhn.) Let that be an object lesson in the danger of mixing disciplines. Anyhow, IRS got to be the fashion in psychology too. Perhaps the main effect of the "cognitive revolution" was that espousing some or other version of IRS became the received way for a psychologist not to be a behaviourist.

So, starting around 1950, practically everybody was saying that the '"Fido"–Fido fallacy' is fallacious,[7] and that concepts (/words) are like chess pieces: just as there can't be a rook without a queen, so there can't be a DOG without an ANIMAL. Just as the value of the rook is partly determined by its relation to the queen, so the content of DOG is partly determined by its relation to ANIMAL. Content is therefore a thing that can only happen internal to *systems* of symbols (or internal to languages, or, on some versions, internal to forms of life). It was left to 'literary theory' to produce the *reductio ad absurdum* (literary theory is good at that): content is constituted *entirely* by intra-symbolic relations; just as there's nothing 'outside' the chess game that matters to the values of the pieces, so too there's nothing outside the text that matters to what it means. Idealism followed, of course.

It is possible to feel that these various ways of motivating IRS, historically effective though they clearly were, are much less than overwhelmingly persuasive. For example, on reflection, it doesn't seem that languages are a lot like games after all: queens and pawns don't mean anything, whereas 'dog' means *dog*. That's why, though you can't translate the queen into French (or, a fortiori, into checkers), you can translate 'dog' into 'chien'. It's perhaps unwise to insist on an analogy that misses so glaring a difference.

Phonemes don't mean anything either, so prima facie, *pace* Saussure, "having a phonological value" and "having a semantic value" would seem to be quite different sorts of properties. Even if it were right that phonemes are individuated by their contrasts and equivalences—which probably they aren't—that wouldn't be much of a reason to claim that words or concepts are also individuated that way.

If, in short, one asks to hear some serious arguments for IRS, one discovers, a bit disconcertingly, that they are very thin upon the ground. I think that IRS is most of what is wrong with current theorizing in cognitive science and the metaphysics of meaning. But I don't suppose for a minute that any short argument will, or should, persuade you to consider junking it. I expect that will need a long argument; hence this long book. Long arguments take longer than short arguments, but they do sometimes create conviction.

Accordingly, my main subject in what follows will be not the history of

---

[7] That is, the "fallacy" of assuming that the meaning of the word is the eponymous dog.

IR semantics, or the niceties of its formulation, or its evidential status, but rather its impact on empirical theories of concepts. The central consideration will be this: If you wish to hold that the content of a concept is constituted by the inferences that it enters into, you are in need of a principled way of deciding *which inferences constitute which concepts*. What primarily distinguishes the cognitive theories we'll consider is how they answer this question. My line will be that, though as far as anybody knows the answers they offer exhaust the options, pretty clearly none of them can be right. Not, NB, that they are incoherent, or otherwise confused; just that they fail to satisfy the empirical constraints on theories of concepts that I've been enumerating, and are thus, almost certainly, false.

At that point, I hope that abandoning IRS in favour of the sort of atomistic, informational semantics that I tentatively endorsed in Chapter 1 will begin to appear to be the rational thing to do. I'll say something in Chapter 6 about what this sort of alternative to IRS might be like.

So much for the first of my two concluding addenda. Here is the second:

I promised you in Chapter 1 that I wouldn't launch yet another defence of RTM; I proposed—aside from my admittedly tendentious endorsement of informational semantics—simply to take RTM for granted as the context in which problems about the nature of concepts generally arise these days. I do mean to stick to this policy. Mostly. But I can't resist rounding off these two introductory chapters by remarking how nicely the pieces fit when you put them all together. I'm going to exercise my hobby-horse after all, but only a little.

In effect, in these introductory discussions, we've been considering constraints on a theory of cognition that emerge from two widely different, and largely independent, research enterprises. On the one hand, there's the attempt to save the architecture of a Fregean—viz. a purely referential—theory of meaning by taking seriously the idea that concepts can be distinguished by their 'modes of presentation' of their extensions. It's supposed to be modes of presentation that answer the question 'How can coreferential concepts be distinct?' Here Frege's motives concur with those of Informational Semantics; since both are referential theories of content, both need a story about how thinking about the Morning Star could be different from thinking about the Evening Star, given that the two thoughts are connected with the same 'thing in the world'.

The project of saving the Frege programme faces two major hurdles. First, 'Mates cases' appear to show that modes of presentations can't be senses. Frege to the contrary notwithstanding, it looks as though practically any linguistic difference between prima facie synonymous expressions, merely syntactic differences distinctly included, can be recruited to block their substitution in some Mates context or other. In the current jargon, the individuation of the propositional attitudes apparently slices them about as thin as the syntactic individuation of forms of words, hence not only thinner than reference can, *but also thinner than sense can*.

The other obstacle to saving the Frege programme was that it took for granted that the semantic question 'How can coreferential concepts fail to be synonyms?' gets the same answer as the psychological question 'How can there be more than one way of grasping a referent?' The postulation of senses was supposed to answer both questions. I argued, however, that given Frege's Platonism about senses, it's by no means obvious why his answer to the first would constitute an answer to the second; in effect, Frege simply stipulates their equivalence. I supposed the moral to be that Frege's theoretical architecture needs to be explicitly psychologized. Modes of presentation need to be 'in the head'.

The short form is: the Frege programme needs something that is both in the head and of the right kind to distinguish coreferential concepts, and the Mates cases suggest that whatever is able to distinguish coreferential concepts is apt for syntactic individuation. Put all this together and it does rather suggest that modes of presentation are syntactically structured mental particulars. Suggestion noted.

The other research programme from which my budget of constraints on theories of concepts derived is the attempt, in cognitive science, to explain how a finite being might have intentional states and capacities that are productive and systematic. This productivity/systematicity problem again has two parts: 'Explain how there can be infinitely many propositional attitudes each with its distinctive propositional object (i.e. each with its own content)' and: 'Explain how there can be infinitely many propositional attitudes each with its distinctive causal powers (i.e. each with its own causal role in mental processes).' Here I have followed what Pylyshyn and I (Fodor and Pylyshyn 1988) called the 'Classical' computational tradition that proceeds from Turing: mental representations are syntactically structured. Their conditions of semantic evaluation and their causal powers both depend on their syntactic structures; the former because mental representations have a compositional semantics that is sensitive to the syntactic relations among their constituents; the latter because mental processes are *computations* and are thus syntactically driven by definition. So the Classical account of productivity/systematicity points in much the same direction as the psychologized Frege programme's account of the individuation of mental states: viz. towards syntactically structured mental particulars whose tokenings are matched, case for case, with tokenings of the de dicto propositional attitudes.

Syntactically structured mental particulars whose tokenings are matched, case for case, with tokenings of the de dicto propositional attitudes are, of course, exactly what RTM has for sale. So RTM seems to be what both the Frege/Mates problems and the productivity/systematicity problems converge on. If beliefs (and the like) are relations to syntactically structured mental representations, there are indeed two parameters of belief individuation, just as Frege requires: Morning Star beliefs have the same conditions of semantic evaluation as Evening Star beliefs, but they implicate the tokening of different syntactic objects and are therefore different beliefs with different causal powers. That believing P and believing Q may be different mental states even if 'P' and 'Q' have the same semantic value shows up in the Mates contexts. That believing P and believing Q may have different causal powers even if 'P' and 'Q' have the same semantic value shows up in all those operas where the soprano dies of mistaken identity.

So RTM looks like a plausible answer to several questions that one might have supposed to be unrelated. I hope that isn't an accident. This book runs on the assumption that it isn't, hence that we need RTM a lot. RTM, in turn, needs a theory of concepts a lot since compositionality says that the contents and causal powers of mental representations are both inherited, eventually, from the contents and causal powers of their minimal constituents; viz. from the primitive concepts that they contain. RTM is simply *no good* without a viable theory of concepts.

So be it, then. Let's see what there might be on offer.

3

The Demise of Definitions, Part I:
The Linguist's Tale

Certain matters would appear to get carried certain distances whether one
wishes them to or not, unfortunately.
                                    —David Markham, *Wittgenstein's Mistress*

Introduction

I WANT to consider the question whether concepts are definitions. And
let's, just for the novelty, start with some propositions that are clearly true:

1. You can't utter the expression 'brown cow' without uttering the word
   'brown'.
2. You can utter the word 'bachelor' without uttering the word
   'unmarried'.

The asymmetry between 1 and 2 will be granted even by those who believe
that the "semantic representation" of 'bachelor' (its representation, as
linguists say, "at the semantic level") is a complex object which contains,
inter alia, the semantic representation of 'unmarried'.
   Now for something that's a little less obvious:

3. You can't entertain the M(ental) R(epresentation) BROWN COW
   without entertaining the MR BROWN.
4. You can't entertain the M(ental) R(epresentation) BACHELOR
   without entertaining the MR UNMARRIED.

I'm going to take it for granted that 3 is true. I have my reasons; they'll
emerge in Chapter 5. Suffice it, for now, that anybody who thinks that 3
and the like are false will certainly think that 4 and the like are false; and
that 4 and the like are indeed false is the main conclusion this chapter aims
at. I pause, however, to remark that 3 is meant to be tendentious. It claims
not just what everyone admits, viz. that anything that satisfies BROWN
COW *inter alia* satisfies BROWN, viz. that brow cows are *ipso facto* brown.

Proposition 3 says, moreover, that to think the content *brown cow* is, *inter alia*, to think the concept BROWN, and that would be false if the mental representation that expresses *brown cow* is atomic; like, for example, BROWNCOW.

What about 4? Here again there is a way of reading what's being claimed that makes it merely truistic: viz. by not distinguishing *concept* identity from *content* identity. It's not, I suppose, unreasonable (for the present illustrative purposes, I don't care whether it's true) to claim that the content *bachelor* and the content *unmarried man* are one and the same. For example, if concepts express properties, then it's not unreasonable to suppose that BACHELOR and UNMARRIED MAN express the *same* property. If so, and if one doesn't distinguish between content identity and concept identity, then of course it follows that you can't think BACHELOR without thinking UNMARRIED (unless you can think UNMARRIED MAN without thinking UNMARRIED. Which let's just concede that you can't).[1]

However, since we *are* distinguishing content identity from concept identity, we're not going to read 4 that way. Remember that RTM is in force, and RTM says that to each tokening of a mental state with the content *so-and-so* there corresponds a tokening of a mental representation with the content *so-and-so*. In saying this, RTM explicitly means to leave open the possibility that different (that is, type distinct) mental representations might correspond to the same content; hence the analogy between mental representations and modes of presentation that I stressed in Chapter 2. In the present case, the concession that being a bachelor and being an unmarried man are the same thing is meant to leave open the question whether BACHELOR and UNMARRIED MAN are the same concept.

RTM also says that (infinitely many, but not all) mental representations have constituent structure; in particular that there are both complex

---

[1] It will help the reader to keep the uses distinct from the mentions, to bear in mind that the expressions appearing in caps. (e.g. 'BACHELOR') are *names*, rather than *structural descriptions*, of mental representations. I thus mean to leave it open that the MR that 'BACHELOR' names might be structurally complex; for example, it might have as constituents the MRs that 'UNMARRIED' and 'MAN' name. By contrast, it's stipulative that no formula is a *structural description* of a mental representation unless it contains names of the MR's constituents. The issues we'll be concerned with can often be phrased either by asking about the structure of mental representations or about the structural descriptions of mental representations. In practice, I'll go back and forth between the two.

The claim that concepts are definitions can be sharpened in light of these remarks. Strictly speaking, it's that the *definiens* is the structural description of the *definiendum*; for example, 'UNMARRIED MAN' is the structural description of the concept BACHELOR.

mental representations and primitive mental representations, and that the former have the latter as proper parts. We are now in a position to make expository hay out of this assumption; we can rephrase the claim that is currently before the house as:

> 5. The M(ental) R(epresentation) UNMARRIED, which is a con-
> stituent of the MR UNMARRIED MAN, is likewise a constituent
> of the MR BACHELOR.

Here's a standard view: the concept BACHELOR is expressed by the word "bachelor", and the word "bachelor" is definable; it means the same as the phrase "unmarried man". In the usual case, the mental representation that corresponds to a concept that corresponds to a definable word is complex: in particular, the mental representation that corresponds to a definable word usually has the same constituent structure as the mental representation that corresponds to its definition. So, according to the present proposal, the constituent structure of the mental representation BACHELOR is something like 'UNMARRIED MAN'.

The thesis that definition plays an important role in the theory of mental representation will be the main concern in this chapter and the next. According to that view, many mental representations work the way we've just supposed that BACHELOR does. That is, they correspond to concepts that are expressed by definable words, and they are themselves structurally complex. This thesis is, to put it mildly, *very* tendentious. In order for it to be true, it must turn out that there are many definable words; and it must turn out, in many cases, that the MRs that correspond to these definable words are structurally complex. I'm going to argue that it doesn't, in fact, turn out in either of those ways.[2]

One last preliminary, and then we'll be ready to go. If there are no definable words, then, of course, there are no complex mental representations that correspond to them. But it doesn't follow that if there are many complex mental representations, then lots of words are definable. In fact, I take it that the view now favoured in both philosophy and cognitive science is that most words aren't definable but do correspond to

---

[2] It's common ground that—idioms excepted—MRs that correspond to phrases (for example, the one that corresponds to "brown cow") are typically structurally complex, so I've framed the definition theory as a thesis about the MRs of concepts that are expressed by lexical items. But, of course, this way of putting it relativizes the issue to the choice of a reference language. Couldn't it be that the very same concept that is expressed by a single word in English gets expressed by a phrase in Bantu, or vice versa? Notice, however, that this could happen only if the English word in question is definable; viz. definable in Bantu. Since it's going to be part of my story that most words are undefinable—not just undefinable in the language that contains them, but undefinable *tout court*—I'm committed to claiming that this sort of case can't arise (very often). The issue is, of course, empirical. So be it.

complex MRs (to something like prototypes or exemplars). Since the case against definitions isn't *ipso facto* a case against complex mental representations, I propose the following expository strategy. In this chapter and the next, I argue that concepts *aren't* definitions even if lots of mental representations *are* complex. Chapter 5 will argue that there are (practically) no complex mental representations at all, definitional or otherwise.[3] At that point, atomism will be the option of last resort.

If we thus set aside, for the moment, all considerations that don't distinguish the claim that mental representations are typically definitional from the weaker claim that mental representations are typically complex, what arguments have we left to attend to? There are two kinds: the more or less empirical ones and the more or less philosophical ones. The empirical ones turn on data that are supposed to show that the mental representations that correspond to definable words are, very often and simply as a matter of fact, identical to the mental representations that correspond to phrases that define the words. The philosophical ones are supposed to show that we need mental representations to be definitions because nothing else will account for our intuitions of conceptual connectedness, analyticity, a prioricity, and the like. My plan is to devote the rest of this chapter to the empirical arguments and all of Chapter 4 to the philosophical arguments. You will be unsurprised to hear what my unbiased and judicious conclusion is going to be. My unbiased and judicious conclusion is going to be that neither the philosophical nor the empirical arguments for definitions are any damned good.

So, then, to business.

Almost everybody used to think that concepts are definitions; hence that having a concept is being prepared to draw (or otherwise acknowledge) the inferences that define it. Prima facie, there's much to be said for this view. In particular, definitions seem to have a decent chance of satisfying all five of the 'non-negotiable' conditions which Chapter 2 said that concepts have to meet. If the meaning-constitutive inferences are the defining ones, then it appears that:

—Definitions can be mental particulars if any concepts can. Whatever the definition of 'bachelor' is, it has the same ontological status as the mental representation that you entertain when you think *unmarried man*. That there is such a mental representation is a claim to which RTM is, of course, independently committed.

—Semantic evaluability is assured; since *all* inferences are semantically

---

[3] i.e. there are no complex mental representations other than those that correspond to concepts that are expressed by phrases; see the preceding footnote. From now on, I'll take this caveat for granted.

evaluable (for soundness, validity, reliability, etc.), defining inferences are semantically evaluable *inter alia*.

—Publicity is satisfied since there's no obvious reason why lots of people might not assign the same defining inferences to a given word or concept. They might do so, indeed, even if there are lots of differences in what they know/believe about the things the concept applies to (lots of differences in the 'collateral information' they have about such things).

—Compositionality is satisfied. This will bear emphasis later. I'm going to argue that, of the various 'inferential role' theories of concepts, only the one that says that concepts are definitions meets the compositionality condition. Suffice it for now that words/concepts do contribute their definitions to the sentences/thoughts that contain them; it's part and parcel of 'bachelor' meaning *unmarried man* that the sentence 'John is a bachelor' means *John is an unmarried man* and does so because it has 'bachelor' among its constituents. To that extent, at least, definitions are in the running to be both word meanings and conceptual contents.

—Learnability is satisfied. If the concept DOG is a definition, then learning the definition should be all that's required to learn the concept. A fortiori, concepts that are definitions don't have to be innate.

To be sure, learning definitions couldn't be the *whole* story about acquiring concepts. Not all concepts could be definitions, since some have to be the primitives that the others are defined in terms of; about the acquisition of the primitive concepts, some quite different story will have to be told. What determines which concepts are primitive was one of the questions that definition theories never really resolved. Empiricists in philosophy wanted the primitive concepts to be picked out by some epistemological criterion; but they had no luck in finding one. (For discussion of these and related matters, see Fodor 1981*a*, 1981*b*.) But, however exactly this goes, the effect of supposing that there are definitions is to reduce the problems about concepts at large to the corresponding problems about primitive concepts. So, if some (complex) concept C is defined by primitive concepts $c_1, c_2, \ldots$, then explaining how we acquire C reduces to explaining how we acquire $c_1, c_2, \ldots$ And the problem of how we apply C to things that fall under it reduces to the problem of how we apply $c_1, c_2, \ldots$ to the things that fall under them. And explaining how we reason with C reduces to explaining how we reason with $c_1, c_2, \ldots$ And so forth. So there is good work for definitions to do if there turn out to be any.

All the same, these days almost nobody thinks that concepts are definitions. There is now something like a consensus in cognitive science that the notion of a definition has no very significant role to play in theories of meaning. It is, to be sure, a weakish argument against definitions that most cognitive scientists don't believe in them. Still, I do want to remind you how general, and how interdisciplinary, the collapse of the definitional theory of content has been. So, here are some reasons why definitions aren't currently in favour as candidates for concepts (/word meanings):

—There are practically no defensible examples of definitions; for all the examples we've got, practically all words (/concepts) are undefinable. And, of course, if a word (/concept) doesn't have a definition, then its definition can't be its meaning. (Oh well, maybe there's one definition. Maybe BACHELOR has the content *unmarried man*. Maybe there are even six or seven definitions; why should I quibble? If there are six or seven definitions, or sixty or seventy, that still leaves a lot of words/concepts undefined, hence a lot of words/concepts of which the definitional theory of meaning is false. The OED lists half a million words, plus or minus a few.)

Ray Jackendoff has suggested that the reason natural language contains so few phrases that are definitionally equivalent to words is that there are "nondiscrete elements of concepts . . . [which] play a role only in lexical semantics and never appear as a result of phrasal combination" (1992: 48). (I guess that "nondiscrete" means something like *analogue* or *iconic*.) But this begs the question that it's meant to answer, since it simply assumes that that there are contents that only nondiscrete symbols can express. Notice that you don't need nondiscrete *symbols* to express nondiscrete *properties*. 'Red' does quite a good job of expressing red. So suppose there is something essentially nondiscrete about the concepts that express lexical meanings. Still, it wouldn't follow that the same meanings can't be expressed by phrases. So, even if nondiscrete elements of concepts never appear as a result of phrasal combination, that *still* wouldn't explain why most words can't be defined.

—It's a general problem for theories that seek to construe content in terms of inferential role, that there seems to be no way to distinguish the inferences that *constitute* concepts from other kinds of inferences that concepts enter into. The present form of this general worry is that there seems to be no way to distinguish the inferences that *define* concepts from the ones that don't. This is, of course, old news to philosophers. Quine shook their faith that 'defining inference' is well defined, and hence their faith in such related notions as analyticity, propositions true in virtue of meaning alone, and so forth. Notice, in particular, that there are grounds for scepticism about *defining* inferences even if you suppose (as, of course, Quine does not) that the notion of *necessary* inference is secure. What's at issue here is squaring the theory of concept individuation with the theory of concept possession. If having a concept requires accepting the inferences that define it, then not all necessities can be definitional. It is, for example, necessary that 2 is a prime number; but surely you can have the concept 2 and not have the concept of a prime; presumably there were millennia when people did. (Similarly, *mutatis mutandis*, for the concept WATER if it's necessary that water is H_2O. I'll come back to this sort of point in Chapter 4.)

It is often, and rightly, said that Quine didn't *prove* that you can't make sense of analyticity, definition, and the like. But so what? Cognitive science doesn't do proofs; it does empirical, non-demonstrative inferences. We have, as things now stand, no account of what makes an inference a defining one, and no idea how such an account might be devised. That's a serious reason to suppose that the theory of content should dispense with definitions if it can.

—Although in principle definitions allow us to reduce all sorts of problems about concepts at large to corresponding problems about concepts in the primitive basis (see above), this strategy quite generally fails in practice. Even if there are definitions, they seem to play no very robust role in explaining what happens when people learn concepts, or when they reason with concepts, or when they apply them. Truth to tell, definitions seem to play no role at all.

For example, suppose that understanding a sentence involves recovering and displaying the definitions of the words that the sentence contains. Then you would expect, all else equal, that sentences that contain words with relatively complex definitions should be harder to understand than sentences that contain words with relatively simple definitions. Various psychologists have tried to get this effect experimentally; to my knowledge, nobody has ever succeeded. It's an iron law of cognitive science that, in experimental environments, definitions always behave exactly as though they weren't there.

In fact, this is obvious to intuition. Does anybody present really think that thinking BACHELOR is harder than thinking UNMARRIED? Or that thinking FATHER is harder than thinking PARENT? Whenever definition is by genus and species, definitional theories perforce predict that concepts for the former ought to be easier to think than concepts for the latter. Intuition suggests otherwise (and so, by the way, do the experimental data; see e.g. Paivio 1971).

Hold-outs for definitions often emphasize that the experimental failures don't *prove* that there aren't any definitions. Maybe there's a sort of novice/expert shift in concept acquisition: (defining) concepts like UNMARRIED MAN get 'compiled' into (defined) concepts like BACHELOR soon after they are mastered. If experiments don't detect UNMARRIED MAN in 'performance' tasks, maybe that's because

BACHELOR serves as its abbreviation.[4] Maybe. But I remind you, once again, that this is supposed to be science, not philosophy; the issue isn't whether there might be definitions, but whether, on the evidence, there actually are some. Nobody has proved that there aren't any little green men on Mars; but almost everybody is convinced by repeated failures to find them.

Much the same point holds for the evidence about concept learning. The (putative) ontogenetic process of compiling primitive concepts into defined ones surely can't be instantaneous; yet developmental cognitive psychologists find no evidence of a stage when primitive concepts exist uncompiled. I appeal to expert testimony; here's Susan Carey concluding a review of the literature on the role of definitions ('conceptual decompositions', as one says) in cognitive development: "At present, there simply is no good evidence that a word's meaning is composed, component by component, in the course of its acquisition. The evidence for component-by-component acquisition is flawed even when attention is restricted to those semantic domains which have yielded convincing componential analyses" (1982: 369). (I reserve the right to doubt that there are any such domains; see below.)

So it goes. Many psychologists, like many philosophers, are now very sceptical about definitions. This seems to be a real case of independent lines of enquiry arriving at the same conclusions for different but compatible reasons. The cognitive science community, by and large, has found this convergence pretty persuasive, and I think it's right to do so. Maybe some version of inferential role semantics will work and will sustain the thesis that most everyday concepts are complex; but, on the evidence, the definitional version doesn't.

I'd gladly leave it here if I could, but it turns out there are exceptions to the emerging consensus that I've been reporting. Some linguists, working in the tradition called 'lexical semantics', claim that there is persuasive distributional (/intuitional) evidence for a level of linguistic analysis at which many words are represented by their definitions. It may be, so the argument goes, that these linguistic data don't fit very well with the results in philosophy and psychology; if so, then that's a problem that cognitive scientists should be worrying about. But, assuming that you're prepared to take distributional/intuitional data seriously at all (as, no doubt, you

---

[4] I am playing very fast and loose with the distinction between concepts and their structural descriptions (see n. 1 above). *Strictu dictu*, it can't both be that the concept BACHELOR *abbreviates* the concept UNMARRIED MAN and that the concept BACHELOR *is* the concept UNMARRIED MAN. But not speaking strictly makes the exposition easier, and the present considerations don't depend on the conflation.

should be) then the evidence that there are definitions is of much the same kind as the evidence that there are nouns.

Just how radical is this disagreement between the linguist's claim that definition is a central notion in lexical semantics and the otherwise widely prevalent view that there are, in fact, hardly any definitions at all? That's actually less clear than one might at first suppose. It is entirely characteristic of lexical semanticists to hold that "although it is an empirical issue [linguistic evidence] supports the claim that the number of primitives is small, significantly smaller than the number of lexical items whose lexical meanings may be encoded using the primitives" (Konrfilt and Correra 1993). Now, one would have thought that if there are significantly fewer semantic primitives than there are lexical items, then there must be quite a lot of definable words (in, say, English). That would surprise philosophers, whose experience has been that there are practically none. However, having made this strong claim with one hand, lexical semanticists often hedge it with the other. For, unlike bona fide (viz. eliminative) definitions, the lexical semanticist's verb "decompositions . . . intend to capture the core aspects of the verb meanings, without implying that all aspects of the meanings are represented" (ibid.: 83).

Whether the definition story about words and concepts is interesting or surprising in this attenuated form depends, of course, on what one takes the "core aspects" of meaning to be. It is, after all, not in dispute that *some* aspects of lexical meanings can be represented in quite an exiguous vocabulary; some aspects of *anything* can be represented in quite an exiguous vocabulary. 'Core meaning' and the like are not, however, notions for which much precise explication gets provided in the lexical semantics literature. The upshot, often enough, is that the definitions that are put on offer are isolated, simply by stipulation, from prima facie counter-examples.[5]

This strikes me as a mug's game, and not one that I'm tempted to play. I take the proper ground rule to be that one expression defines another only if the two expressions are synonymous; and I take it to be a necessary condition for their synonymy that whatever the one expression applies to, the other does too. To insist on taking it this way isn't, I think, merely persnickety on my part. Unless definitions express semantic equivalences, they can't do the jobs that they are supposed to do in, for example, theories

---

[5] It's important to distinguish the idea that definitions typically capture only the core meaning of a univocal expression from the idea that definitions typically capture only one sense of an ambiguous expression. The latter is unobjectionable because it is responsive to pretheoretic intuitions that are often pretty emphatic: surely 'bank' has more than one meaning. But who knows how many "aspects" the meaning of an *un*ambiguous word has? A fortiori, who knows when a theory succeeds in capturing some but not all of them?

of lexical meaning and theories of concept acquisition. The idea is that its definition is what you acquire when you acquire a concept, and that its definition is what the word corresponding to the concept expresses. But how could "bachelor" and "unmarried male" express the same concept— viz. UNMARRIED MALE—if it's not even true that "bachelor" and "unmarried male" apply to the same things? And how could acquiring the concept BACHELOR be the same process as acquiring the concept UNMARRIED MALE if there are semantic properties that the two concepts don't share? It's supposed to be *the main virtue* of definitions that, in all sorts of cases, they reduce problems about the defined concept to corresponding problems about its primitive parts. But that won't happen unless each definition has *the very same content* as the concept that it defines.

I propose now to consider some of the linguistic arguments that are supposed to show that many English words have definitions, where, however, "definitions" means *definitions*. I think that, when so constrained, none of these arguments is any good at all. The lexical semantics literature is, however, enormous and I can't prove this by enumeration. What I'll do instead is to have a close look at some typical (and influential) examples. (For discussions of some other kinds of 'linguistic' arguments for definitions, see Fodor 1970; Fodor and Lepore, forthcoming *a*; Fodor and Lepore, forthcoming *b*.)

Jackendoff

Here's a passage from Jackendoff 1992. (For simplification, I have omitted from the quotation what Jackendoff takes to be some parallel examples; and I've correspondingly renumbered the cited formulas.)

The basic insight . . . is that the formalism for encoding concepts of spatial location and motion, suitably abstracted, can be generalized to many verbs and prepositions in two or more semantic fields, forming intuitively related paradigms. [J1–J4] illustrates [a] basic case.

  [J1 Semantic field:] Spatial location and motion: 'Harry kept the bird in the cage.'
  [J2 Semantic field:] Possession: 'Susan kept the money.'
  [J3 Semantic field:] Ascription of properties [*sic*]:[6] 'Sam kept the crowd happy.'

---

[6] Wherein does this semantic field differ from any other? If I say that Harry kept the bird in the cage, don't I thereby ascribe a property—viz. the property of keeping the bird in the cage—to Harry? Jackendoff has a lot of trouble deciding what to call his semantic fields. This might well be because they're gerrymandered.

[J4 Semantic field:] Scheduling of activities: 'Let's keep the trip on Satur-
    day.' . . .

The claim is that the different concepts expressed by 'keep'. . . are not unrelated:
they share the same functional structure and differ only in the semantic field
feature. (1992: 37–9).

I think the argument Jackendoff has in mind must be something like this:
'Keep' is "polysemous". On the one hand, there's the intuition that the
very same word occurs in J1–J4; 'keep' isn't ambiguous like 'bank'. On
the other hand, there's the intuition that the sense of 'keep' does somehow
differ in the four cases. The relation between Susan and the money in J2
doesn't seem to be quite the same as the relation between John and the
crowd in J3. How to reconcile these intuitions?

Well, suppose that 'keep' sentences "all denote the causation of a state
that endures over a period of time" (37).[7] That would account for our
feeling that 'keep' is univocal. The intuition that there's something
different, all the same, between keeping the money and keeping the crowd
happy can now also be accommodated by reference to the differences
among the semantic fields, each of which "has its own particular
inferential patterns"(39). So Jackendoff "accounts for [the univocality of
'keep' in J1–J4] by claiming that they are each realizations of the basic
conceptual functions" (specified by the putative definition) (37). What
accounts for the differences among them is "a semantic field feature that
designates the field in which the Event [to which the analysis of 'keep'
refers] . . . is defined" (38). So if we assume that 'keep' has a definition, and
that its definition is displayed at some level of linguistic/cognitive
representation, then we can see how it can be true both that 'keep' means
what it does and that what it means depends on the semantic field in which
it is applied.[8]

So much for exposition. I claim that Jackendoff's account of polysemy
offers no good reason to think that there are definitions. As often happens
in lexical semantics, the problem that postulating definitions is supposed
to solve is really only begged; it's, as it were, kicked upstairs into the
metalanguage. The proposed account of polysemy works only because it

---

[7] This analysis couldn't be exhaustive; cf. 'keep an appointment/ promise' and the like.
But perhaps 'keep' is ambiguous as well as polysemous. There's certainly something
zeugmatic about 'He kept his promises and his snowshoes in the cellar'.

[8] On the West Coast of the United States, much the same sort of thesis is often held in
the form that lexical analysis captures the regularities in a word's behaviour by exhibiting a
core meaning together with a system of 'metaphorical' extensions. See, for example, the
putative explanation of polysemy in Lakoff (1988) and in many other treatises on "cognitive
semantics". As far as I can tell, the arguments against Jackendoff that I'm about to offer
apply without alteration to Lakoff as well.

takes for granted a theoretical vocabulary whose own semantics is, in the crucial respects, unspecified.[9] Since arguments from data about polysemy to the existence of definitions have been widely influential in linguistics, and since the methodological issues are themselves of some significance, I'm going to spend some time on this. Readers who are prepared to take it on faith that such arguments don't work are advised to skip.

The proposal is that whatever semantic field it occurs in, 'keep' always means (expresses the concept) CAUSE A STATE THAT ENDURES OVER TIME. Notice, however, that this assumption would explain the intuitive univocality of 'keep' only if it's also assumed that 'CAUSE', 'STATE', 'TIME', 'ENDURE', and the rest are themselves univocal across semantic fields. A's always entailing B doesn't argue for A's being univocal if B means sometimes one thing and sometimes another when A entails it. So, then, let's consider the question whether, for example, 'CAUSE' is univocal in, say, 'CAUSE THE MONEY TO BE IN SUSAN'S POCKET' and 'CAUSE THE CROWD TO BE HAPPY'? My point will be that Jackendoff is in trouble whichever answer he gives.

On the one hand, as we've just seen, if 'CAUSE' is polysemic, then BLAH, BLAH, CAUSE, BLAH, BLAH is itself polysemic, so the assumption that 'keep' always means BLAH, BLAH, CAUSE, BLAH, BLAH doesn't explain why 'keep' is intuitively univocal, and Jackendoff looses his argument for definitions. So, suppose he opts for the other horn. The question now arises what explains the univocality of 'CAUSE' across semantic fields? There are, again, two possibilities. Jackendoff can say that what makes 'CAUSE' univocal is that it has the definition BLAH, BLAH, X, BLAH, BLAH where 'X' is univocal across fields. Or he can give up and say that what makes 'CAUSE' univocal across fields isn't that it has a univocal definition but just that it always means *cause*.

Clearly, the first route leads to regress and is therefore not viable: if the univocality of 'CAUSE' across fields is required in order to explain the univocality of 'keep' across fields, and the univocality of 'X' across fields

---

[9] Examples of this tactic are legion in the literature. Consider the following, from Higginbotham 1994. "[T]he meanings of lexical items systematically infect grammar. For example . . . it is a condition of object-preposing in derived nominal constructions in English that the object be in some sense 'affected' in the events over which the nominal ranges: that is why one has (1) but not (2)" (renumbered):
    1. algebra's discovery (by the Arabs)
    2. *algebra's knowledge (by the Arabs).
Note that 'in some sense' is doing all the work. It is what distinguishes the striking claim that preposing is sensitive to the meanings of verbs from the rather less dramatic thought that you can prepose with some verbs (including 'discover') and not with others (including 'know'). You may suppose you have some intuitive grasp of what 'affecting' amounts to here, but I think it's an illusion. Ask yourself *how much* algebra was affected by its discovery? More or less, would you say, than the light bulb was affected by Edison's inventing it?

is required in order to explain the univocality of 'CAUSE' across fields, then presumably there's got to be a '*Y*' whose univocality explains the univocality of '*X*' across fields. From there it's turtles all the way up.

But the second route is equally embarrassing since it tacitly admits that you don't, after all, need to assume that a word (/concept) has a definition in order to explain its being univocal across semantic fields; 'CAUSE' would be a case to the contrary. But if that is admitted, then how does the fact that 'keep' is univocal across semantic fields argue that 'keep' has a definition? Why not just say that 'keep' is univocal because it always means *keep*; just as, in order to avoid the regress, Jackendoff is required to say that 'CAUSE' is univocal because it always means *cause*. Or, quite generally, why not just say that *all* words are univocal across semantic fields because semantic fields don't affect meaning. This 'explanation' is, of course, utterly empty; for all words to be univocal across semantic fields *just is* for semantic fields not to affect meaning. But Jackendoff's 'explanation' is empty too, and for the same reason. As between "'keep' is univocal because it is field invariant' and "'keep' is univocal *because its definition* is field invariant' there is, quite simply, nothing to choose.

In short: Suppose 'CAUSE' is *ambiguous* from field to field; then the fact that 'keep' always entails 'CAUSE' is not sufficient to make 'keep' univocal from field to field. Well then, suppose 'CAUSE' is *univocal* from field to field; then the fact that 'keep' (like 'CAUSE') occurs in many different fields doesn't explain its intuitive polysemy. Either way, Jackendoff loses.

A recent letter from Jackendoff suggests, however, that he has yet a third alternative in mind: "I'm not claiming", he writes, "that keep is univocal, nor that cause is. Rather, the semantic field feature varies among fields, the rest remaining constant. AND THE REST IS ABSTRACT AND CANNOT BE EXPRESSED LINGUISTICALLY, BECAUSE YOU HAVE TO CHOOSE A FIELD FEATURE TO SAY ANY-THING" (*sic*; Jackendoff's caps. Personal communication, 1996). This suggestion strikes me as doubly ill-advised. In the first place, there is no obvious reason why its being "abstract", ineffable, and so on, should make a concept univocal (/field invariant); why shouldn't abstract, ineffable concepts be polysemic, just like concrete concepts that can be effed? Unless Jackendoff has an answer to this, he's back in the old bind: 'CAUSE' is field invariant only by stipulation. Secondly, this move leaves Jackendoff open to a charge of seriously false advertising. For it now turns out that 'cause a state that endures over time' doesn't really express the definition of 'keep' after all: 'Keep' means something that can't be said. A less misleading definition than the one Jackendoff offers might thus be "'keep' means @#&$(*]', which has the virtue of not even *appearing* to say anything. The same, *mutatis mutandis*, for the rest of English, of course, so lexical semantics, as Jackendoff understands it, ends in silence. The methodological moral is, surely, Frank Ramsey's: 'What can't be said can't be said, and it can't be whistled either.'

I should add that Jackendoff sometimes writes as though all accounts that agree that keeping is a kind of causing are *ipso facto* "notational variants" of the definition theory. (I suppose this means that they are also *ipso facto* notational variants of the non-definitional theory, since the relation *notational variant of* is presumably symmetrical.) But I would have thought that the present disagreement is not primarily about whether keeping is a kind of causing; it's about whether, if it is, it follows that sentences with 'keep' in their surface structures have 'CAUSE' in their semantic representations. This inference is, to put it mildly, not trivial since the conclusion entails that the meaning of 'keep' is structurally complex, while the premise is compatible with 'keep' being an atom. (By the way, what exactly *is* a notational variant?)

The moral of this long polemic is, I'm afraid, actually not very interesting. Jackendoff's argument that there are definitions is circular, and circular arguments are disreputable. To the best of my knowledge, all extant arguments that there are definitions are disreputable.

Auntie: Anyone can criticize. Nice people try to be constructive. We've heard a very great deal from you of 'I don't like this' and 'I think that won't work'. Why don't you tell us *your* theory about why 'keep' is intuitively polysemic?

—: Because you won't like it. Because you'll say it's silly and frivolous and shallow.

Auntie: I think you don't have a theory about why 'keep' is intuitively polysemic.

—: Yes I do, yes I do, yes I do! Sort of.

My theory is that there is no such thing as polysemy. The appearance that there is a problem is generated by the assumption that there are definitions; if you take the assumption away, the problem disappears. As they might have said in the '60s: definitions don't *solve* the problem of polysemy; definitions *are* the problem of polysemy.

Auntie: I don't understand a word of that. And I didn't like the '60s.

—: Well, here's a way to put it. Jackendoff's treatment of the difference between, say, 'NP kept the money' and 'NP kept the crowd happy' holds that, in some sense or other, 'keep' means different things in the two sentences. There is, surely, another alternative; viz. to say that 'keep' means the same thing in both—it expresses the same relation—but that, in one case, the relation it expresses holds between NP and the crowd's being happy, and in the other case it holds between NP and the money. Since, on anybody's story, the money and the crowd's being happy are quite different sorts of things, why do we also need a difference between the meanings of 'keep' to explain what's going on in the examples?

People sometimes used to say that 'exist' must be ambiguous because look at the difference between 'chairs exist' and 'numbers exist'. A familiar reply goes: the difference between the existence of chairs and the existence of numbers seems, on reflection, strikingly like the difference between numbers and chairs. Since you have the latter to explain the former, you don't also need 'exist' to be polysemic.

This reply strikes me as convincing, but the fallacy that it exposes dies awfully hard. For example, Steven Pinker (personal communication, 1996) has argued that 'keep' can't be univocal because it implies possession in sentences like J2 but not in sentences like J3. I think Pinker is right that 'Susan kept the money' entails that something was possessed and that 'Sam kept the crowd happy' doesn't. But (here we go again) it just begs the question to assume that this difference arises from a polysemy in 'keep'.

For example: maybe 'keep' has an underlying complement in sentences like (2) and (3); so that, roughly, 'Susan kept the money' is a variant of *Susan kept having the money* and 'John kept the crowd happy' is a variant of *John kept the crowd being happy*. Then the implication of possession in the former doesn't derive from 'keep' after all; rather, it's contributed by material in the underlying complement clause. On reflection, the difference between keeping the money and keeping the crowd happy does seem strikingly like the difference between *having* the money and the crowd *being* happy, a fact that the semantics of (2) and (3) might reasonably be expected to capture. This modest analysis posits no structure inside lexical items, and it stays pretty close to surface form. I wouldn't want to claim that it's apodictic, but it does avoid the proliferation of lexical polysemes and/or semantic fields and it's quite compatible with the claim that 'keep' means neither more nor less than *keep* in all of the examples under consideration.[10]

Auntie: Fiddlesticks. Consider the case where language *A* has a single unambiguous word, of which the translation in language *B* is either of two words, depending on context. Everybody who knows anything knows that happens all the time. Whenever it does, the language-*A* word is *ipso*

---

[10] Fodor and Lepore (forthcoming *a*) provides some independent evidence for the analysis proposed here. Suppose, however, that this horse won't run, and the asymmetry Pinker points to really does show that 'keep' is polysemous. That would be no comfort to Jackendoff, since Jackendoff's account of the polysemy doesn't predict the asymmetry of entailments either: that J2 but not J3 belongs to the semantic field "possession" in Jackendoff's analysis is pure stipulation.

But I won't stress this. Auntie says I should swear off ad hominems.

facto polysemous. If you weren't so embarrassingly monolingual, you'd have noticed this for yourself. (As it is, I'm indebted to Luca Bonatti for raising the point.)

—: No. Suppose English has two words, 'spoiled' and 'addled,' both of which mean *spoiled*, but one of which is used only of eggs. Suppose also that there is some other language which has a word 'spoilissimoed' which means *spoiled* and is used both of spoiled eggs and of other spoiled things. The right way to describe this situation is surely *not* that 'spoiled' is *ipso facto* polysemous. Rather the thing to say is: 'spoiled' and 'addled' are synonyms and are (thus) *both* correctly translated 'spoilissimoed'. The difference between the languages is that one, but not the other, has a word that means *spoiled* and is context restricted to eggs; hence one language, but not the other, has a word for *being spoiled* whose possession condition includes having the concept EGG. This is another reason for distinguishing questions about meaning from questions about possession conditions (in case another reason is required. Remember WATER and H_2O).

Auntie (*who has been catching a brief nap during the preceding expository passage*) *wakes with a start*: Now I've got you. You say 'keep' is univocal. Well, then, what is the relation that it univocally expresses? What is the relation such that, according to you, Susan bears it to the money in J2 and Sam bears it to the crowd's being happy in J3?

—: I'm afraid you aren't going to like this.

Auntie: Try me.

—: It's (sigh!) *keeping*. (Cf: "What *is it* that "exist" expresses in both 'numbers exist' and 'chairs exist'?" Reply: "It's (sigh!) *existing*.")

In effect, what I'm selling is a *disquotational* lexicon. Not, however, because I think semantic facts are, somehow, merely pleonastic; but rather because I take semantic facts with full ontological seriousness, and I can't think of a better way to say what 'keep' means than to say that it means *keep*. If, as I suppose, the concept KEEP is an atom, it's hardly surprising that there's no better way to say what 'keep' means than to say that it means *keep*.

I know of no reason, empirical or a priori, to suppose that the expressive power of English can be captured in a language whose stock of morphologically primitive expressions is interestingly smaller than the lexicon of English. To be sure, if you are committed to 'keep' being definable, and to its having the same definition in each semantic field, then you will have to face the task of saying, in words other than 'keep', what relation it is that keeping the money and keeping the crowd happy both instance. But, I would have thought, saying what relation they both instance is precisely what the word 'keep' is for; why on earth do you suppose that you *can* say it 'in other words'? I repeat: assuming that 'keep' has a definition is what makes the problem about polysemy; take away that assumption and 'what do keeping the money and keeping the crowd happy share?' is easy. They're both *keeping*.

Auntie: I think that's silly, frivolous, and shallow! There is no such thing as keeping; there isn't anything that keeping the money and keeping the crowd happy share. It's all just made up.[11]

—: Strictly speaking, that view isn't available to Aunties who wish also to claim that 'keep' has a definition that is satisfied in all of its semantic fields; by definition, such a definition would express something that keeping money and keeping crowds happy have in common. Still, I do sort of agree that ontology is at the bottom of the pile. I reserve comment till the last two chapters.

Pinker

There is, as I remarked at the outset, a very substantial linguistic literature on lexical semantics; far more than I have the space or inclination to review. But something needs to be said, before we call it quits, about a sustained attempt that Steven Pinker has been making (Pinker 1984; 1989) to co-opt the apparatus of lexical semantics for employment in a theory of how children learn aspects of syntax. If this project can be carried through, it might produce the kind of reasonably unequivocal support for definitional analysis that I claim that the considerations about polysemy fail to provide.

Pinker offers, in fact, two kinds of ontogenetic arguments for definitions; the one in Pinker 1984 depends on a "semantic bootstrapping" theory of syntax acquisition; the one in Pinker 1989, turns on an analysis

---

[11] Auntie's not the only one with this grumble; Hilary Putnam has recently voiced a generalized version of the same complaint. "[O]n Fodor's theory . . . the *meaning* of . . . words is not determined, even in part, by the conceptual relations among the various notions I have mastered—e.g., between 'minute' and my other time concepts—but depends *only* on 'nomic relations' between the words (e.g. minute) and the corresponding universals (e.g. minutehood). These 'universals' are just word-shaped objects which Fodor's metaphysics projects out into the world for the words to latch on to via mysterious 'nomic relations'; the whole story is nothing but a 'naturalistic' version of the Museum Myth of Meaning" (1995: 79; italics and scare-quotes are Putnam's). This does seem to me to be a little underspecified. Since Putnam provides no further exposition (and, endearingly, no arguments at all), I'm not sure whether I'm supposed to worry that there aren't *any* universals, or only that there aren't the universals that my semantics requires. But if Putnam thinks saying "'takes a minute' expresses the property of *taking a minute*" all by itself puts me in debt for a general refutation of nominalism, then he needs to have his methodology examined.

Still, it's right that informational semantics needs an ontology, and that the one it opts for had better not beg the questions that a semantic theory is supposed to answer. I'll have a lot to say about all that in Chapters 6 and 7.

of a problem in learnability theory known as "Baker's Paradox". Both arguments exploit rather deep assumptions about the architecture of theories of language development, and both have been influential; sufficiently so to justify taking a detailed look at them. Most of the rest of this chapter will be devoted to doing that.

The Bootstrapping Argument

A basic idea of Pinker's is that some of the child's knowledge of syntactic structure is "bootstrapped" from knowledge about the semantic properties of lexical items; in particular, from knowledge about the semantic structure of verbs. The details are complicated but the outline is clear enough. In the simplest sorts of sentences (like 'John runs', for example), if you can figure out what syntactic classes the words belong to (that 'John' is a noun and 'runs' is an intransitive verb) you get the rest of the syntax of the sentence more or less for free: intransitive verbs have to have NPs as subjects, and 'John' is the only candidate around.

This sort of consideration suggests that a significant part of the child's problem of breaking into sentential syntax is identifying the syntax of lexical items. So far so good. Except that it's not obvious how properties like being a noun or being an intransitive verb might signal their presence in the learner's input since they aren't, in general, marked by features of the data that the child can unquestion-beggingly be supposed to pick up. There aren't, for example, any acoustic or phonetic properties that are characteristic of nouns as such or of verbs as such.

The problem with almost every nonsemantic property that I have heard proposed as inductive bases [*sic*] is that the property is itself defined over configurations . . . that are not part of the child's input, that themselves have to be learned . . . [By contrast] how the child comes to know such things, which are not marked explicitly in the input stream, is precisely what the semantic bootstrapping hypothesis is designed to explain. (Pinker 1984: 51)

Here's how the explanation goes. Though (by assumption) the child can't detect being a noun, being a verb, being an adjective, etc. in the "input stream", he can (still by assumption) detect such putative reliable semantic correlates of these syntactic properties as being a person or thing, being an action or change of state, and being an attribute. (For more of Pinker's suggested pairings of syntactic properties with their semantic correlates, see 1984: 41, table 2.1.) Thus, "when the child hears 'snails eat leaves,' he or she uses the actionhood of 'eat' to infer that it is a verb, the agenthood of 'snails' to infer that it plays the role of subject, and so on" (ibid.: 53). In effect, the semantic analysis of the input sentence is supposed somehow to be perceptually given; and the correspondence between such semantic features as *expressing a property* and such syntactic features as *being an adjective* are assumed to be universal. Using the two together provides the child with his entering wedge.

Now, prima facie at very least, this seems to be a compact example of two bad habits that lexical semanticists are prone to: kicking the problem upstairs ('How does the child detect whatever property it is that 'attribute' denotes?' replaces 'How does the child detect whatever property it is that 'adjective' denotes?'); and a partiality for analyses that need more analysis than their analysands. One sort of knows what an adjective is, I guess. But God only knows what's an attribute, so God only knows what it is for a term to express one.

The point isn't that 'attribute' isn't well defined; I suppose theoretical terms typically aren't. Rather, the worry is that Pinker has maybe got the cart before the horse; perhaps the intuition that 'red' and '12' both express "attributes" (the first of, as it might be, hens (cf. 'red hens'), and the second of, as it might be, sets (cf. 'twelve hens')) isn't really semantical at all; perhaps it's just a hypostatic misconstrual of the syntactic fact that both words occur as modifiers of nouns.[12] It's undeniable that 'red' and 'twelve' are more alike than, as it might be, 'red' and 'of'. But it's a fair question whether their similarity is semantic or whether it consists just in the similarity of their syntactic distributions. Answering these questions in the way that Pinker wants us to (viz. 'Yes' to the first, 'No' to the second) depends on actually cashing notions like object, attribute, agent, and the rest; on saying what exactly it is that the semantics of two words have in common in so far as both words 'denote attributes'. So far, however, there is nothing on offer. Rather, at this point in the discussion, Pinker issues a kind of disclaimer that one finds very often in the lexical semantics literature: "I beg the thorny question as to the proper definition of the various semantic terms I appeal to such as 'agent,' 'physical object', and the like" (ibid.: 371 n. 12). Note the tactical similarity to Jackendoff, who, as we've seen, says that 'keep' means CAUSE A STATE TO ENDURE, but is unprepared to say much about what 'CAUSE A STATE TO ENDURE' means (except that it's ineffable).

Digression on method. You might suppose that in "begging the thorny question", Pinker is merely exercising a theorist's indisputable right not to

---

[12] For an account of language acquisition in which the horse and cart are assigned the opposite configuration—syntax bootstraps semantics—see Gleitman 1990. To the extent that we have some grasp on what concepts terms like 'S', 'NP', 'ADJ' express, the theory that children learn by syntactic boostrapping is at least better defined than Pinker's. (And to the extent that we don't, it's not.)

provide a formal account of the semantics of the (meta)language in which he does his theorizing. But that would misconstrue the logic of intentional explanations. When Pinker says that the child represents the snail as an agent, 'agent' isn't just a term of art that's being used to express a concept of the theorist's; it's also, simultaneously, being used to express a concept that the theorist is attributing *to the child*. It serves as part of a de dicto characterization of the intentional content of the *child*'s state of mind, and the burden of the theory is that it's the child's being in a state of mind with *that* content that explains the behavioural data. In this context, to refuse to say *what state of mind* it is that's being attributed to the child simply vitiates the explanation. Lacking some serious account of what 'agent' means, Pinker's story and the following are closely analogous:

—Why did Martha pour water over George?
—Because she thinks that *George is flurg*.
—What do you mean, *George is flurg*?
—I beg that thorny question.

If a physicist explains some phenomenon by saying 'blah, blah, blah, because it was a proton . . .', *being a word that means proton* is not a property his explanation appeals to (though, of course, *being a proton* is). That, basically, is *why* it is not part of the physicist's responsibility to provide a linguistic theory (e.g. a semantics) for 'proton'. But the intentional sciences are different. When a psychologist says 'blah, blah, blah, because the child represents the snail as an agent . . .', the property of *being an agent-representation* (viz. *being a symbol that means agent*) is appealed to in the explanation, and the psychologist owes an account of what property that is. The physicist is responsible for *being a proton* but not for *being a proton-concept*; the psychologist is responsible for *being an agent-concept* but not for *being an agent-concept-ascription*. Both the physicist and the psychologist is required to theorize about the properties he ascribes, and neither is required to theorize about the properties of the language he uses to ascribe them. The difference is that the psychologist is working one level up. I think confusion on this point is simply rampant in linguistic semantics. It explains why the practice of 'kicking semantic problems upstairs' is so characteristic of the genre.

We've encountered this methodological issue before, and will encounter it again. I do hate to go on about it, but dodging the questions about the individuation of semantic features (in particular, about what semantic features denote) lets lexical semanticists play with a stacked deck. If the examples work, they count them for their theory. If they don't work, they count them as metaphorical extensions. I propose that we spend a couple of pages seeing how an analysis of this sort plays out.

Consider the following, chosen practically at random. It's a sketch of Pinker's account of how the fact that a verb has the syntactic property of being 'dativizable' (of figuring in alternations like 'give Mary a book'/'give a book to Mary') can be inferred from the child's data about the semantics of the verb.

> Dativizable verbs have a semantic property in common: they must be capable of denoting prospective possession of the referent of the second object by the referent of the first object . . . [But] possession need not be literal . . . [V]erbs of communication are treated as denoting the transfer of messages or stimuli, which the recipient metaphorically possesses. This can be seen in sentences such as 'He told her the story,' 'He asked her a question,' and 'She showed him the answer' [all of which have moved datives]. (Pinker 1989: 48)

What exactly Pinker is claiming here depends quite a lot on what relation "prospective possession" is, and on what is allowed as a metaphor for that relation; and, of course, we aren't told either. If John sang Mary a song, does Mary metaphorically prospectively possess the song that John sang to her? If so, does she also metaphorically prospectively possess a goodnight in "John wished Mary a goodnight?" Or consider:

> Zen told his story to the judge/Zen told the judge his story

but

> Zen repeated his story to the judge/*Zen repeated the judge his story.

I *think* this is a counter-example to Pinker's theory about datives. Could the difference really be that the judge was a prospective possessor of the story when Zen told it the first time, but not when he repeated it? On the other hand, since who knows what prospective possession is, or what might express it metaphorically, who knows whether such cases refute the analysis?

Or consider:

> John showed his etchings to Mary/John showed Mary his etchings.

but

> John exhibited his etchings to Mary/*John exhibited Mary his etchings.

Is it that Mary is in metaphorical possession of etchings that are shown to her but not of etchings that are exhibited to her? How is one to tell? More to the point, *how is the child to tell*? Remember that, according to Pinker's story, the child figures out that 'exhibit' doesn't dative-move when he decides that it doesn't—even metaphorically—express prospective possession. But how on earth does he decide that?[13]

I should emphasize that Pinker is explicitly aware that there are egregious exceptions to his semantic characterization of the constraints on dative movement, nor does he suppose that appeals to "metaphorical possession" and the like can always be relied on to get him off the hook. At least one of the things that he thinks is going on with the double-object construction is a *morphological* constraint on dative movement: polysyllabic verbs tend to resist it (notice show/*exhibit; tell/*repeat in the examples above). But though Pinker remarks upon the existence of such non-semantic constraints, he appears not to see how much trouble they make for his view.

Remember the architecture of Pinker's argument. What's on offer is an inference from ontogenetic considerations to the conclusion that there are definitions. What shows that there are definitions is that there is a semantic level of linguistic representation at which verbs are lexically decomposed. What shows that there are semantic-level representations is that you need semantic vocabulary to formulate the hypotheses that the child projects in the course of learning the lexicon; and that's because, according to Pinker, these hypotheses express correlations between certain semantic properties of lexical items, on the one hand, and the grammatical structures that the items occur in, on the other. Double-object constructions, as we've seen, are supposed to be paradigms.

But it now appears that the vocabulary required to specify the conditions on such constructions isn't *purely* semantic after all; not even according to Pinker. To predict whether a verb permits dative movement,

---

[13] When Pinker's analyses are clear enough to evaluate, they are often just wrong. For example, he notes in his discussion of causatives that the analysis $PAINT_{VTR}$ = *cover with paint* is embarrassed by such observations as this: although when Michelangelo dipped his paintbrush in his paint pot he thereby covered the paintbrush with paint, nevertheless he did not, thereby, paint the paintbrush. (The example is, in fact, borrowed from Fodor 1970.) Pinker explains that "stereotypy or conventionality of manner constrains the causative . . . This might be called the 'stereotypy effect'" (1984: 324). So it might, for all the good it does. It is possible, *faut de mieux*, to paint the wall with one's handkerchief; with one's bare hands; by covering oneself with paint and rolling up the wall (in which last case, by the way, though covering the wall with the paint counts as painting the wall, covering oneself with the paint does not count as painting oneself even if one does it with a paintbrush; only as getting oneself covered with paint).

Whether you paint the wall when you cover it with paint depends not on how you do it but on what you have in mind when you do it: you have to have in mind not merely to cover the wall with paint but to paint the wall. That is, "$paint_{vtr}$" apparently can't be defined even in terms of such closely related expressions as "$paint_n$". Or, if it can, none of the decompositional analyses suggested so far, Pinker's included, comes even close to showing how.

you need to know *not only* whether it expresses (literally or metaphorically) 'prospective possession', but also the pertinent facts about its morphology. What account of the representation of lexical structure does this observation imply? The point to notice is that there isn't, on *anybody's* story, any *one* level of representation that specifies both the semantic *and* the morphological features of a lexical item. In particular, it's a defining property of the (putative) semantic level that it *abstracts from* the sorts of (morphological, phonological, syntactic, etc.) properties that distinguish between synonyms. For example, the semantic level is supposed *not* to distinguish the representation of (e.g.) "bachelor" from the representation of "unmarried man", the representation of "kill" from the representation of "cause to die", and so forth.

Well, if that's what the semantic level is, and if the facts about morphological constraints on double-object structures are as we (and Pinker) are supposing them to be, then the moral is that there is *no* level of linguistic representation at which the constraints on dative movement can be expressed: not the morphological level because (assuming that Pinker's story about "prospective possession" is true) morphological representation abstracts from the semantic properties on which dative movement is contingent. And, precisely analogously, *not the semantic level* because semantic level representation abstracts from the morphological properties of lexical items on which dative movement is also contingent.

Time to pull this all together and see where the argument has gotten. Since heaven only knows what "prospective possession" is, there's no seriously evaluating the claim that dative movement turns on whether a verb expresses it. What does seem clear, however, is that even if there are semantic constraints on the syntactic behaviour of double-object verbs, there are also morphological constraints on their syntactic behaviour. So to state such generalizations at a single linguistic level, you would need to postulate not *semantic* representations but *morpho*semantic representations. It is, however, common ground that there is no level of representation in whose vocabulary morphological and semantic constraints can be simultaneously imposed.

This isn't a paradox; it is perfectly possible to formulate conditions that depend, simultaneously, on semantic and morphological properties of lexical items without assuming that there is a semantic level (and, for that matter, without assuming that there is a morphological level either). The way to do so is to suppose that lexical entries specify *semantic features* of lexical items.

Linguistic discussions of lexical semantics just about invariably confuse two questions we are now in a position to distinguish: *Are there semantic features?* and *Is there a semantic level?* It is, however, important to keep these questions distinct if you care about the structure of concepts. It's especially important if what you care about is whether "kill", "eat", and the like have definitions; i.e. whether KILL, EAT, and the like are complex concepts or conceptual primitives. To say, in the present context, that there are semantic *features* is just to say that semantic facts can have syntactic reflexes: what an expression means (partially) determines the contexts in which it is syntactically well-formed. To say that there is a semantic *level* is to make a very much stronger claim: viz. that there is a level of representation at which *only* the semantic properties of expressions are specified, *hence at which synonymous expressions get the same representations*, hence at which the surface integrity of lexical items is not preserved. I am, as no doubt the reader will have gathered, much inclined to deny *both* these claims; but never mind that for now. My present concern is just to emphasize the importance of the difference between them.

For many of the familiar tenets of lexical semantics flow from the stronger claim *but not from the weaker one*. For example, since everybody thinks that the concepts expressed by *phrases* are typically complex, and since, by definition, representations at the semantic level abstract from the lexical and syntactic properties that distinguish phrases from their lexical synonyms, it follows that if there is a semantic level, then the concepts expressed by single words are often complex too. However, this conclusion does *not* follow from the weaker assumption: viz. that lexical entries contain semantic features. Linguistic features can perfectly well attach to a lexical item that is none the less primitive at *every* level of linguistic description.[14] And it's only the weaker assumption that the facts about dative movement and the like support, since the most these data show is that the syntactic behaviour of lexical items is determined by their semantics *inter alia*; e.g. by their semantic features together with their morphology. So Pinker's argument for definitions doesn't work *even on the assumption that 'denotes a prospective possession' and the like are bona fide semantic representations*.

THE MORAL: AN ARGUMENT FOR LEXICAL SEMANTIC FEATURES IS NOT IPSO FACTO *AN ARGUMENT THAT THERE IS LEXICAL SEMANTIC DECOMPOSITION!!!* Pardon me if I seem to shout; but people do keep getting this wrong, and it does make a litter of the landscape.

---

[14] Compare: no doubt, the lexical entry for 'boy' includes the syntactic feature +Noun. This is *entirely* compatible with 'boy' being a lexical primitive at *every level* of linguistic description.

Saying that lexical items *have features* is one thing; saying that lexical items *are feature bundles* is quite another. *Do not conflate these claims.*

Well, but has Pinker made good even the weaker claim? Suppose we believe the semantic bootstrapping story about language learning; and suppose we pretend to understand notions like *prospective possession*, *attribute*, and the like; and suppose we assume that these are, as it were, really semantic properties and not mere shadows of distributional facts about the words that express them; and suppose we take for granted the child's capacity for finding such semantic properties in his input; and suppose that the question we care about is *not* whether there's a semantic level, but just whether the mental lexicon (ever) represents semantic features of lexical items. Supposing all of this, is there at least a bootstrapping argument that, for example, part of the lexical entry for 'eat' includes the semantic feature ACTION.

Well, no. Semantic bootstrapping, even if it really is semantic, doesn't require that lexical entries ever specify semantic properties. For even if the child uses the knowledge that 'eat' denotes an action to bootstrap the syntax of 'snails eat leaves', it doesn't follow that "denoting an action" is a property that "eat" has in virtue of what it *means*. All that follows— hence all the child needs to know in order to bootstrap—is that 'eat' denotes eating and that eating is a kind of acting. (I'm indebted to Eric Margolis for this point.) Indeed, mere *reliability* of the connection between eating and acting would do perfectly well for the child's purposes; "semantic bootstrapping" does not require the child to take the connection to be semantic or even *necessary*. The three-year-old who thinks (perhaps out of Quinean scruples) that 'eating is acting' is true but contingent will do just fine, so long as he's prepared to allow that contingent truths can have syntactic reflexes.

So much for the bootstrapping argument. I really must stop this grumbling about lexical semantics. And I will, except for a brief, concluding discussion of Pinker's handling of (what he calls) 'Baker's Paradox' (after Baker 1979). This too amounts to a claim that ontogenetic theory needs lexical semantic representations; but it makes quite a different sort of case from the one we've just been looking at.

The 'Baker's Paradox' Argument

Pinker thinks that, unless children are assumed to represent 'eat' as an action verb (*mutatis mutandis*, 'give' as a verb of prospective possession, etc.). Baker's Paradox will arise and make the acquisition of lexical syntax unintelligible. I'll tell you what Baker's Paradox is in a moment, but I want to tell you what I think the bottom line is first. I think that Baker's Paradox is a red herring in the present context. In fact, I think that it's two red herrings: on Pinker's own empirical assumptions, there probably isn't a

Baker's Paradox about learning the lexicon; and, anyhow, assuming that there is one provides no argument that lexical items have semantic structure. Both of these points are about to emerge.

Baker's Paradox, as Pinker understands it, is a knot of problems that turn on the (apparent) fact that children (do or can) learn the lexical syntax of their language without much in the way of overt parental correction. Pinker discerns, "three aspects of the problem [that] give it its sense of paradox", these being the child's lack of negative evidence, the productivity of the structures the child learns ("if children simply stuck with the argument structures that were exemplified in parental speech . . . they would never make errors . . . and hence would have no need to figure out how to avoid or expunge them"), and the "arbitrariness" of the linguistic phenomena that the child is faced with (specifically "near synonyms [may] have different argument structures" (1989: 8–9)). If, for example, the rule of dative movement is productive, and if it is merely arbitrary that you can say 'John gave the library the book' but not *'John donated the library the book', how, except by being corrected, could the child learn that the one is OK and the other is not?

That's a good question, to be sure; but it bears full stress that the three components do not, as stated and by themselves, make Baker's Paradox paradoxical. The problem is an unclarity in Pinker's claim that the rules the child is acquiring are 'productive'. If this means (as it usually does in linguistics) just that the rules are general (they aren't mere lists; they go 'beyond the child's data') then we get no paradox but just a standard sort of induction problem: the child learns more than the input shows him, and something has to fill the gap. To get a paradox, you have to throw in the assumption that, by and large, children don't overgeneralize; i.e. that, by and large, they don't apply the productive rules they're learning to license usages that count as mistaken by adult standards. For suppose that assumption is untrue and the child does overgeneralize. Then, on *anybody's* account, there would have to be some form of correction mechanism in play, endogenous or otherwise, that serves to expunge the child's errors. Determining what mechanism(s) it is that serve(s) this function would, of course, be of considerable interest; especially on the assumption that it isn't parental correction. But so long as the child *does something* that shows the world that he's got the wrong rule, there is nothing paradoxical in the fact that information the world provides ensures that he eventually converges on the right one.

To repeat, Baker's Paradox is a paradox only if you add 'no over-generalizations' to Pinker's list. The debilitated form of Baker's Paradox that you get without this further premiss fails to do what Pinker very much wants Baker's Paradox to do; viz. "[take] the burden of explaining learning out of the environmental input and [put] it back into the child" (1989: 14–15). Only if the child does not overgeneralize lexical categories is there evidence for his "differentiating [them] *a priori*" (ibid.: 44, my emphasis); viz. prior to environmentally provided information.

Pinker's argument is therefore straightforwardly missing a premiss. The logical slip seems egregious, but Pinker really does make it, as far as I can tell. Consider:

[Since there is empirical evidence against the child's having negative information, and there is empirical evidence for the child's rules being productive,] the only way out of Baker's Paradox that's left is . . . rejecting arbitrariness. Perhaps the verbs that do or don't participate in these alterations do not belong to arbitrary lists after all . . . [Perhaps, in particular, these classes are specifiable by reference to semantic criteria.] . . . If learners could acquire and enforce criteria delineating the[se] . . . classes of verbs, they could productively generalize an alternation to verbs that meet the criteria without overgeneralizing it to those that do not. (ibid.: 30)

Precisely so. If, as Pinker's theory claims, the lexical facts are non-arbitrary and children are sensitive to their non-arbitrariness, then the right prediction is that *children don't overgeneralize the lexical rules.*

Which, however, by practically everybody's testimony, including Pinker's, children reliably do. On Pinker's own account, children aren't "conservative" in respect of the lexicon (see 1989: 19–26, sec. 1.4.4.1 for lots and lots of cases).[15] This being so, there's got to be something wrong with the theory that the child's hypotheses "differentiate" lexical classes a priori. A priori constraints would mean that false hypotheses *don't even get tried.* Overgeneralization, by contrast, means that false hypotheses do get tried but are somehow expunged (presumably by some sort of information that the environment supplies).

At one point, Pinker almost 'fesses up to this. The heart of his strategy for lexical learning is that "if the verbs that occur in both forms have some [e.g. semantic] property . . . that is missing in the verbs that occur [in the input data] in only one form, bifurcate the verbs . . . so as to expunge nonwitnessed verb forms generated by the earlier unconstrained version of the rule if they violate the newly learned constraint" (1989: 52). Pinker admits that this may "appear to be using a kind of indirect negative evidence: it is sensitive to the nonoccurrence of certain kinds of verbs". To be sure; it sounds an awful lot like saying that there is no Baker's Paradox for the learning of verb structure, hence no argument for a priori semantic

---

[15] Though the facts are a little labile, to be sure. For some recent data, see Marcus *et al.* 1992.

constraints on the child's hypotheses about lexical syntax. What happens, on this view, is that the child overgeneralizes, just as you would expect, but the overgeneralizations are inhibited by lack of positive supporting evidence from the linguistic environment and, for this reason, they eventually fade away. This would seem to be a perfectly straightforward case of environmentally determined learning, albeit one that emphasizes (as one might have said in the old days) 'lack of reward' rather than 'punishment' as the signal that the environment uses to transmit negative data to the learner. I'm not, of course, suggesting that this sort of story is right. (Indeed Pinker provides a good discussion of why it probably isn't, see section 1.4.3.2.) My point is that Pinker's own account seems to be no more than a case of it. *What is crucial to Pinker's solution of Baker's Paradox isn't that he abandons arbitrariness; it's that he abandons 'no negative data'.*

Understandably, Pinker resists this diagnosis. The passage cited above continues as follows:

This procedure might appear to be using a kind of indirect negative evidence; it is sensitive to the nonoccurrence of certain kinds of forms. It does so, though, only in the uninteresting sense of acting differently depending on whether it hears X or doesn't hear X, which is true of virtually any learning algorithm . . . It is not sensitive to the nonoccurrence of particular sentences or even verb-argument structure combinations in parental speech; rather it is several layers removed from the input, looking at broad statistical patterns across the lexicon. (1989: 52)

I don't, however, think this comes to anything much. In the first place, it's not true (in any unquestion-begging sense) that "virtually any learning algorithm [acts] differently depending on whether it hears X or doesn't hear X". To the contrary, it's a way of putting the productivity problem that the learning algorithm must somehow converge on treating infinitely many *un*heard types in the same way that it treats finitely many of the *heard* types (viz. as grammatical) and finitely many heard types in the same way that it treats a different infinity of the unheard ones (viz. as ungrammatical). To that extent, the algorithm must not assume that either being heard or not being heard is a projectible property of the types.

On the other hand, every treatment of learning that depends on the feedback of evidence at all (whether it supposes the evidence to be direct or indirect, negative or positive, or all four) must "be several layers removed from the input, looking at broad statistical patterns across the lexicon"; otherwise the presumed feedback won't generalize. It follows that, on *anybody's* account, the negative information that the environment provides can't be "the nonoccurrence of *particular* sentences" (my emphasis); it's got to be the non-occurrence of certain *kinds* of sentences.

This much is common ground to any learning theory that accounts for the productivity of what is learned.

Were we've gotten to now: probably there isn't a Baker's Paradox about lexical syntax; you'd need 'no overgeneralization' to get one, and 'no overgeneralization' is apparently false of the lexicon. Even if, however, there were a Baker's Paradox about the lexicon, that would show that the hypotheses that the child considers when he makes his lexical inductions must be tightly endogenously constrained. But it wouldn't show, or even suggest, that they are hypotheses about semantic properties of lexical items. No more than the existence of a bona fide Baker's Paradox for *sentential* syntax—which it does seem that children hardly ever over-generalize—shows, or even suggests, that it's in terms of the semantic pro-perties of sentences that the child's hypotheses about their syntax are defined.

So much for Pinker's two attempts at ontogenetic vindications of lexical semantics. Though neither seems to work at all, I should emphasize a difference between them: whereas the 'Baker's Paradox' argument dissolves upon examination, there's nothing wrong with the *form* of the bootstrapping argument. For all that I've said, it could still be true that lexical syntax is bootstrapped from lexical semantics. Making a convincing case that it is would require, at a minimum, identifying the straps that the child tugs and showing that they are bona fide semantic; specifically, it would require showing that the lexical properties over which the child generalizes are typically among the ones that semantic-level lexical representations specify. In principle, we could get a respectable argument of that form tomorrow; it's just that, so far, there aren't any. So too, in my view, with the other 'empirical' or 'linguistic' arguments for lexical decomposition; all that's wrong with them is that they aren't sound.

Oh, well, so be it. Let's go see what the philosophers have.

4

The Demise of Definitions, Part II: The Philosopher's Tale

[A] little thing affects them. A slight disorder of the stomach makes them cheats. [They] may be an undigested bit of beef, a blot of mustard, a crumb of cheese, a fragment of underdone potato.

—Scrooge

IT's a sad truth about definitions that even their warm admirers rarely loved them for themselves alone. Cognitive scientists (other than linguists; see Chapter 3) cared about definitions because they offered a handy construal of the thesis that many concepts are complex; viz. *the concepts in a definition are the constituents of the concept it defines.* And cognitive scientists liked many concepts being complex because then many concepts could be learned by assembling them from their parts. And cognitive scientists liked many concepts being learned by assembling them from their parts because then only the primitive parts have to be *un*learned. We'll see, in later chapters, how qualmlessly most of cognitive science dropped definitions when it realized that it could have complex concepts without them.

Something like that went on in philosophy too. Philosophers cared about definitions because they offered a handy construal of the thesis that inferential connections are sometimes intrinsic to the concepts that enter into them: viz. *complex concepts are constituted by their inferential relations to the concepts in their definitions.* Correspondingly, philosophical affection for definitions waned when intrinsic conceptual connectedness fell into disrepute (as it did in the US in consequence of Quine's strictures on analyticity) and when epistemological construals of intrinsic conceptual connectedness bade fare to displace semantic ones (as they did in the UK in the criteriological philosophy of Wittgenstein and his followers).

Philosophers do like the idea of there being lots of intrinsic connections among concepts; even philosophers who think there aren't any often sort of wish that there were. The idea is that an inference that constitutes the concepts which enter into it can be known a priori to be sound. And inferences that can be known a priori to be sound are prized by philosophers because they are useful for bopping sceptics over the head with. Thus:

> *Sceptic*: You can't ever infer with certainty from how things look to how they are.
>
> *Antisceptic*: Can too, because there is an *intrinsic conceptual connection* between how-things-look concepts and how-things-are concepts (between behaviour-concepts and mind-concepts; between is-concepts and ought-concepts, etc. etc.). Bop. I win.
>
> *Sceptic*: I don't acknowledge such intrinsic connections.
>
> *Antisceptic*: *Then you don't have the concepts!* Bop. I still win.

And even philosophers who don't care much about scepticism sometimes get hooked on intrinsic conceptual connectedness out of their concern for full employment. What else but constitutive connections among concepts is there for a philosophical analysis to be the philosophical analysis of? And, if there are no philosophical analyses, what are analytic philosophers *for*?

In short, when philosophers opt for definitions it's usually less because they're independently convinced that the theory of language or the theory of mind requires them than because constitutive conceptual connectedness seems worth having if buying into definitions is the cost. There may be some other way to get such connections (see Appendix 5A), but definitions are a convenient way, and one which, unlike criteriology, can be scrupulous about keeping epistemology out of semantics.

So, if you're interested in what philosophers have to say that bears on whether concepts are definitions, it's their discussions of conceptual connectedness that are most likely to be relevant. These days, what one often hears listening in on such discussions is some version of the following line of thought:

> —It's right that you can't infer that there are intrinsic conceptual connections simply from the premiss that if there were, they would be useful for antisceptical employment.
>
> —However, Quine's arguments that there are no such connections aren't conclusive; in fact, nobody seems to be able to agree about exactly what Quine's arguments are.
>
> —There is a field of data for the explanation of which the notion of intrinsic conceptual connection appears to be well suited. These data include intuitions that certain propositions are analytic (hence necessary, hence a priori). Paradigms are *no bachelors are married*, *Tuesdays precede Wednesdays*, and so on. There are, as you'd expect,

also the corresponding intuitions about concept *possession*; no one who lacked the concept MARRIED could have the concept BACHELOR; no one who lacked the concept WEEKDAY or the concept WEDNESDAY could have the concept TUESDAY, and so on. This is all as it should be. If a connection between two concepts is constitutive, you can't have the one unless you have the other.

—Given that there are these intuitions, we are justified in appealing to a notion of intrinsic conceptual connectedness as a sort of theoretical posit, even if we can't produce a satisfactory account of such connections cash in hand.

—Maybe whatever explication of *intrinsic conceptual connection* proves, eventually, to account for these intuitions will correspondingly elucidate such notions as *definition*, *analyticity*, *a prioricity*, and the rest. Maybe it will even do some work against sceptics, who knows? Anyhow, since the intuitions are strong and the a priori arguments against analyticity aren't conclusive, it's *not* reasonable to take for granted that there are no intrinsic conceptual connections. And, given the intimate relation between intrinsic conceptual connections and definitions, perhaps we had also better not take for granted that there are none of the latter.

There is quite a lot that one might say here, both on matters of exegesis and on matters of substance. I am, myself, inclined to think it's pretty clear after all how Quine's main argument against analyticity is supposed to run: namely, that nobody has been able to draw a serious and unquestion-begging distinction between conceptual connections that are reliable because they are intrinsic/constitutive and conceptual connections that are reliable although they aren't; and that it would explain the collapse of this project if there were, in fact, no such distinction. Moreover, since I suppose informational semantics to be more or less true, I think we can now see *why* Quine was right about there not being an analytic/synthetic distinction. Informational semantics is atomistic; it denies that the grasp of *any* interconceptual relations is constitutive of concept possession. (More on this below.)

I don't, however, propose to refight these old battles here. Rather, I want to concentrate on the argument that the very fact that we *have* intuitions of analyticity makes a formidable case for there being intrinsic conceptual connections. I am sympathetic to the tactics of this argument. First blush, it surely does seem plausible that *bachelors are unmarried* is a different kind of truth from, as it might be, *it often rains in January*; and it's not implausible, again first blush, that the difference is that the first truth, but not the second, is purely conceptual. I agree, in short, that assuming that they can't be otherwise accounted for, the standard intuitions offer respectable evidence for there being cases of intrinsic conceptual connectedness. Sheer goodness of heart prompts me also to concede the stipulation that if a conceptual connection is *constitutive*, then it constrains concept possession. (Note that it doesn't follow, and that I don't concede, that if a conceptual connection is *necessary* it constrains concept possession. More about this presently too.)

I also agree that the standard deflationary account of analyticity intuitions, viz. Quine's appeal to 'theoretical centrality,' is unpersuasive for many cases. If '$F = MA$' strikes one as true by definition, that *may* be because so much of one's favourite story about the mechanics of middle-sized objects depends on it. But appeal to centrality doesn't seem nearly so persuasive to explain why we're conservative about bachelors being unmarried and Tuesdays coming before Wednesdays. Quite the contrary; if one is inclined to think of these as 'merely' conceptual truths, that's precisely because *nothing* appears to hang on them. It is, to speak with the vulgar, just a matter of what you mean by 'bachelor' and by 'Tuesday'.

So, here's what I take the geography to be: on the one hand, concepts can't be definitions unless some sense can be made of *intrinsic conceptual connection*, *analyticity*, and the like; and there are the familiar Quinean reasons to doubt that any sense can be. But, on the other hand, there are lots of what would seem to be intuitions of intrinsic conceptual connectedness, and that's a prima face argument that perhaps there are intrinsic conceptual connections after all. If there are, then a crucial necessary condition for concepts to be definitions is in place. If there aren't, then what are usually taken to be intuitions of intrinsic conceptual connectedness must really be intuitions of something else and they will have to be explained away. As between these options, you pay your money and you place your bets.

I propose, in the rest of this chapter, to try to explain the intuitions away. I'll sketch an account of them which, like Quine's story about centrality, is loosely epistemic, but which seems to me to work well just where appealing to centrality doesn't. The next to the bottom line will be that *soi-disant* intuitions of conceptual connectedness are perhaps a mixed bag, sometimes to be explained by appealing to centrality, sometimes to be explained by appealing to my Factor X, but rarely, if ever, to be explained by appealing to the constitutive conditions for concept possession. The bottom line will be that the existence of the putative intuitions of analyticity offers no very robust evidence that conceptual connectedness can be made sense of, so probably the Quinean arguments hold good, so probably notions like *definition* can't be sustained, so probably the conclusion that we should draw from the available philosophical evidence is that concepts aren't definitions. Which, according to me, is also the conclusion that we should draw from the available *non*philosophical evidence. Convergence is bliss.

This story I'm about to tell you needs, however, some heavy duty assumptions whose status is itself much in dispute. I propose to set these out in a relatively leisurely and extended way, hoping thereby to illuminate several aspects of conceptual atomism as well as the present issues about the nature of analyticity intuitions. I claim for my assumptions only that none of them is *known* to be false. Beyond that, it's the usual methodological situation: if my story is plausible, that argues for my assumptions; if my assumptions are plausible, that argues for my story. For the moment, all I ask is the temporary suspension of your disbelief.

First Assumption: Informational Semantics

I continue to take for granted, as I've been doing all along of course, that semantic facts are somehow constituted by nomic relations. To a zero'th approximation, the fact that DOG means *dog* (and hence the fact "dog" does) is constituted by a nomic connection between two properties of dogs; viz. *being dogs* and *being causes of actual and possible DOG tokenings in us*.[1] As those of you who follow the literature on informational semantics will be aware, it's a little tricky to get the details of this nomological story about content just right. Never mind. My point will be the modest one that *if* informational semantics can be sustained, that would give us a leg up on accounting for such intuitions as that it's analytic that bachelors are unmarried and that Tuesdays come before Wednesdays.

I hope you will find even this modest claim surprising. It's generally thought that, because informational semantics is inherently atomistic, intuitions of intrinsic conceptual connectedness are among its chief embarrassments. Informational semantics denies that "dog" means *dog* because of the way that it is related to other linguistic expressions ("animal" or "barks", as it might be). Correspondingly, informational semantics denies that the concept DOG has its content in virtue of its position in a network of conceptual relations. So, then, the intuition that there are other concepts that anybody who has DOG must also have is

---

[1] Since "dog" means *dog*, informational semantics requires that there *be* such a property as *being a dog*. *Mutatis mutandis*, since "Tuesday" means *Tuesday*, informational semantics requires that there be such a property as *being a Tuesday* (a highly mind-dependent, highly relational property, presumably, of certain segments of space-time). I sympathize if you're inclined to gag on this rich ontology. But that one should do the ontology last is among my religious principles, so please hold on till Chapter 6.

one that informational semantics can make no sense of. *Intuitions of conceptual connection are the bane of informational semantics*; so goes the usual account of the geography. But, I want to redraw the map a little: it's one question whether informational semantics rules out conceptual connections that are constitutive of concept possession. It does, and therefore so do I. But it's quite a different question whether informational semantics rules out there being intuitions *as of* such conceptual connections. It doesn't, and I don't either. In fact, I think that there clearly are such intuitions and that informational semantics helps explain them.

I pause, while I'm at it, to rub in a distinction that keeps coming up, and that's once again germane. What *surely* doesn't embarrass informational semantics, not even prima facie, is the intuition that there is a *necessary* connection *between being a dog* and *being an animal*, or between *being a bachelor* and *being unmarried*, or between *being a Tuesday* and *being the day before Wednesday*. For informational semantics is a theory of *content*, and these necessities might all be viewed as *metaphysical* rather than semantic. (For example, they might be supposed to arise out of property identities.)

The problem for informational semantics comes not from intuitions that the connection between *being Tuesday* and *coming before Wednesday* is *necessary*, but from intuitions that it's *constitutive* in the sense that one can't have one of the concepts unless one has the other. Compare *water is H_2O* and *two is prime*. Presumably though both are necessary, neither is constitutive. Accordingly, it's possible to have the concept WATER but not the concept HYDROGEN, and it's possible to have the concept TWO but not the concept PRIME. All of that is perfectly OK as far as informational semantics is concerned. It's perfectly consistent to claim that concepts are individuated by the properties they denote, and that *the properties* are individuated by their necessary relations to one another, but to deny that knowing about the necessary relations among the properties is a condition for having the concept.

Whether it is a *virtue* of informational semantics that it proposes to distance the metaphysics of modality from the metaphysics of concept possession is a large issue; one that I don't propose to discuss here at all. Clearly, if you think there's any serious chance that part/whole relations among concepts might *explain* what makes propositions necessary, then informational semantics isn't likely to be your dish; qua atomistic, informational semantics denies that the reason cats have to be animals is that ANIMAL is a constituent of CAT. As the reader will have gathered, I doubt that explanations of that sort will be forthcoming, but I won't argue the general issue here. Suffice it that *the* difference between *mere* necessity (which informational semantics is perfectly happy about) and *conceptual* necessity (over which informational semantics weeps) is that the latter, but not the former, constrains concept possession.

Second Assumption: Semantic Access

So far we have it, by assumption, that 'dog' and DOG mean *dog* because 'dog' expresses DOG, and DOG tokens fall under a law according to which they reliably are (or would be) among the effects of instantiated *doghood*. I now add the considerably less tendentious assumption that if there are such meaning-making laws, they surely couldn't be basic. Or, to put it another way, if there is a nomic connection between *doghood* and *cause-of-DOG-tokeninghood*, then there must be a causal process whose operation mediates and sustains this connection. Or, to put it a third way, if informational semantics is right about the metaphysics of meaning, there must be mechanisms *in virtue of which* certain mental (-cum-neural) structures 'resonate' to *doghood* and *Tuesdayhood*.[2] Or, to put it a last way, informational semantics is untenable unless there's an answer to questions like: '*how* does (or would) the instantiation of *doghood* cause tokenings of DOG?' I propose to call whatever answers such a question a mechanism of '*semantic access*'. Mechanisms of semantic access are what sustain our ability to think *about* things.

What such mechanism might there be in the case of dogs? Unsurprisingly, the sort of inventory that suggests itself looks a lot like what you'd get if you asked for the mechanisms that mediate our *epistemic* access to dogs. Unsurprisingly because there can be no epistemic access without semantic access; what you can't *think* about, you can't *know* about.[3] Informational semantics says that it's because the mediation

---

[2] I borrow J. J. Gibson's phrase (see e.g. 1966) but not his metaphysics. Roughly, informational semantics is Gibsonian semantics, but without the ban on mental processes; just as, roughly, it is Skinnerian semantics without the behaviourism. (See below and Fodor 1990.)

[3] Cf. Antony (1995: 433): "no device can be said to have *epistemic* access to any aspect of its environment unless it is a device that *represents* its environment". This doesn't go the other way around, of course: semantic access doesn't guarantee epistemic warrant. With any luck, all of this ought to come out right if your semantics is informational and your theory of knowledge is reliabilist. Since content supervenes on purely nomic relations—that is, on certain lawful relations among properties—and since lawful relations can presumably hold among properties that are, de facto, uninstantiated, the metaphysical conditions for content can in principle be met entirely counterfactually: no actual tokens of DOG have actually to be caused by dogs for the counterfactuals that its content supervenes on to be in place. Epistemic warrant, by contrast, has to do with the causal *history* of one or another actual belief token: the warranted belief has to have been acquired by reliable means. So it should turn out that the conditions for epistemic access include, but aren't exhausted by, the conditions that semantic access imposes.

between dogs and DOG-tokens is reliable that there is a community of *dog*-thinkers, creatures whose mental processes fall under the intentional laws about *dog*-thoughts. Just so, epistemologists (have been known to) say that it's the reliability of the mediation between dogs and one's *dog*-thoughts that *justifies* one's knowledge claims about dogs. This convergence of views is all to the good, of course; the requirements that epistemology places upon epistemic warrant ought to be ones that the theory of content allows many of one's beliefs actually to meet.

The psychological and physiological mechanisms that mediate the perception of middle-sized events and objects must surely head the list of the mechanisms of semantic access. It's about as reliable as the empirical generalizations of intentional psychology ever get that if you put a DOG-owner, eyes open, in a dog-filled environment and you turn up the lights, *dog*-thoughts will ensue. Or, to say it the way that RTM wants us to, the mechanisms of visual perception normally function to insure that 'IT'S DOGGING' gets tokened in the subject's belief box in such well-lit, doggy situations. De facto, our capacities for thinking about dogs, and hence our possibilities for knowing about them, both depend heavily on the reliability with which the mechanisms of visual perception do this.

Note, however, that I did *not* just claim that one's possession of the concept DOG is *constituted* by the fact that seeing dogs causes tokens of DOG in one's belief box. To the contrary: one's possession of that concept is constituted by there being the appropriate, meaning-making lawful relations between instantiated *doghood* and one's neural-cum-mental states. It's *that* your mental structures contrive to resonate to *doghood*, not *how* your mental structures contrive to resonate to *doghood*, that is constitutive of concept possession according to the informational view. This too is all to the good since it helps with satisfying the publicity constraint on concept possession that was endorsed in Chapter 2. For Helen Keller, it was *not* visual perception that sustained the meaning-making dog–DOG relation. Yet she and I, each in our way, can both satisfy the conditions for DOG-possession according to the present account of those conditions.

Just as I did not say that having perceptual mechanisms that connect dog sightings with DOG-tokens-in-the-belief-box constitutes your *having* the concept DOG, so I also did not say that the character of these mechanisms determines the *content* of your concept. How a concept achieves semantic access is one thing, what content the concept has is quite another. It is a chief virtue of informational semantics to distinguish between these two (just as it was the besetting vice of operationalism to conflate them). You tell that a thing's a dog by, *inter alia*, looking and listening; dog-shaped sights and woof-shaped sounds are among the reliable things to look and listen for. It does not follow either that there are perceptual 'criteria' for *doghood* or that, if there are, these criteria are constitutive of the content of the concept DOG. What's metaphysically pertinent to the *content* of DOG is the same thing that's metaphysically pertinent to your *possession* of DOG; namely, that it's *doghood* (and not, as it might be, *cathood*) that your DOG tokenings are under the lawful control of.

I've said that, de facto, perceptual mechanisms head the list of the ones that mediate our semantic access to *doghood*. But I now want to emphasize that that list is very long; in fact, that it's open-ended in a way that is important both for semantics and for epistemology. Here are some routes, *other than* perceiving dogs, that do, or might, sustain the meaning-making causal connection between dogs and their mental representations:

— *Dog bells.* Someone may rig things so that a bell goes off when the dog shakes its head. If I know how things are rigged, hearing the bell may reliably cause me to think *dog*.[4] Similarly for my hearing the door bell when the dog pushes the button.

In fact, I may myself rig things this way, thereby insuring that if the bell rings, thus indicating that *doghood* is locally instantiated, I will be caused to think *dog*, and thus come to be in a cognitive condition that is appropriate to my environmental situation. That we do, routinely and successfully, pursue policies intended to engineer our mind–world correlations in this sort of way strikes me as one of the most characteristic and remarkable things about us. (See Fodor 1994.)

— *Gossip.* Somebody may tell me things about dogs—including dogs far away, and dogs long dead and gone—and that too may cause me to think *dog*. Gossip is like perception in that it offers a permanent possibility of semantic access. Only, unlike perception, its range of operation isn't local.

I include, under this general head, cases where semantic access is achieved by exploiting a linguistic division of labour. Hilary Putnam and Tyler Burge have argued (though they don't put it quite this way) that sometimes *all* that's needed to effect semantic access is that I'm properly disposed to rely on experts to decide what my concept applies to. In effect, dogs make the expert think *dog*, and the expert's thinking *dog* makes me

---

[4] This is what philosophers call a 'thought experiment'. But I gather, from opera libretti, that the sort of arrangement I've envisaged actually is employed by artless shepherdesses and other light sopranos to keep their flocks from straying. How they manage to make their trills heard in such a din, I simply cannot imagine.

think *dog* in so far as I am prepared to rely on him. So my *dog*-thoughts are reliably (though indirectly) connected with dogs. Relying on experts to mediate semantic access is a lot like relying on perception to mediate semantic access, except that the perceptions you are using belong to someone else. (Who may in turn rely on someone else's still . . . and so on, though not ad infinitum.) Gossips, experts, witnesses, and, of course, written records have it in common that each extends, beyond the sorts of limits that merely perceptual sensitivity imposes, the causal chains on which achieving and sustaining semantic access—hence conceptual content—depends. (With, however, a corresponding increase of the likelihood that the chain may become degraded. Testimony one takes with a grain of salt; it's *seeing* that's supposed to be believing.)

—*Theoretical inference.* The merest ripple in dog-infested waters may suffice to cause *dog*-thoughts in the theoretically sophisticated. Analogously: because they left their tooth marks on bones some archaeologists dug up, *and because I've done my homework*, I can know about, a fortiori think about, dogs that lived in Sumer a very long while ago. Here semantic and epistemic access are sustained by a mixture of perception and inference. I think that is quite probably the typical case.

—*High tech.* Including dog detection by radar, sonar, telescopes, microscopes, hearing aids, bifocal lenses, and other apparatus. The open-endedness of this list, is, I suppose, pretty obvious.

The first moral that's to be drawn from this (surely fragmentary) survey is that, as often as not, the mechanisms whereby semantic access is achieved themselves involve the operation of intentional processes. This may well be so even where semantic access is sustained just by perception; whether it is, is what the argument about whether perception is 'inferential' is an argument about. Anyhow, it's patent that applying some concepts mediates applying others wherever semantic access is sustained by gossip, theoretical inference, expertise, deployment of instruments of observation, and the like. This consideration would, of course, be devastating if the present project were somehow to use the notion of semantic access to define, or otherwise to analyse, such notions as content or intentionality. But it's not. What meaning is, is a metaphysical question to which, I'm supposing, informational semantics is the answer. The current question, by contrast, is about not metaphysics but engineering: how are certain lawful mind–world correlations (the ones that informational semantics says are content-constituting) achieved and sustained? Answers to this engineering question can unquestion-beggingly appeal to the operation of semantic and intentional mechanisms, since 'semantic' and 'intentional' are presumed to be independently defined.

A second moral I want to draw is the *multiplicity* of the means of semantic access. Prima facie there are *all sorts* of mechanisms, physiological, psychological, cultural, and technological, that can, and do, sustain the meaning-making nomic connections that constitute the contents of one's concepts. To be sure, it may be that all the non-perceptual mechanisms that sustain semantic access to *doghood* depend, 'in the long run', on one's having and exercising perceptual capacities. But not, according to the present view, on one's having any *particular* perceptual capacity (remember Helen Keller). Nor could the dependence of concept possession upon perceptual capacities turn out to be principled. Informational semantics says that a (certain kind of) nomic relation between DOGs and *doghood, however mediated*, suffices for content. But 'however mediated' should be read to include, in principle, nomic relations that aren't mediated at all. There is nothing in informational semantics that stops content-making laws from being basic. For that matter, I suppose there's nothing in metaphysics that stops *any* law from being basic; it's just a fact about the world that the ones that are and the ones that aren't aren't. That being so, the centrality of perceptual mechanisms in mediating the meaning-making laws is also just a fact about the world, and not a fact about the metaphysics of content. Presumably God's thoughts could have *immediate* semantic access to dogs: The law according to which His DOG-tokens are controlled by instantiated *doghood* could be basic for all that informational theology cares.

I pause to underline this last point: it is, I think, a great virtue of informational semantics that, unlike any version of Empiricism, it denies a constitutive status to the relation between content and perception. If you try to list the sorts of perceptual environments in which *dog*-thoughts are *likely* to arise in a perceiver if he has the concept DOG at all, you will find that the list is, on the one hand, open-ended and, on the other hand, closely dependent on what the perceiver happens to know about, believe about, or want from, dogs. And if you try to list the sorts of perceptual environments in which *dog*-thoughts *must* arise if a creature has the concept DOG, you will find that there aren't any: no landscape is either so barren, or so well lit, that it is *metaphysically* impossible to fail to notice whether it contains a dog. That, in some circumstances, perception primitively compels one to think of dogs is a *psychophysical* fact of capital significance: perception is one of the core mechanisms by which one's semantic access to dogs is sustained. But the necessity of the connection between having the concept and having perceptually driven *dog*-thoughts is itself empirical, not metaphysical. It entails no constitutive constraints either on the content of one's concept, or on the conditions for possessing it. If informational semantics is anywhere near to being right, Empiricism is *dead*.

OK; kindly hold onto all that. There's one more ingredient I want to add.

'One-Criterion' Concepts

Back in 1983, Putnam wrote a paper about analyticity that one can see in retrospect to have been motivated by many of the same considerations that I've been discussing here. Putnam was an early enthusiast for Quine's polemic against analyticities, definitions, constitutive conceptual connections, and the like. But he was worried about bachelors being unmarried and Tuesdays coming before Wednesdays. These struck Putnam as *boringly* analytic in a way that $F = MA$, or even *dogs are animals*, is not. So Putnam had trouble viewing *Tuesday before Wednesday* and the like as bona fide cases of theoretical centrality; and, as remarked above, theoretical centrality was all Quine had on offer to explain why some truths seem to be conceptual. Putnam therefore proposed to tidy up after Quine.

Strictly speaking, according to Putnam, there are definitions, analyticities, and constitutive conceptual connections after all. But that there are isn't philosophically interesting since they won't do any of the heavy duty epistemological or metaphysical work that philosophers have had in mind for them, and that they won't is intrinsic to the nature of conceptual connection. According to Putnam's story, analyticity works only for concepts that *lack* centrality; only for concepts that *fail* to exhibit any substantial intricacy of attachment to the rest of the web of belief; in short, only for concepts that lack precisely what philosophers care about about concepts. The very facts that permit there to be conceptual truths about bachelors and Tuesdays prohibit there being such truths in the case of more amusing concepts like DOG, CAUSE, or TRIANGLE; to say nothing of PHYSICAL OBJECT, GOD, PROTON, or GOOD. So, anyhow, Putnam's story was supposed to make it turn out.

Putnam's idea was that, out at the edge of the web, and hence connected to nothing very much, there is a fringe of 'one-criterion' concepts. Criteria are ways of telling, so you're a one-criterion concept only if there is just one way to tell that you apply. BACHELOR qualifies because the only way to tell whether Jones is a bachelor is by finding out if he's an unmarried man. TUESDAY qualifies because the only way to tell that it's

Tuesday is by finding out if it's the second day of the week. And so on. Well, according to Putnam, if a concept has, in this sense, only one criterion, then it is conceptually necessary (viz. constitutive of the content of the concept) that if the criterion is satisfied then the concept applies. So there is, after all, an *epistemic* clause in the theory of concept constitutivity. Old timers will recognize this treatment of BACHELOR and the like as close kin to the then-popular theory that DOG, CAUSE, PAIN, FORCE, WATER, INFLUENZA, and the like are "cluster" concepts. In effect, a cluster concept is one for whose application there are *lots* of criteria.

So, then, according to Putnam, analyticity just *is* one-criterionhood. The problems with this account by now seem pretty obvious; we'll return to them in a moment. First, however, a word or two in its praise.

To begin with, it deconfounds analyticity from centrality, thereby freeing embarrassed Quineans from having to assimilate *bachelors are unmarried* to $F = MA$. It also deconfounds analyticity from mere necessity in a way that intuition applauds. As I remarked above, it's necessary that bachelors are unmarried, and it's again necessary that two is prime, but only the first seems to be a good candidate for a *conceptual* necessity since one isn't much tempted by the thought that not having the concept PRIME entails not having the concept TWO. Putnam's story works very well here. It is precisely because *two* is enmeshed in a rich—indeed an infinite—network of necessities that one hesitates to choose among them the ones that constitute the content of the concept. Given the plethora of necessary inferences that TWO can mediate, who's to say which ones your having the concept *requires* that you acknowledge? Similarly with the logical particles. And similarly, too, for FORCE and DOG (though the necessities that embed these concepts are characteristically metaphysical and/or nomic rather than mathematical or logical). In short, the less work a concept does, the stronger the analyticity intuitions that it is able to support; just as Putnam's account of conceptual connectedness predicts.

And since being well connected to the web, like being near the web's centre, is a matter of degree, Putnam's story explains straight off why intuitions of analyticity are graded. Nobody seriously doubts that bachelors being unmarried is a better candidate for analyticity than dogs being animals, which is in turn a better candidate than F's being MA, which is in turn at least as bad a candidate as two's being prime. The gradedness of analyticity intuitions suggests some sort of epistemic construal if the alternative explanation is that they arise from such structural relations among concepts as containment. Containment, unlike criteriality, doesn't plausibly come in more or less.

So there are nice things to be said for Putnam's account of analyticity, and I suppose that Quine's sympathizers would have jumped at it except that it is, alas, hopelessly circular. Putnam's 'one criterion' test does no work unless a way to count criteria is supplied. But you can't count what you can't individuate, and there looks to be no principle of individuation for criteria that doesn't *presuppose* the notion of analyticity. Does 'bachelor' have one criterion (viz. *unmarried man*) or two (viz. *unmarried man* and *not married man*)? That depends, *inter alia*, on whether "unmarried man" and "not married man" are synonyms. But if there are troubles about understanding analyticity there are the same troubles about understanding synonymy, the two being trivially interdefinable (as Quine rightly remarked in "Two dogmas"). So, it looks as though Putnam's construal of *analytic connection* in terms of *one-criterion concept* leaves us back where we started; in a tight circle of interdefined semantic-cum-conceptual vocabulary. I first heard this objection to Putnam's proposal from Jerry Katz when we were both graduate students. It struck me then as conclusive, and it continues to do so now.

So, then, the notion of a one-criterion term does nothing to clarify the metaphysics of analyticity. But I think it can perhaps be co-opted for a less ambitious purpose. Because I'm into atomistic informational semantics, I have to tell a story that explains what the object of our *soi-disant* intuitions of analyticity and intrinsic conceptual connectedness is, and explains why we have such intuitions, without admitting that there are analytic truths or intrinsically connected concepts. Since, moreover, the robustness of the intuitions seems undeniable, I want my story to make them intuitions of something *real*. *Being a one-criterion concept* is a godsend for my purpose; it's my candidate for Factor X. Notice that since what I'm aiming for is not an account of the individuation of meanings, but just a diagnosis of some faulty intuitions, telling my story doesn't presuppose a prior or a principled account of the individuation of criteria. Unlike Putnam, I can make do with what I imagine everyone will grant: that for some concepts there are, de facto, lots of ways of telling that they apply and for other concepts there are, de facto, very few.

Auntie (back again): I'm back again. Tell me just *why* am I supposed to grant that for some concepts there are lots of ways of telling that they apply and that for others there are very few. Isn't it rather that if there's any way at all to tell, there's sure to be a lot? If I can tell that the dog is at the door by listening for the bell to ring, then I can tell that the dog is at the door by getting Jones to listen for the bell to ring. And if I can tell that the dog is at the door by getting Jones to listen for the bell to ring, then I can tell that the dog is at the door by getting Jones to ask Smith to listen for the bell to ring . . . And so on. There aren't, even de facto, any one-criterion terms according to *my* way of counting.

—: Yes, all right, but not a sympathetic reading. What Putnam must have had in mind, and what I too propose to assume, is that some ways of telling pretty clearly depend on others. It's the latter—the pretty clearly *in*dependent ones—that you are supposed to count when you decide whether something's a one-criterion concept, or a cluster concept, or whatever. In your example, one's own listening for the bell to ring is pretty clearly at the bottom of the heap.

Auntie: Why do you keep saying 'pretty clearly' in that irritating way?

—: Because I want to emphasize that the kind of dependence I have in mind isn't metaphysical, or conceptual, or even nomic, but just epistemic. What rationalizes your asking Jones to ask Smith to listen for the bell is your knowledge that Smith has ways of telling that don't depend on *his* asking *Jones* to listen for the bell. Compare the sort of contrast cases that Putnam had in mind: the so-called cluster concepts. You can tell, pretty reliably, whether stuff is water by, for example, how it looks, how it tastes, where it's located, its specific heat, its specific gravity, what it says on the bottle, which tap it came from, and so on and on. No doubt, the fact that all these ways of telling work depends on a bundle of metaphysical and nomic necessities; but your employing the tests doesn't depend on, and isn't usually rationalized by, your knowing that this is so; pretty clearly, the various tests for *being water* are largely epistemically independent.

I agree that this is all quite loose and unprincipled; but, as remarked, it's not required to bear much weight. All I need it for is to explain away some faulty intuitions. Can I proceed?

Auntie: You may try.

Then here's my story in a nutshell: suppose you think the only epistemic route from the concept C to the property that it expresses depends on drawing inferences that involve the concept C^*. Then you will find it intuitively plausible that the relation between C and C^* is conceptual; specifically, that you can't have C unless you also have C^*. And the more you think that it is *counterfactual supporting* that the only epistemic route from C to the property it expresses depends on drawing inferences that involve the concept C^*, the stronger your intuition that C and C^* are conceptually connected will be.[5]

---

[5] Sober (1984: 82) makes what amounts to the converse point: "In general, we expect theoretical magnitudes to be *multiply accessible*; there should be more than one way of finding out what their values are in a given circumstance. This reflects the assumption that theoretical magnitudes have multiple causes and effects. There is no such thing as the only possible effect or cause of a given event; likewise, there is no such thing as the only possible way of finding out whether it occurred. I won't assert that this is somehow a necessary feature of all theoretical magnitudes, but it is remarkably widespread." Note the suggestion that the phenomena in virtue of which a "theoretical magnitude" is multiply epistemically accessible are naturally construed as its "causes and its effects". In the contrasting case, when there is only one access path (or, anyhow, only one access path that one can think of)

The best way to see how this account of analyticity intuitions is supposed to work is to consider some cases where it *doesn't* apply. Take the concepts DOG and ANIMAL; and let's suppose, concessively, that *dogs are animals* is necessary. Still, according to the present story, 'dogs are animals' should be a relatively poorish candidate for *analyticity* as necessities go. Why? Well, because there are lots of plausible scenarios where your thoughts achieve semantic access to *doghood* but *not* via your performing inferences that deploy the concept ANIMAL. Surely it's likely that perceptual identifications of dogs work that way; even if dog perception is always inferential, there's no reason to suppose that that ANIMAL is always, or even often, deployed in drawing the inferences. To the contrary, perceptual inferences from *doggish-looking* to *dog* are no doubt direct in the usual case. So, then, deploying ANIMAL is pretty clearly not a necessary condition for getting semantic access to *dog*; so the strength of the intuition that *dogs are animals* is analytic ought to be pretty underwhelming according to the present account. Which, I suppose, it is.

I suppose, to continue the previous example, that the same holds for concepts like WATER and H_2O. No doubt, *water is H_2O* is metaphysically necessary. But, there's a plethora of reliable ways of determining that stuff is water; outside the laboratory, one practically never does so by inference from its being H_2O. So, even if they express the same property, my story says that the relation between the concepts ought not to strike one's intuition as plausibly constitutive. Which, I suppose, it doesn't. (See also the old joke about how to tell how many sheep there are: you count the legs and divide by four. Here too the crucial connection is necessary; presumably it's a *law* that sheep have four legs. But the necessity isn't intuitively conceptual, even first blush. That's because there are lots of other, and better, ways to get epistemic (a fortiori, semantic) access to the cardinality of one's flock.)

But offhand, I can't imagine how I might determine whether John is a bachelor except by determining that he's male and un- (viz. not) married. Or by employing some procedure that I take to be a way of determining that he is male and unmarried . . . etc. Just so, offhand, I can't imagine how I might determine whether it's Tuesday except by determining that it's the second day of the week; e.g. by determining that yesterday was Monday and/or that tomorrow will be Wednesday. Hence the intuitive analyticity of *bachelors are unmarried, Tuesday just before Wednesday*, and the like. I'm suggesting that it's the *epistemic* property of being a one-criterion concept—not a modal property, and certainly not a semantic property—

the intuition is generally that the magnitude at issue isn't bona fide theoretical, and that its connection to the criterion is conceptual rather than causal.

that putative intuitions of analyticity detect. A fortiori, such intuitions do not detect the constituent structure of complex concepts.

TUESDAY is especially engaging in this respect. It pays to spend some time on TUESDAY. I suppose the intuition that needs explaining is that "Tuesday" is conceptually connected to a small circle of mutually interdefinable terms, at least some of which you must have to have it. This kind of thing is actually a bit embarrassing for the standard, semantic account of analyticity intuitions. Since there's no strong intuition about *which* of the *Tuesday*-related concepts you have to have to have "Tuesday", it's correspondingly unclear which of the concepts deployed in the various necessary truths about Tuesdays should count as constitutive; i.e. which of them should be treated as part of the *definition* of "Tuesday". (Correspondingly, there's no clear intuition about which of this galaxy of concepts should be *constituents* of TUESDAY, assuming you hold a containment theory of definition.)

And Tuesday-intuitions raise another embarrassing question as well: suppose you could somehow decide which *Tuesday*-involving necessities are definitional and which aren't. You would still have the worry which *Tuesday*-related concepts are primitive and which are defined. Is it that Tuesday is the second day of the week (in which case TUESDAY is the definiendum and . . . WEEK . . . is the definiens)? Or is it that a week is seven consecutive days, of which the second is Tuesday (in which case, the primitive/defined relation goes the other way around)? The same sort of question crops up, of course, with regard to kinship terms, chess terms, and the like. Whenever you get a little family of jargon vocabulary, the intuition is that the application of some of the terms depends on inferences from the applicability of others, but that it doesn't matter much which you take as primitive. It used to be that philosophers thought this decision might be made on the principle that the relatively primitive concept is the one that's closer to sensations. These days, however, not even the friends of definitions think that this project has a prayer.[6]

My story about this says what I really do think one's story ought to say: such questions haven't got answers. What's being delivered by (e.g.) the intuition that pawns are conceptually connected to queens is not the internal structure of a concept (it's not that the concept QUEEN has the concept PAWN as a constituent or vice versa). What you're intuiting is really something epistemic: that the usual ways that PAWN gets semantic access to *pawnhood* all run via inferences involving one or other member of quite a small family. In consequence, although the connections of

---

[6] There are a few, lonely exceptions; but they are mostly in AI, so perhaps they don't count. See, for example, Woods 1975.

PAWN to the other members of this family no doubt strike one as conceptual, none of these connections is intuited as clearly definitional rather than merely necessary; and none of the concepts involved is clearly intuited as primitive rather than defined. This situation would be paradoxical if the intuitions were detecting definitional relations. But they aren't, so it isn't.

I'm suggesting that intuitions of conceptual connectedness are a sort of normal illusion; they depend on an understandable conflation between an epistemic property and a semantic one. In this respect, what I say about analyticity intuitions is, of course, a lot like what Quine says; except that he takes the epistemic property to be centrality whereas I think it's one-criterionhood. I doubt that either story covers all the cases, and there's no obvious reason why they shouldn't both be true. After all, the moral of both is that intuitions of analyticity are *misguided*; and, as Aristotle pointed out a while ago, there are generally *lots* of ways for an arrow to miss the target.

Conclusion

So, then, where have we got to? The best philosophical argument for analyticity used to be necessity/a prioricity (the tradition I have in mind generally didn't distinguish between them). Positivism, in particular, took it for granted that a priori truths must be necessary, and that if there is necessity, it has to be linguistic/conceptual. Carnap and Quine split the available options between them. According to Carnap, some truths are necessary and a priori, so some must be analytic. According to Quine, no truths are analytic, so none can be either necessary or a priori. It was, quite distinctly, a family squabble. Over the last several decades, however, it has come to seem increasingly implausible that necessary truths could be analytic in the general case. Correspondingly, the best defence of analyticity now turns on a direct appeal to intuition: some necessities strike one as conceptual; the analytic truths are the ones that elicit intuitions of that sort.

No doubt, intuitions deserve respect. As Grice and Strawson pointed out (1956), if people agree that *A*s are different from *B*s, and if they agree on which is which in novel cases, that's strong prima facie evidence *A*s and *B*s really are different in some way or other. But *that A*s and *B*s are different is one thing; what they differ *in* is quite another. And, in fact, the difference often turns out to be not at all what informants suppose. Informants, oneself included, can be quite awful at saying what it is that drives their intuitions; sometimes it's just a fragment of underdone potato.

This holds all the way from chicken sexing to judgements of grammaticality and modality. Good Quinean that I am, I think that it is *always* up for grabs what an intuition is an intuition of. At a minimum, it is surely *sometimes* up for grabs, and I don't see why *soi-disant* intuitions of conceptual connectedness shouldn't be of this unapodictic kind.

I think that raw intuitions of conceptual connectedness can plausibly be explained away by appealing to some mixture of centrality and Factor X. And, as far as I know, there is nothing in philosophy aside from these raw intuitions that seriously suggests that content constituting conceptual connections exist. So I think it's reasonable, on the philosophical evidence, to suppose that such conceptual connections *don't* exist. Quine was likely right about conceptual connections, even though he was wrong about necessity and a prioricity, both of which are, so I suppose, very important and perfectly real. If all of that is so, then from the philosopher's point of view the bottom line is that necessity, a prioricity and the like are very mysterious: they are, in general, not by-products of analyticity; and they are, in general, things that we do not understand. What else is new?

And the bottom line for the purposes of the theory of concepts is this: if there are no constitutive conceptual connections, then there are also no definitions; and, if there are no definitions, then there are no definitions for concepts to be.

5

Prototypes and Compositionality[1]

A Good Apple tree or a bad, is an Apple tree still: a Horse is not more a
Lion for being a Bad Horse.

—William Blake

Introduction

The definition theory says that concepts are complex structures which
entail their constituents. By saying this, it guarantees both the connection
between content and necessity and the connection between concept
individuation and concept possession. On the one hand, since definitions
entail their constituents, it follows that whatever belongs to a concept's
definition is thereby true of everything, actual or possible, that the concept
subsumes. On the other hand, since what definitions entail are their
constituents, it follows that a definition of a concept specifies its canonical
(viz. individuating) structural description. And finally, whatever else
concept possession may amount to, you can't have a thing unless you have
its parts; hence the connection between concept possession and concept
individuation according to the definition story. This metaphysical synthesis
of a theory of concept individuation with theories of modality and
concept possession was no small achievement. In some respects it has yet
to be bettered, as we're about to see.

By and large, it's been the modal properties of definitions that
philosophers have cared about since, as previously remarked, the
semantical truths that definitions generate recommend themselves for

---

[1] Terminological conventions with respect to the topics this chapter covers are unsettled.
I'll use 'stereotype' and 'prototype' interchangeably, to refer to mental representations of
certain kinds of properties. So, 'the dog stereotype' and 'the dog prototype' designate some
such (complex) concept as: BEING A DOMESTIC ANIMAL WHICH BARKS, HAS A
TAIL WHICH IT WAGS WHEN IT IS PLEASED, . . . etc. I'll use 'exemplar' for the
mental representation of a kind, or of an individual, that instantiates a prototype; so
'sparrows are the exemplars of birds' and 'Bambi is Smith's exemplar of a deer' are both
well-formed. 'Sparrows are stereotypic birds' (/'Bambi is a prototypic deer') are also OK;
they mean that a certain kind (/individual) exhibits certain stereotypic (/prototypic)
properties to a marked degree.

antisceptical employment. By contrast, it's their being *complex* that primarily makes definitions interesting to psychologists and linguists. With complex things, there's always the hope that their behaviour can be predicted from the behaviour of their parts; with primitive things, since there are no parts, there is no such hope. In particular (for the linguists), if words have definitions, then arguably words have the syntax of phrases "at the semantic level"; so perhaps lexical grammar can be unified with phrasal grammar. Likewise (for the psychologists), if lexical concepts are *tacitly* structurally complex, perhaps they can be brought under the same psychological generalizations that govern concepts that are *manifestly* complex; if the concept BACHELOR is the concept UNMARRIED MAN, then learning or thinking with the one can't differ much from learning or thinking with the other.[2]

So the definition theory was a fusion of disparate elements; in particular, the idea that concepts are complex and the idea that their constitutive inferences are typically necessary are in principle dissociable. And, for better or worse, they have been coming unstuck in the recent history of cognitive science. The currently standard view is that the definition story was right about the complexity of typical lexical concepts, but wrong to claim that complex concepts typically *entail* their constituents. According to the new theory, it's not the *necessity* of an inference but its *reliability* that determines its relevance to concept individuation.

How this is supposed to work, and why it doesn't work the way that it's supposed to, and where its not working the way that it's supposed to leaves us in the theory of concepts, will be the substance of this chapter.

Statistical Theories of Concepts

The general character of the new theory of concepts is widely known throughout the cognitive science community, so the exegesis that follows will be minimal.

Imagine a hierarchy of concepts ordered by relations of dominance and sisterhood, where these obey the intuitive axioms (e.g. dominance is antireflexive, transitive and asymmetric; sisterhood is antireflexive, transitive, and symmetric, etc.). Figure 5.1 is a sort of caricature.

---

[2] The structural complexity of definitions was of some use to philosophers too: it promised the (partial?) reduction of conceptual to logical truth. So, for example, the conceptual truth that if John is a bachelor then John is unmarried, and the logical truth that if John is unmarried and John is a man then John is unmarried, are supposed to be indistinguishable at the 'semantic level'.

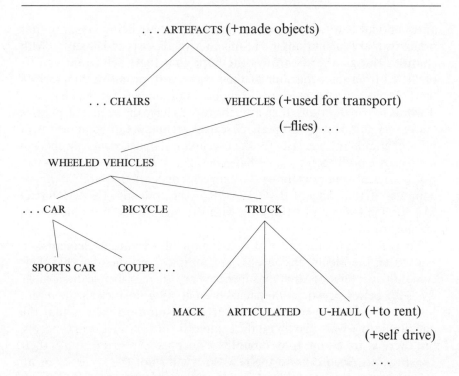

FIG. 5.1 An entirely hypothetical 'semantic hierarchy' showing the position and features of some concepts for vehicles.

The intended interpretation is that, on the one hand, if something is a truck or a car, then it's a vehicle; and, on the other hand, if something is a vehicle, then it's either a truck, or a car, or . . . etc. (Let's, for the moment, take for granted that these inferences are sound but put questions about their modal status to one side.) As usual, expressions in caps ('VEHICLE' and the like) are the *names* of concepts, not their structural descriptions. We continue to assume, as with the definition theory, that lexical concepts are typically complex. In particular, a lexical concept is a tree consisting of names of taxonomic properties together with their features (or 'attributes'; for the latter terminology, see Collins and Quillian 1969), which I've put in parentheses and lower case.[3] In a hierarchy like 5.1, each concept inherits the features of the concepts by which it is dominated.

---

[3] What, exactly, the distinction between semantic features and taxonomic classes is supposed to come to is one of the great mysteries of cognitive science. There is much to be said for the view that it doesn't come to anything. I shall, in any case, not discuss this issue here; I come to bury prototypes, not to exposit them.

Thus, vehicles are artefacts that are mobile, intended to be used for transport, . . . etc.; trucks are artefacts that are mobile, intended to be used for transport of freight (rather than persons), . . . etc. U-Haul trucks are artefacts that are mobile, intended to be rented to be used for transport of freight (rather than persons), . . . and so forth.

The claims of present interest are that when conceptual hierarchies like 5.1 are mentally represented:

i. There will typically be a *basic level* of concepts (defined over the dominance relations);

and

ii. There will typically be a *stereotype structure* (defined over the sisterhood relations).

Roughly, and intuitively: the *basic level concepts* are the ones that receive relatively few features from the concepts that immediately dominate them but transmit relatively many features to the concepts that they immediately dominate. So, for example, that it's a car tells you a lot about a vehicle; but that it's a sports car doesn't add a lot to what 'it's a car' already told you. So CAR and its sisters (but not VEHICLE or SPORTS CAR and their sisters) constitute a basic level category. Correspondingly, the *prototypical sister* at a given conceptual level is the one which has the most features in common with the rest of its sisterhood (and/or the least in common with non-sisters at its level). So, cars are the prototypical vehicles because they have more in common with trucks, buses, and bicycles than any of the latter do with any of the others.

Such claims should, of course, be relativized to an independently motivated account of the individuation of semantic features (see n. 3). Why, for example, isn't the feature bundle for VEHICLE just the unit set {+vehicle}? Well may you ask. But statistical theories of concepts are no better prepared to be explicit about what semantic features are than definitional theories used to be; in practice, it's all just left to intuition. That's scandalous, to be sure; but fortunately it doesn't matter a lot for the issues that will concern us here. As we're about to see, prototype concepts and basic object concepts exhibit a cluster of reliably correlated properties which allow us to pick them out pretty well even though, lacking a theory of features, we have no respectable account of what their basicness or their prototypicality consists in.

That concepts are organized into hierarchies isn't, of course, anything that definitional theories need deny. What primarily distinguishes the new story about concepts from its classical predecessor is the nature of the glue that's supposed to hold a feature bundle together. Defining features were supposed to exhibit severally necessary and jointly sufficient conditions for a thing's inclusion in a concept's extension. On the present account, by contrast, whether a feature is in the bundle for a given concept is primarily a question of *how likely it is* that something in the concept's extension has the property that the feature expresses. Being able to fly isn't a *necessary* condition for being a bird (*vide* ostriches); but it is a property that birds are quite reliably found to have. So, *ceteris paribus*, +*flies* belongs to the feature bundle for BIRD. The effect, is to change from a kind of metaphysics in which the concept-constitutive inferences are distinguished by their *modal* properties to a kind of metaphysics in which they're picked out *epistemically*.[4]

Notice that the thesis that concepts are individuated by their inferential roles (specifically by their inferential relations to their constituents) survives this shift. It's just that the individuating inferences are now supposed to be statistical.[5] A fortiori, we're still working within a cognitivist account of concept possession: to have a concept is, at least *inter alia*, to believe certain things (e.g. in the case of BIRD, that generally birds fly). Notice also that the new story about concepts has claims to philosophical good repute that its definitional predecessor arguably lacked. Maybe, as Quine says, conceptual entailment isn't all that much clearer than the psychological and semantic notions that it was traditionally supposed to reconstruct. But if there's something philosophically wrong with statistical reliability, *everybody* is in trouble.

So, then, consider the thesis that concepts are bundles of statistically reliable features, hence that having a concept is knowing which properties the things it applies to reliably exhibit (together, perhaps, with enough of the structure of the relevant conceptual hierarchy to at least determine how basic the concept is).

A major problem with the definition story was the lack of convincing examples; nobody has a bullet-proof definition of, as it might be, 'cow' or 'table' or 'irrigation' or 'pronoun' on offer; not linguists, not philosophers,

---

[4] Elanor Rosche, who invented this account of concepts more or less single-handed, often speaks of herself as a Wittgensteinian; and there is, of course, a family resemblance. But I doubt that it goes very deep. Rosche's project was to get modality out of semantics by *substituting* a probabilistic account of content-constituting inferences. Whereas I suppose Wittgenstein's project was to offer (or anyhow, make room for) an epistemic *reconstruction* of conceptual necessity. Rosche is an eliminativist where Wittgenstein is a reductionist. There is, in consequence, nothing in Rosche's theory of concepts that underwrites Wittgenstein's criteriology, hence nothing that's of use for bopping sceptics with.

[5] Just as it's possible to dissociate the idea that concepts are complex from the claim that meaning-constitutive inferences are necessary, so too it's possible to dissociate the idea that concepts are constituted by their roles in inferences from the claim that they are complex. See Appendix 5A.

least of all English-speakers as such. By contrast, the evidence that people know (and agree about) concerning the prototype structure of words and concepts is ubiquitous and robust.[6] In fact, you can hardly devise a concept-possession test on which prototype structure fails to have an appreciable effect. Ask a subject to tell you the first —— that comes into his head, and it's good odds he'll report the prototype for the category — —: cars for vehicles, red for colours, diamonds for jewels, sparrows for birds, and so on. Ask which vehicle-word a child is likely to learn first, and prototypicality is a better predictor than even very good predictors like the relative frequency of the word in the adult corpus. Ask an experimental subject to evaluate the truth of 'a —— is a vehicle' and he'll be fastest where a word for the basic level prototype fills the blank. And so forth. Even concepts like ODD NUMBER, which clearly do have definitions, often have prototype structure as well. The number 3 is a 'better' odd number than 27 (and it's a better prime than 2) (see Armstrong, Gleitman, and Gleitman 1983). The discovery of the massive presence of prototypicality effects in all sorts of mental processes is one of the success stories of cognitive science. I shall simply take it for granted in what follows; but for a review, see Smith and Medin 1981.

So prototypes are practically everywhere and definitions are practically nowhere. So why not give up saying that concepts are definitions and start saying instead that concepts are prototypes? That is, in fact, the course that much of cognitive science has taken in the last decade or so. But it is not a good idea. Concepts can't be prototypes, *pace* all the evidence that everybody who has a concept is highly likely to have its prototype as well. I want to spend some time rubbing this point in because, though it's sometimes acknowledged in the cognitive science literature, it has been very much less influential than I think that it deserves to be. Indeed, it's mostly because it's clear that concepts can't be prototypes that I think that concepts have to be atoms.[7]

---

[6] For a dissenting opinion, see Barsalou 1985 and references therein. I find his arguments for the instability of typicality effects by and large unconvincing; but if you don't, so much the better for my main line of argument. Unstable prototypes *ipso facto* aren't public (see Chapter 2), so they are *ipso facto* unfitted to be concepts.

[7] Some of the extremist extremists in cognitive science hold not only that concepts are prototypes, but also that thinking is the 'transformation of prototype vectors'; this is the doctrine that Paul Churchland calls the "assimilation of 'theoretical insight' to 'prototype activation'" (1995, 117; for a review, see Fodor 1995a). But that's a minority opinion prompted, primarily, by a desire to assimilate a prototype-centred theory of concepts to a Connectionist view about cognitive architecture. In fact, the identification of concepts with prototypes is entirely compatible with the "Classical" version of RTM according to which concepts are the constituents of thoughts and mental processes are defined on the constituent structure of mental representations.

But though prototypes are neutral with respect to the difference between classical and

In a nutshell, the trouble with prototypes is this. Concepts are productive and systematic. Since compositionality is what explains systematicity and productivity, it must be that concepts are compositional. But it's as certain as anything ever gets in cognitive science that prototypes don't compose. So it's as certain as anything ever gets in cognitive science that concepts can't *be* prototypes and that the glue that holds concepts together can't be statistical.

Since the issues about compositionality are, in my view, absolutely central to the theory of concepts, I propose to go through the relevant considerations with some deliberation. We'll discuss first the status of the arguments for the compositionality of concepts and then the status of the arguments against the compositionality of prototypes.

The Arguments for Compositionality

Intuitively, the claim that concepts compose is the claim that the syntax and the content of a complex concept is normally determined by the syntax and the content of its constituents. ('Normally' means something like: *with not more than finitely many exceptions*. 'Idiomatic' concepts are allowed, but they mustn't be productive.) A number of people (see e.g. Block 1993; Zadrozny 1994) have recently pointed out that this informal characterization of compositionality can be trivialized, and there's a hunt on for ways to make the notion rigorous. But we can bypass this problem for our present purposes. Since the argument that concepts compose is primarily that they are productive and systematic, we can simply stipulate that the claim that concepts compose is true only if the syntax and content of complex concepts is derived from the syntax and content of their constituents *in a way that explains their productivity and systematicity*. I do so stipulate.

The Productivity Argument for Compositionality

The traditional argument for compositionality goes something like this. There are infinitely many concepts that a person can entertain. (*Mutatis*

---

connectionist architectures, it doesn't follow that the difference between the architectures is neutral with respect to prototypes. For example, in so far as Connectionism is committed to statistical learning as its model of concept acquisition, it may well *require* that concepts have statistical structure on pain of their being unlearnable. If, as I shall argue, the structure of concepts *isn't* statistical, then Connectionists have yet another woe to add to their collection.

mutandis in the case of natural languages: there are infinitely many expressions of *L* that an *L*-speaker can understand.) Since people's representational capacities are surely finite, this infinity of concepts must itself be finitely representable. In the present case, the demand for finite representation is met if (and, as far as anyone knows, only if) all concepts are individuated by their syntax and their contents, and the syntax and contents of each complex concept is finitely reducible to the syntax and contents of its (primitive) constituents.

This seems as good an opportunity as any to say something about the current status of this line of thought. Of late, the productivity argument has come under two sorts of criticism that a cognitive scientist might find persuasive:

—*The performance/competence argument*. The claim that conceptual repertoires are typically productive requires not just an idealization to infinite cognitive capacity, but the kind of idealization that presupposes a memory/program distinction. This presupposition is, however, tendentious in the present polemical climate. No doubt, if your model for cognitive architecture is a Turing machine with a finite tape, it's quite natural to equate the concepts that a mind could entertain with the ones that its program could enumerate *assuming that the tape supply is extended arbitrarily*. Because the Turing picture allows the size of the memory to vary while the program stays the same, it invites the idea that machines are individuated by their programs.

But this way of drawing a 'performance/competence' distinction seems considerably less natural if your model of cognitive architecture is (e.g.) a neural net. The natural model for 'extending' the memory of a network (and likewise, *mutatis mutandis*, for other finite automata) is to add new nodes. However, the idea of adding nodes to a network while preserving its identity is arguably dubious in a way that the idea of preserving the identity of a Turing machine tape while adding to its tape is arguably not.[8] The problem is precisely that the memory/program distinction isn't available for networks. A network is individuated by the totality of its nodes, and the nodes are individuated by the totality of their connections, direct and indirect, to one another.[9] In consequence, 'adding' a node to a network changes the identity of all the other nodes, and hence the identity

---

[8] If the criterion of machine individuation is I(nput)/O(utput) equivalence, then a finite tape Turing machine *is* a finite automaton. This doesn't, I think, show that the intuitions driving the discussion in the text are incoherent. Rather it shows (what's anyhow independently plausible) that I/O equivalence isn't what's primarily at issue in discussions of cognitive architecture. (See Pylyshyn 1984.)

[9] Nodes may have intrinsic properties over and above their connectivity (e.g. their rest level of excitation). The discussion in the text abstracts from such niceties.

of the network itself. In this context, the idealization from a finite cognitive performance to a productive conceptual capacity may strike the theorist as begging precisely the architectural issues that he wants to stress.

— *The finite representation argument.* If a finite creature has an infinite conceptual capacity, then, no doubt, the capacity must be finitely *determined*; that is, there must be a finite set of sufficient conditions, call it *S*, such that a creature has the capacity if *S* obtains. But it doesn't follow by any argument I can think of that satisfying *S* depends on the creature's representing the compositional structure of its conceptual repertoire; or even that the conceptual repertoire *has* a compositional structure. For all I know, for example, it may be that sufficient conditions for having an infinite conceptual capacity can be finitely specified in and only in the language of neurology, or of particle physics. And, presumably, notions like *computational state* and *representation* aren't accessible in these vocabularies. It's tempting to suppose that one has one's conceptual capacities in virtue of some act of intellection that one has performed. And then, if the capacity is infinite, it's hard to see what act of intellection that could be other than grasping the primitive basis of a system of representations; of Mentalese, in effect. But talk of grasping is tendentious in the present context. It's in the nature of intentional explanations of intentional capacities that they have to run out sooner or later. It's entirely plausible that explaining what determines one's conceptual capacities (figuratively, explaining one's mastery of Mentalese) is *where* they run out.

One needs to be sort of careful here. I'm not denying that Mentalese *has* a compositional semantics. In fact, I can't actually think of any other way to explain its productivity, and writing blank checks on neurology (or particle physics) strikes me as unedifying. But I do think we should reject the following argument: 'Mentalese *must have* a compositional semantics because mastering Mentalese requires *grasping* its compositional semantics.' It isn't obvious that mastering Mentalese requires grasping *anything*.

The traditional locus of the inference from finite determination to finite representation is, however, not Mentalese but English (see Chomsky 1965; Davidson 1967). Natural languages are learned, and learning is an 'act of intellection' par excellence. Doesn't that show that English has to have a compositional semantics? I doubt that it does. For one thing, as a number of us have emphasized (see Chapter 1; Fodor 1975; Schiffer 1987; for a critical discussion, see Lepore 1997), if you assume that thinking is computing, it's natural to think that acquiring a natural language is learning how to translate between it and the language you compute in. Suppose that language learning requires that the translation procedure be 'grasped' and grasping the translation procedure requires that it be finitely and explicitly represented. Still, there is no obvious reason why translation between English and Mentalese requires having a compositional theory of *content* for either language. Maybe translation to and from Mentalese is a syntactical process: maybe the Mentalese translation of an English sentence is fully determined given its canonical structural descriptions (including, of course, lexical inventory).

I don't really doubt that English and Mentalese are both productive; or that the reason that they are productive is that their semantics is compositional. But that's faith in search of justification. The polemical situation is, on the one hand, that minds are productive only under a tendentious idealization; and, on the other hand, that productivity doesn't literally entail semantic compositionality for either English or Mentalese. Somebody sane could doubt that the argument from productivity to compositionality is conclusive.

The Systematicity Argument for Compositionality

'Systematicity' is a cover term for a cluster of properties that quite a variety of cognitive capacities exhibit, apparently as a matter of nomological necessity.[10] Here are some typical examples. If a mind can grasp the thought that $P \rightarrow Q$, it can grasp the thought that $Q \rightarrow P$; if a mind can grasp the thought that $\sim(P \& Q)$, it can grasp the thought that $\sim P$ and the thought that $\sim Q$; if a mind can grasp the thought that Mary loves John, it can grasp the thought that John loves Mary . . . etc. Whereas it's by no means obvious that a mind that can grasp the thought that $P \rightarrow Q$ can also grasp the thought that $R \rightarrow Q$ (not even if, for example, $(P \rightarrow Q) \rightarrow (R \rightarrow Q)$). That will depend on whether it is the kind of mind that's able to grasp the thought that R. Correspondingly, a mind that can think *Mary loves John* and *John loves Mary* may none the less be unable to think *Peter loves Mary*. That will depend on whether it is able to think about Peter.

It seems pretty clear why the facts about systematicity fall out the way they do: mental representations are compositional, and compositionality explains systematicity.[11] The reason that a capacity for *John loves Mary*

[10] It's been claimed that (at least some) facts about the systematicity of minds are *conceptually* necessary; 'we wouldn't call it thought if it weren't systematic' (see e.g. Clark 1991). I don't, in fact, know of any reason to believe this, nor do I care much whether it is so. If it's *conceptually* necessary that thoughts are systematic, then it's *nomologically* necessary that creatures like us have thoughts, and this latter necessity still wants explaining.

[11] It's sometimes replied that compositionality doesn't *explain* systematicity since compositionality doesn't *entail* systematicity (e.g. Smolensky 1995). But that only shows that explanation doesn't entail entailment. Everybody sensible thinks that the theory of

thoughts implies a capacity for *Mary loves John* thoughts is that the two kinds of thoughts have the same constituents; correspondingly, the reason that a capacity for John loves Mary thoughts does *not* imply a capacity for *Peter loves Mary* thoughts is that they *don't* have the same constituents. Who could really doubt that this is so? Systematicity seems to be one of the (very few) organizational properties of minds that our cognitive science actually makes some sense of.

If your favourite cognitive architecture doesn't support a productive cognitive repertoire, you can always argue that since minds are really finite, they aren't *literally* productive. But systematicity is a property that even quite finite conceptual repertoires can have; it isn't remotely plausibly a methodological artefact. If systematicity needs compositionality to explain it, that strongly suggests that the compositionality of mental representations is mandatory. For all that, there has been an acrimonious argument about systematicity in the literature for the last ten years or so. One does wonder, sometimes, whether cognitive science is worth the bother.

Some currently popular architectures *don't* support systematic representation. The representations they compute with lack constituent structure; a fortiori they lack compositional constituent structure. This is true, in particular, of 'neural networks'. Connectionists have responded to this in a variety of ways. Some have denied that concepts are systematic. Some have denied that Connectionist representations are inherently unstructured. A fair number have simply failed to understand the problem. The most recent proposal I've heard for a Connectionist treatment of systematicity is owing to the philosopher Andy Clark (1993). Clark says that we should "bracket" the problem of systematicity. "Bracket" is a technical term in philosophy which means *try not to think about*.

I don't propose to review this literature here. Suffice it that if you assume compositionality, you can account for both systematicity and productivity; and if you don't, you can't. Whether or not productivity and systematicity *prove* that conceptual content is compositional, they are clearly substantial straws in the wind. I find it persuasive that there are

---

continental drift explains why (e.g.) South America fits so nicely into Africa. It does so, however, not by *entailing* that South America fits into Africa, but by providing a theoretical background in which the fact that they fit comes, as it were, as no surprise. Similarly, *mutatis mutandis*, for the explanation of systematicity by compositionality.

Inferences from systematicity to compositionality are 'arguments to the best explanation', and are (of course) *non-demonstrative*; which is (of course) not at all the same as their being implausible or indecisive. Compare Cummins 1996, which appears to be confused about this.

quite a few such straws, and they appear all to be blowing in the same direction.

The Best Argument for Compositionality

The best argument for the compositionality of mental (and linguistic) representation is that its traces are ubiquitous; not just in very general features of cognitive capacity like productivity and systematicity, but also everywhere in its details. Deny productivity and systematicity if you will; you still have these particularities to explain away.

Consider, for example: the availability of (definite) descriptions is surely a universal property of natural languages. Descriptions are nice to have because they make it possible to talk (*mutatis mutandis*, to think) about a thing even if it isn't available for ostension and even if you don't know its name; even, indeed, if it doesn't *have* a name (as with ever so many real numbers). Descriptions can do this job because they pick out unnamed individuals *by reference to their properties*. So, for example, 'the brown cow' picks out a certain cow; viz. the brown one. It does so by referring to a property, viz. *being brown*, which that cow has and no other cow does that is contextually relevant. Things go wrong if (e.g.) there are no contextually relevant cows; or if none of the contextually relevant cows is brown; or if more than one of the contextually relevant cows is brown . . . And so forth.

OK, but just how does all this work? Just what is it about the syntax and semantics of descriptions that allows them to pick out unnamed individuals by reference to their properties? Answer:

i. Descriptions are complex symbols which have *terms that express properties* among their syntactic constituents;

and

ii. These terms contribute the properties that they express to determine what the descriptions that contain them specify.

It's because 'brown' means *brown* that it's the brown cow that 'the brown cow' picks out. Since you can rely on this arrangement, you can be confident that 'the brown cow' will specify the local brown cow *even if you don't know which cow the local brown cow is*; even if you don't know that it's Bossie, for example, or that it's *this* cow. That, however, is just to say that descriptions succeed in their job *because* they are compositional. If English didn't let you use 'brown' context-independently to mean *brown*, and 'cow' context-independently to mean *cow*, it couldn't let you use 'the brown cow' to specify a brown cow without naming it.

Names, by contrast, succeed in their job because they *aren't*
compositional; not even when they are syntactically complex. Consider
'the Iron Duke', to which 'Iron' does *not* contribute *iron*, and which you
can therefore use to specify the Iron Duke even if you don't know what he
was made of. Names are nicer than descriptions because you don't have to
know much to specify their bearers, although you *do* have to know what
their bearers are called. Descriptions are nicer than names because,
although you do have to know a lot to specify their bearers, you *don't* have
to know what their bearers are called. What's nicer than having the use of
either names or descriptions is having the use of both. I agree that, as a
piece of semantic theory, this is all entirely banal; but that's my point, so
don't complain. There is, to repeat, no need for *fancy* arguments that the
representational systems we talk and think in are in large part
compositional; you find the effects of their compositionality just about
wherever you look.

I must apologize for having gone on at such length about the arguments
pro and con conceptual compositionality; the reason I've done so is that,
in my view, the status of the statistical theory of concepts turns, practically
entirely, on this issue. And statistical theories are now the preferred
accounts of concepts practically throughout cognitive science. In what
follows I will take the compositionality of conceptual repertoires for
granted, and try to make clear how the thesis that concepts are prototypes
falls afoul of it.

Why Concepts Can't Be Prototypes[12]

Here's why concepts can't be prototypes: whatever conceptual content is,
compositionality requires that complex concepts inherit their contents
from those of their constituents, and that they do so in a way that explains
their productivity and systematicity. Accordingly, whatever is *not* inherited
from its constituents by a complex concept is *ipso facto* not the content of
that concept. But: (i) indefinitely many complex concepts have no
prototypes; a fortiori they do not inherit their prototypes from their
constituents. And, (ii) there are indefinitely many complex concepts whose
prototypes aren't related to the prototypes of their constituents in the ways
that the compositional explanation of productivity and systematicity
requires. So, again, if concepts are compositional then they can't be
prototypes.

[12] Some of the next several pages is condensed from Fodor and Lepore 1994, q.v. for a
more extended treatment.

In short, *prototypes don't compose*. Since this is the heart of the case against statistical theories of concepts, I propose to expatiate a bit on the examples.

(i) *The Uncat Problem*

For indefinitely many "Boolean" concepts,[13] *there isn't any prototype* even though:

— their primitive constituent concepts all have prototypes,

and

— the complex concept itself has definite conditions of semantic evaluation (definite satisfaction conditions).

So, for example, consider the concept NOT A CAT (*mutatis mutandis*, the predicate 'is not a cat'); and let's suppose (probably contrary to fact) that CAT isn't vague; i.e. that 'is a cat' has either the value S or the value U for every object in the relevant universe of discourse. Then, clearly, there is a definite semantic interpretation for NOT A CAT; i.e. it expresses the property of *not being a cat*, a property which all and only objects in the extension of the complement of the set of cats instantiate.

However, although NOT A CAT is semantically entirely well behaved on these assumptions, it's pretty clear that it hasn't got a stereotype or an exemplar. For consider: a bagel is a pretty good example of a NOT A CAT, but a bagel couldn't be NOT A CAT's prototype. Why not? Well, if bagels are the prototypic NOT A CATs, it follows that the more a thing is like a bagel the less it's like a cat; *and the more a thing isn't like a cat, the more it's like a bagel.* But the second conjunct is patently not true. Tuesdays and erasers, both of which are very good examples of NOT A CATs, aren't at all like bagels. An Eraser is not more a Bagel for being a bad Cat. Notice that the same sort of argument goes through if you are thinking of stereotypes in terms of features rather than exemplars. There is nothing that non-cats qua non-cats as such are likely to have in common (except, of course, not being cats).[14]

---

[13] To simplify the exposition, I'll use this notion pretty informally; for example, I'm glossing over the distinction between Boolean *sentences* and Boolean *predicates*. But none of this corner-cutting is essential to the argument.

[14] This is not to deny that there are typicality effects for negative categories; as Barsalou remarks, "with respect to *birds*, *chair* is a better nonmember than is *butterfly*" (1987: 101). This observation does not, however, generalize to Boolean functions at large. I doubt that there are more and less typical examples of *if it's a chair, then it's a Windsor* or of *chair or butterfly*.

The moral seems clear enough: the mental representations that correspond to complex Boolean concepts specify *not their prototypes but their logical forms*. So, for example, NOT A CAT has the logical form *not*(*F*), and the rule of interpretation for a mental representation of that form assigns as its extension the complement of the set of *F*s. To admit this, however, is to abandon the project of using prototype structure to account for the productivity (/systematicity) of complex Boolean predicates. So be it.

(ii) *The Pet Fish Problem*

Prototype theories want to explicate notions like *falling under a concept* by reference to notions like *being similar to the concept's exemplar*. Correspondingly, prototype theories can represent conceptual repertoires as compositional only if (barring idioms) a thing's similarity to the exemplar of a complex concept is determined by its similarity to the exemplars of its constituents. However, this condition is not satisfied in the general case. So, for example, a goldfish is a poorish example of a fish, and a poorish example of a pet, but it's a prototypical example of a pet fish. So similarity to the prototypic pet and the prototypic fish doesn't predict similarity to the prototypical pet fish. It follows that if meanings were prototypes, then you could know what 'pet' means and know what 'fish' means and still not know what 'pet fish' means. Which is just to say that if meanings were prototypes, then the meaning of 'pet fish' wouldn't be compositional. Various solutions for this problem are on offer in the literature, but it seems to me that none is even close to satisfactory. Let's have a quick look at one or two.

Smith and Osherson (1984) take prototypes to be matrices of weighted features (rather than exemplars). So, for example, the prototype for APPLE might specify a typical shape, colour, taste, size, ripeness, . . . etc. Let's suppose, in particular, that the prototypical apple is red, and consider the problem of constructing a prototype for PURPLE APPLE. The basic idea is to form a derived feature matrix that's just like the one for APPLE, except that the feature *purple* replaces the feature *red* and the weight of the new colour feature is appropriately increased. PET FISH would presumably work the same way.

It's pretty clear, however, that this treatment is flawed. To see this, ask yourself *how much* the feature *purple* weighs in the feature matrix for PURPLE APPLE. Clearly, it must weigh more than the feature *red* does in the matrix for APPLE since, though there can be apples that aren't red, there can't be purple apples that aren't purple; any more than there can be red apples that aren't red, or purple apples that aren't apples. In effect, *purple* has to weigh *infinitely* much in the feature matrix for PURPLE APPLE because *purple apples are purple*, unlike *typical apples are red*, is a *logical* truth.

So the Smith/Osherson proposal for composing prototypes faces a dilemma: either treat the logical truths as (merely) extreme cases of statistically reliable truths, or admit that the *weights* assigned to the features in derived matrices aren't compositional *even if the matrices themselves are*. Neither horn of this dilemma seems happy. Moreover, it's pretty clear what's gone wrong: what really sets the weight of the *purple* in PURPLE APPLE isn't the concept's prototype; *it's the concept's logical form*. But prototypes don't have logical forms.

Another way to put the pet fish problem is that the 'features' associated with the As in AN constructions are not, in the general case, independent of the features associated with the Ns. So, suppose that the prototype for NURSE includes the feature *female*. Pace Smith and Osherson's kind of proposal, you can't derive the prototype for MALE NURSE just by replacing *female* with *male*; all sorts of other things have to change too. This is true even though the concept MALE NURSE is 'intersective'; i.e. even though the set of male nurses is the overlap of the set of males with the set of nurses (just as the set of pet fish is the overlap of the set of pets with the set of fish). I want to stress this point because prototype theorists, in their desperation, are sometimes driven to suggest that MALE NURSE, PET FISH, and the like *aren't* compositional after all, but it's all right that they aren't, since they are idioms. But surely, *surely*, not. What could be stronger evidence against PET FISH being an idiom or for its being compositional than that it entails PET and FISH and that {PET, FISH} entails it?

It's perhaps worth mentioning the most recent attempt to salvage the compositionality of prototypes from pet fish, male nurses, striped apples, and the like (Kamp and Partee 1995). The idea goes like this: maybe good examples of striped apples aren't good examples of striped things *tout court* (compare zebras). But, plausibly, a prototypic example of a striped apple would *ipso facto* be as good an example of something striped *as an apple can be*. That is a way of saying that the relevant comparison class for judging the typicality of a sample of apple stripes is not the stripes on things at large but rather the stripes on other apples; it's these that typical apple stripes are typical *of*. In effect, then, what you need to do to predict whether a certain example of apple stripes is a good example of apple stripes, is to "recalibrate" STRIPES to apples.

A fair amount of algebra has recently been thrown at the problem of how, given the appropriate information about a reference set, one might calculate the typicality of one of its members (for discussion, see Kamp and Partee 1995; Osherson and Smith 1996). But, as far as I can see, the undertaking is pointless. For one thing, it bears emphasis that the appropriate information for recalibrating a complex concept comes from the world, not from the content of its constituents. If it happens that they paint fire engines in funny shades of red, then typical fire engine red won't be typical red. To decide whether the colour of a certain engine is typical, you'd therefore need to recalibrate RED to FIRE ENGINE; and to do that, you'd need to know the facts about what shades of red fire engines are painted. Nothing about the concepts RED or FIRE ENGINE, per se, could tell you this; so nothing about these concepts, per se, could predict the typicality of a given sample of fire-engine red. In this sense, "recalibrated" compositionality, even if we knew how to compute it, wouldn't really *be* compositionality. Compositionality is the derivation of the content of a complex concept *just* from its structure and the content of its constituents; *that's why* compositionality explains productivity and systematicity.

Still worse, if possible: identifying the relevant reference set for a complex concept itself depends on a prior grasp of its compositional structure. In the case of STRIPED APPLE, for example, the reference set for the recalibration of STRIPE is the striped apples. How do we know that? Because we know that STRIPED APPLE applies to is the intersection of the striped things and the apple things. And how do we know *that*? Because we know the compositional semantics of STRIPED APPLE. Computing typicality for a complex concept by "recalibrating" its constituents thus *presupposes* semantic compositionality; it presupposes that we already know how the content of the concept depends on the content of the concept's constituents. So, recalibration couldn't be what makes concepts compositional, so it couldn't be what makes them systematic and productive. So what is recalibration *for*? Search me.

By the way, these pet fish sorts of arguments ramify in ways that may not be immediately apparent; compositionality is a sharp sword and cutteth many knots.[15] For example, it's very popular in philosophical circles (it's the last gasp of Empiricist semantics) to suppose that there are such things as 'recognitional concepts'; RED and SQUARE, for example, and likewise, I suppose, DOG and TREE, and many, many others. Peacocke 1992 is a *locus classicus* for this thesis, but any philosopher who says there are 'criteria' for the application of a concept is likely to be intending to claim that the concept is recognitional. All told, that includes quite a lot of philosophers and quite a lot of concepts.

---

[15] An expanded version of the argument I'm about to sketch can be found in Fodor forthcoming *a*; q.v.

A concept is recognitional, in the intended sense, only if the ability to identify its instances in favourable circumstances is among its concept-constitutive possession conditions. Thus, being able to identify squares is part and parcel of having the concept SQUARE; it's constitutive of the content—hence of the identity—of the concept. So the story goes. Notice that having SQUARE doesn't require the ability to identify any and every square (consider a square as big as the universe). Likewise, somebody could be thoroughly a possessor of the concept BIRD and none the less not know whether to apply it to ostriches (to say nothing of pterodactyls). So the story must be (indeed, is) that having a recognitional concept requires being able to recognize good (clear, paradigmatic, etc.) instances of the concept. You don't have BIRD unless you are inclined to take sparrows and the like to be birds.

But, now, the pet fish/striped apple/male nurse worries return full force. If, in particular, nothing is constitutive of conceptual content unless it composes, then recognitional capacities can't be constitutive of conceptual content. For someone could have the appropriate recognitional capacities with respect to FISH (he sees at a glance that trout, tuna, and the like are fish) and could have the appropriate recognitional capacities with respect to PET (he sees at a glance that poodles, Siamese kittens, and the like are pets), but be quite at a loss to identify even paradigmatic pet fish (e.g. even goldfish) as such. Because *being a paradigm* doesn't compose, recognitional capacities don't compose either. So the same argument that shows that paradigms aren't constituents of content shows that recognitional capacities aren't either; hence that there aren't any recognitional concepts. Compositionality is a sharp sword which cutteth many knots. (Or have I mentioned that?)

The long and short: either concepts qua prototypes aren't compositional or, if they are, their compositionality is parasitic upon concepts qua something other than prototypes. Conceptual contents, however, *must* be compositional; nothing else could explain why concepts are systematic and productive. So concepts aren't prototypes. This is too sad for words. A theory of concepts has two things to explain: how concepts function as categories, and how a finite mind can have an infinite and systematic conceptual capacity. Prototypes do a not-bad job of explaining the first (though, notoriously, they're not so good at penguins and ostriches being birds). Anyhow, they do noticeably better than definitions. But they are *hopeless* at the second job; so I am claiming.

It may occur to you, however, that my evidence for this claim has thus far consisted exhaustively of the enumeration of counter-examples; and it may likewise strike you that that kind of evidence isn't ultimately persuasive. No doubt, there are technical problems about uncats and pet fish; but it's a profound methodological principle (owing, I believe, to Jim Higginbotham) that for technical problems there are technical solutions. Maybe there is, after all, some way around the apparent failures of prototypes to compose? Given all the evidence that people do have prototypes, isn't the identification of prototypes with concepts a programme that's worth persisting in? Surely, the proper response to a counter-example is to explain it away? Or simply to ignore it?

That is a methodology with which I am deeply sympathetic. But it doesn't apply in the present case since there is independent reason to doubt that the examples of failures of prototypes to compose are merely apparent. It's not just that, prima facie, the identification of contents with prototypes fails for certain cases; it's that there's a pretty convincing diagnosis of the failures which, if correct, shows why the project *can't* succeed. Here's the diagnosis.

Prototype theories of conceptual content are, as we've seen, instances of inferential role theories of conceptual content. Their only fundamental argument with the classical, definitional version of IRS is over *which* inferences are content-constitutive: classical theorists say it's the defining ones, prototype theories say that it's the statistically reliable ones. But so long as IRS is common ground for everyone concerned, this is an argument that the classical theorists are bound to win. That's because, except for definitional inferences, *inferential roles themselves don't compose*.

Compositionality says that, whatever content is, constituents must yield theirs to their hosts and hosts must derive theirs from their constituents. Roughly, the first half is required because whatever is true of cows as such or of brown things as such is *ipso facto* true of brown cows. And the second half is required because, if the content of BROWN COW is *not* fully determined by the content of BROWN and the content of COW (together with syntactic structure), then grasping BROWN and COW isn't sufficient for grasping BROWN COW, and the standard explanation of productivity is undone.

Now, complying with the first half of this constraint is easy for IRS since BROWN contributes to BROWN COW not only its *content-constitutive* inferences (whichever those may be), but *every* inference that holds of brown things in general.[16] If whatever is a cow is an animal, then brown cows are animals a fortiori. If whatever is brown is square, then, a fortiori, every brown cow is a square cow.

But the second half of the compositionality constraint is tricky for an

---

[16] If *all* of BROWN's inferential role is content-constitutive, so be it; BROWN contributes its whole inferential role to BROWN COW, so compositionality isn't violated. Holism is compatible with compositionality. As far as I know, that's its only virtue.

IRS. If nothing can belong to the content of BROWN COW except what it inherits either from BROWN or from COW, then the content of BROWN COW *can't* be its *whole* inferential role. For, of course, all sorts of inferences can hold of brown cows (not qua brown or qua cows but) simply as such. That's because all sorts of things can be true of brown cows that aren't true either of brown things in general or of cows in general; that they are brown cows is an egregious example.

If an *X*-kind of inference is required to be such that constituents contribute all their *X*-inferences to their hosts, and hosts inherit their *X*-inferences only from their constituents, then only *defining* inferences will do as candidates for *X*: the inferential role of a complex concept is exhaustively determined by the inferential roles of its constituents *only* with respect to its defining inferences.[17] That statistical inferences fail to compose is just a special case of this general truth. The pet fish problem is therefore not a fluke. Either the classical, definitional version of IRS is right, or no version can be.

So here's the impasse: prototypes are public (i.e. they are widely shared) and they are psychologically real, so they do meet two of the non-negotiable conditions that concepts are required to meet; but they aren't compositional. Definitions would be compositional if there were any, but there aren't, so they're not. As things stand, *there is no version of the inferential role theory of conceptual content for which compositionality and psychological reality can both be claimed.* I think there must be something wrong with inferential role theories of content.

A modest proposal:

—"All right, all right; but if constituent concepts don't contribute their definitions or their prototypes to their complex hosts, what *do* they contribute?"

—Duck soup. *They contribute what they mean*; e.g. the properties that they express. What PET contributes to PET FISH is the property of *being a pet*; what FISH contributes to PET FISH is the property of *being a fish*. It's because PET contributes *pet* to PET FISH and FISH contributes *fish* to PET FISH that PET FISH entails PET and FISH. And it's because *pet* and *fish* exhaust the content of PET FISH that {PET, FISH} entails PET FISH. There are, to be sure, hard cases for this sort of analysis (what do RISING and TEMPERATURE contribute to THE RISING

[17] More precisely, only with respect to *conceptually necessary* inferences. (Notice that neither nomological nor metaphysical necessity will do; there might be laws about brown cows per se, and (who knows?) brown cows might have a proprietary hidden essence.) I don't know what a Classical IRS theorist should say if it turns out that conceptually necessary inferences aren't *ipso facto* definitional or vice versa. That, however, is his problem, not mine.

TEMPERATURE?), but they are just the cases that are hard for compositionality on *any* known view.

—"Oh bother, why didn't *I* think of that?"

—Presumably because the metaphysics that you had in mind says that meaning is constituted by inferential roles; in which case, the present proposal is no better off than the ones that we've just been discussing. By contrast, informational semantics contemplates the metaphysical possibility that there should be something that a concept means (e.g. a property that it expresses) even though the concept enters into *no constitutive inferential relations at all*. My advice is, therefore: if you want to say what compositionality appears to require you to—that what a concept contributes to its hosts is what it means—you'd better mean by 'what it means' not its inferential role but something like *the information that it carries*, where, by assumption, RED carries information about *redness*.

Inferential role semantics is bankrupt. Because cognitive science has swallowed Inferential Role Semantics whole, its treatment of concepts is bankrupt too; it keeps writing cheques on a theory of meaning that isn't there. It is *very naughty* to write cheques that you can't cash, and it's past time for cognitive science to kick the habit. Chapters 6 and 7 will be about that.

APPENDIX 5A
Meaning Postulates

Prototypes dissociate two issues that definition theories treat together: *What is the structure of a lexical concept?* and *What modal inferences do you have to accept to have the lexical concept X?* On the definition story, both these questions get answered by reference to the relations between concepts and their parts: lexical concepts typically have constituent structure, much like phrasal concepts; and if the concept *C* is a constituent of the concept *X*, then you don't have *X* unless you believe that *X*s are *necessarily C*s. The argument between definitions and prototypes is over the second of these claims.

But it's worth noting that the question whether lexical concepts have constituent structure can be dissociated from *both* the question whether inferences constitute content and whether what makes an inference content-constitutive is something about its modality. *Inferential role semantics doesn't have to claim that lexical concepts are structurally complex* if it doesn't want to. In particular, it doesn't have to claim that the inferences which constitute a concept's content are defined over its constituent structure.

There may be several motivations for separating the question whether (and which) inferences constitute content from the question whether typical lexical concepts are structurally complex. Some philosophers do so because they want to hold on to intuitions of analyticity in face of the mounting empirical evidence that lexical concepts generally behave like atoms by either linguistic or psychological criteria. And there's an independent, semantical argument as well; it's known in the lexical semantics literature as the 'residuum problem'.

In the most familiar cases, lexically governed inferences are supposed to follow from definitions by an analogue to simplification of conjunction. Thus, 'bachelor' entails *unmarried* because its definition is '*male and unmarried*' and the 'and' works in the usual truth-conditional way. This treatment fits naturally with the idea that concepts are bundles of semantic features, each of which express a property of the (actual or possible) things that the concept subsumes.

Now, it's natural to assume that if there is a property corresponding to the feature bundle '$F_1, F_2, \ldots, F_n$', then there should also be a property corresponding to the bundle '$F_1, F_2, \ldots, F_{n-1}$'. So, for example, what's left when you take the *unmarried* out of the definition of 'bachelor' is the definition of 'male'; and what's left when you take the *male* out of the definition of 'bachelor' is the definition of 'unmarried'. Just as the result of simplifying a conjunctive predicate is always itself a predicate, so the result of simplifying a feature bundle is always itself a feature bundle.

But there are cases of lexically governed entailment which appear not to follow this model; 'red → colour' is a paradigm. According to the definition story, this inference should be the simplification of a complex concept (the definition of 'red') which has the form: '$F_1, \ldots,$ COLOUR, $\ldots$'; but, on reflection, it's hard to see what could go in for the 'F_1'. A male is something that is just like a bachelor but not necessarily married; but what is just like red but not necessarily a colour? If you take the 'COLOUR' out of the definition of 'red', what you're left with *doesn't seem to be a possible meaning*; the residuum of 'red → coloured' is apparently a surd. Or, to put it the other way round, it looks like the only thing that could combine with 'COLOURED' to mean *red* is 'RED'. That, however, can't be what the lexical semanticist is proposing. To have 'RED' in the definition of 'red' would make 'COLOUR' redundant, since if 'RED' means *red*, it *thereby* entails 'COLOUR'. If the definition of 'red' includes RED, that's *all* it includes, so in effect the proposal that it does concedes the concept to atomism.

It might be possible to treat such cases as mere curiosities specific to sensory concepts. It's sometimes suggested that they illustrate the presence of an "iconic" element in concepts like RED (see the discussion above of Jackendoff 1992). Maybe 'red' means something like 'similar in respect of colour to this' where the 'this' ostensively introduces a red sample. The trouble with taking this line, however, is that the pattern RED and the like exemplify actually appears to be quite general: lots of lexical concepts for which *definitions* are very hard to find nevertheless appear to enter into the same sort of "one way" entailments that hold between 'red' and 'colour'. It's plausible that 'dog' means *animal*, but there doesn't seem to be any F (except DOG) such that 'F + ANIMAL' means *dog*. 'Chair' means *furniture*, but what and FURNITURE means *chair*? Notice that it won't do to appeal to 'iconic elements' in these non-sensory cases. Maybe 'red' means '*similar in colour to this*', but 'dog' doesn't mean '*similar in X to this*' for any X that I can think of except *dog*hood. It appears that, contrary to traditional Empiricist doctrine, many lexical items are not independent but not definable either; 'red' entails 'colour' but can't be defined in terms of it.

A natural way to accommodate the residuum problem is to allow that some content-constitutive inferences don't arise from definitions after all. It's not that RED entails COLOUR because the definition of 'red' is COLOUR & F; rather, RED just entails COLOUR full stop. Following the historical usage, I'll call a principle of inference that institutes a 'one way' relation of entailment between lexical concepts a "meaning postulate". Rules of lexically governed inference that happen to be biconditional, like 'bachelor ↔ unmarried man', have no special status according to the theory that meaning postulates are what license lexically governed inferences. This version of Inferential Role Semantics is therefore *weaker* than the definitional account; the latter allows a lexical concept to enter into constitutive inferential relations *only if it is definable*.

From our perspective, the important consequence of this liberalization is that it disconnects the question whether an inference from C to C_1 is content-constitutive from the question whether C_1 is a syntactic part of C. Notice that it was only because definitions were required to be biconditional that they *could* be viewed as exhibiting the structural description of a concept. UNMARRIED MAN can't be the structural description of BACHELOR unless 'BACHELOR' and 'UNMARRIED MAN' denote the same concept. But BACHELOR and UNMARRIED MAN can't be the same concept unless 'BACHELOR ↔ UNMARRIED MAN' is true.

Detaching the question whether RED entails COLOUR from the question whether COLOUR is a constituent of RED has its virtues, to be sure. We've been seeing how weakly the empirical evidence supports claims for the internal structure of lexical concepts. Meaning postulates allow one to give up such claims while holding onto both "'red' means *colour* is analytic' and 'you don't have RED unless you know that red is a colour'. On the meaning postulate story, RED → COLOUR could be meaning-constitutive even if neither RED nor COLOUR have *any* internal structure; i.e. even if it's atomic.

But no free lunch, of course. We started out this chapter by remarking that one of the nicest things about the definition story was that it explains an otherwise striking and perplexing symmetry between the metaphysics of meaning and the metaphysics of concept possession: *the very inferences that are supposed to define a concept are also the ones you have to accept in order to possess the concept.* This really is striking and perplexing and not at all truistic; remember, it isn't (can't be) true of *all* necessary inferences—or even of all a priori inferences—that they determine the conditions for possessing the concepts involved in them. Well, the theory that concepts are definitions gets this symmetry for free; it follows from the fact that definitions relate concepts *to their constituents*. If C is literally a part of C_1, then *of course* you can't have C_1 unless you also have C. Notice that this explanation turns on precisely the idea that meaning postulates propose to abandon: viz. that the content-constitutive inferences are the ones that relate a concept to its parts.

In short, if you are *independently* convinced *both* that there are meaning-constitutive inferences *and* that most lexical concepts behave like primitives, you've got a residuum problem to which meaning postulates may indeed offer a solution. But at a price, since the solution weakens the architecture of your overall theory: it breaks the connection between the structure of a concept and its possession conditions.

Partee has tried bravely to make a virtue of this necessity:

Meaning postulates might be a helpful tool . . . since they make the *form* [*sic*] of some kinds of lexical information no different in kind from the form of some kinds of general knowledge. That would make it possible to hypothesize that the very same 'fact'—for example, whales are mammals—could be stored in either of two 'places,' a storehouse of lexical knowledge or a storehouse of empirical knowledge; whether it's part of the meaning of 'whale' or not need not be fixed once and for all. (1995: 328)

But it is inadvisable for a theory to recognize degrees of freedom that it is unable to interpret. Exactly because meaning postulates break the 'formal' relation between belonging to the structure of a concept and being among its constitutive inferences, *it's unclear why it matters* which box a given such 'fact' goes into; i.e. whether a given inference is treated as meaning-constitutive. Imagine two minds that differ in that 'whale → mammal' is a meaning postulate for one but is 'general knowledge' for the other. Are any further differences between these minds entailed? If so, which ones? Is this wheel attached to anything at all?

It's a point Quine made against Carnap that the answer to 'When is an inference analytic?' can't be just 'Whenever I feel like saying that it is'. Definition versions of IR Semantics can hold that an inference is analytic when and only when it follows from the structure of a concept. If the meaning postulate version has an alternative proposal on offer, it's not one that I've heard of.

APPENDIX 5B
The 'Theory Theory'[18] of Concepts

The theories of concepts discussed so far all presuppose Inferential Role Semantics, so they all owe an account of which inferences determine conceptual content. The big divides are between holism (which says that all inferences do) and some sort of molecularism (which says that only some inferences do); and, within the latter, between classical theories (according to which it is modality that matters to content constitution) and prototype theories (according to which it's empirical reliability that does). In effect, the various theories of concepts we've reviewed are versions of IRS distinguished, primarily, by what they say about the problem of individuating content.

Now, a quite standard reading of the history of cognitive science has the reliability-based versions of IRS displacing the modality-based versions and in turn being displaced, very recently, by theory theories.[19] But that way of telling the story is, I think, mistaken. Though theory theories do propose a view about what concepts are (or, anyhow, about what concepts are like; or, anyhow, about what a lot of concepts are like), they don't, as far as I can tell, offer a distinct approach to the content individuation problems. Sometimes they borrow the modality story from definitional theories, sometimes they borrow the reliability story from prototype theories, sometimes they share the holist's despair of individuating concepts at all. So, for our purposes at least, it's unclear that theory theories of concepts differ substantially from the kinds of theories

[18] I'm not crazy about this terminology, if only because it invites conflation with the quite different issue whether "folk psychology" is a (tacit) theory (see, for example, Gordon 1986). But it's standard in the cognitive science literature so I'll stick with it, and from here on I'll omit the shudder-quotes.

[19] For a relatively clear example of a discussion where theory theories are viewed as *alternatives* to probabilistic accounts of concepts, see Keil 1987. See also Keil 1991, where the primary contrast is between theory theories and "associative" models of concept structure. For a critical survey of the recent history, see Margolis 1994.

of concepts that we've already reviewed. Hence the relatively cursory treatment they're about to receive.

The basic idea is that concepts are like theoretical constructs in science *as the latter are often construed by post-Empiricist philosophers of science*. The caveat is important. For example, it's not unusual (see Carey 1991; Gopnik 1988) among theory theorists to postulate 'stage-like discontinuities' in conceptual development, much as Piagetians do. But, unlike Piaget, theory theorists construe the putative stage changes on the analogy of—perhaps even as special cases of—the kinds of discontinuities that 'paradigm shifts' are said to occasion in the history of science. The usual Kuhnian morals are often explicitly drawn:

the concepts of the new and old theory and of the evidential description are incommensurab[le].(Gopnik 1988: 199)

Asking whether or not the six-month-old has a concept of object-permanence in the same sense that the 18-month-old does is like asking whether or not the alchemist and the chemist have the same concept of gold, or whether Newton had the same concept of space as Einstein. These concepts are embedded in complex theories and there is no simple way of comparing them. Moreover, particular concepts are inextricably intertwined with other concepts in the theory. (Ibid.: 205)

It should be clear how much this account of conceptual ontogenesis relies on a Kuhnian view of science. It isn't just that if Kuhn is wrong about theory change, then Gopnik is wrong about the analogy between the history of science and conceptual development. It's also that key notions like *discontinuity* and *incommensurability* aren't explicated within the ontogenetic theory; the buck is simply passed to the philosophers. "It may not resolve our puzzlement over the phenomena of qualitative conceptual change in childhood to point out that there are exactly parallel paradoxes of incommensurability in science, but at this stage we may see the substitution of a single puzzling phenomenon for two separate puzzling phenomena as some sort of progress" (Gopnik 1988: 209). Correspondingly, however, if you find the idea that a scientific theory-change is a paradigm shift less than fully perspicuous, you will also be uncertain what exactly it is that the ontogenetic analogy asserts about stages of conceptual development. Your response will then be a sense less of illumination than of *déjà vu*.

If Gopnik finds some solace in this situation, that's because, like Kuhn, she takes IRS not to be in dispute.[20] The putative "problem of incommens-

_____

[20] They aren't the only ones, of course. For example, Keil remarks that "Theories . . . make it impossible . . . to talk about the construction of concepts solely on the basis of

urability" is that *if* the vocabulary of a science is implicitly defined by the theories it endorses, it's hard to see how the theories can correct or contradict each other. This state of affairs might be supposed to provide a precedent for psychologists to appeal to who hold that the minds of young children are incommensurably different from the minds of adults. Alternatively, it might be taken as a reductio of the supposition that the vocabulary of a science is implicitly defined by its theories. It's hard to say which way one ought to take it barring some respectable story about *how* scientific theories implicitly define their vocabularies; specifically, an account that makes clear which of the inferences that such a theory licenses are constitutive of the concepts it deploys. And there's no point in cognitive scientists relying on the philosophy of science for an answer to this question; the philosophy of science hasn't got one. It seems that we're back where we started.

In short, it may be that the right moral to draw from the putative analogy between scientific paradigms and developmental stages is that the ontogenesis of concepts is discontinuous, just like scientific theory-change. Or the right moral may be that, by relativizing the individuation of concepts to the individuation of theories, IRS makes a hash of *both* cognitive development *and* the history of science.

If there is any positive account of conceptual content that most theory theorists are inclined towards, I suppose that it's holism.[21] I don't, however, know of any attempt they have made seriously to confront the objections that meaning holism is prone to. Two of these are particularly relevant. The first is familiar and quite general (see Chapter 1 and Fodor and Lepore 1992) and I won't go on about it here. Suffice it that if the individuation of concepts is literally relativized to whole belief systems, then no two people, and no two time slices of a given person, are ever subsumed by the same intentional generalizations, and the prospects for robust theories in intentional psychology are negligible.

---

probabilistic distributions of properties in the world" (1987: 196). But that's true only on the assumption that theories somehow constitute the concepts they contain. Ditto Keil's remark that "future work on the nature of concepts . . . must focus on the sorts of theories that emerge in children and how these theories come to influence the structure of the concepts that they embrace" (ibid.).

[21] There are exceptions. Susan Carey thinks that the individuation of concepts must be relativized to the theories they occur in, but that only the basic 'ontological' commitments of a theory are content constitutive. (However, see Carey 1985: 168: "I assume that there is a continuum of degrees of conceptual differences, at the extreme end of which are concepts embedded in incommensurable conceptual systems.") It's left open how basic ontological claims are to be distinguished from commitments of other kinds, and Carey is quite aware that problems about drawing this distinction are depressingly like the analytic/synthetic problems. But in so far as Carey has an account of content individuation on offer, it does seem to be some version of the Classical theory.

But I do want to say a word or so about the second objection, which is that holism about content individuation doesn't square with key principles of the theory theory itself. Consider, in particular, the idea that new concepts get introduced, in the course of theory change, by a kind of implicit theoretical definition. In all the examples I've heard of, a theory can be used to effect the implicit definition of a new term only if at least some of its vocabulary is *isolated* from meaning changes of the sorts that holists say that concept introduction brings about. That's hardly surprising. Intuitively, implicit definition determines the meaning of a new term by determining its inferential relations to terms in the host theory that are *presumed to be previously understood*. It is, to put it mildly, hard to see how this could work if introducing a new concept into a theory *ipso facto* changes what all the old terms mean. For then the expressions by reference to which the neologism is introduced aren't 'previously understood' after all: they are just *homophones* of the previously understood expressions.[22]

Consider, for a familiar example, the introduction by implicit definition of a logical constant like '∨'. The idea is that to determine that '∨' has the same sense as the (truth conditional, inclusive) English 'or', it's sufficient to stipulate that:

$$P \rightarrow P \vee Q$$
$$(P \vee Q) \, \& \sim P \rightarrow Q$$

But the plausibility of claiming that these stipulations determine that '∨' means 'or' depends on supposing that they preserve the standard interpretations of '&' (= conjunction), '∼' (= negation), and '→' (= truth-functional implication). That, however, implies that the interpretation of '&', '∼', and '→' must be assumed to be isolated from whatever meaning changes adding '∨' to the host theory is supposed to bring about; an assumption that is contrary, apparently, to the holist thesis that the semantic effects of theory change reverberate throughout the vocabulary of the theory. (I say that it's 'apparently' contrary to the holist thesis because I know of no formulation of semantic holism that is precise enough to yield unequivocal entailments about which changes of theory effect which changes of meaning.)

---

[22] This point is related, but not identical, to the familiar worry about whether implicit definition can effect a 'qualitative change' in a theory's expressive power: the worry that definitions (implicit or otherwise) can only introduce concepts whose contents are already expressible by the host theory. (For discussion, see Fodor 1975.) It looks to me that implicit definition is specially problematic for meaning holists *even if* it's granted that an implicit definition can (somehow) extend the host theory's expressive power.

This isn't just a technical problem; texts that flout it tend to defy coherent exegesis. Consider, for one example among very many, Gopnik's suggestion[23] that

An 'object' is a theoretical entity which explains sequences of what (for lack of a better term) we might call object-appearances at the evidential level . . . At the very earliest stage infants seem to have a few rules about the relations between their own actions and object-appearances, for example, infants seem to know that objects disappear when you turn away from them and reappear when you turn back to them. (1988: 205)

(and so forth, *mutatis mutandis*, for further 'rules' that the child gets later).

How are we to interpret this passage? Notice the tell-tale aporia (where are you, Jacques Derrida, now that we need you?). The rule with which the infants are credited is said to be about "relations between their own actions and object-*appearances*" (my emphasis). But, when an instance of such a rule is offered, it turns out to be that "*objects* [my emphasis] disappear when you turn away from them". Question: what does 'objects' mean in this rule? In particular, *what does it mean to the infant* who, we're supposing, learns the concept OBJECT by a process that involves formulating and adopting the rule?[24] If it means object-*appearances*, then (quite aside from traditional worries about how an *appearance* could *reappear*) it doesn't do what Gopnik wants; since it specifies a relation *among* object-appearances, it doesn't give the infant information about the relation between *objects* and object-appearances.

So, maybe 'object' means *theoretical entity which explains sequences of what (for lack of a better term) we might call object-appearances at the evidential level*. I rush past the implausibility of claiming that infants have to have that much ontology (in particular, that much *dubious* ontology) in order to learn quotidian object-concepts like CHAIR. I'm a nativist too, after all. The more pressing problem for a theory theorist is: if *that's* what 'object' means in the infant's rule, *in what sense are there discontinuities in the development of the infant's object-concept*? On this reading of the text, it looks like what the infant has—right from the start and right to the finish—is a concept of an object that's much like Locke's: objects are unobservable kinds of things that cause experiences. Correspondingly, cognitive development consists of learning more and more about things of

---

[23] I don't particularly mean to pick on Gopnik; the cognitive science literature is full of examples of the mistake that I'm trying to draw attention to. What's unusual about Gopnik's treatment is just that it's clear enough for one to see what the problem is.

[24] As usual, it's essential to keep in mind that when a de dicto intentional explanation attributes to an agent knowledge (rules, etc.), it *thereby credits the agent* with the concepts involved in formulating the knowledge, and thus incurs the burden of saying what concepts they are. See the 'methodological digression' in Chapter 2.

this kind (e.g. that when you turn your back on one, it ceases to cause appearances in you . . . etc.).[25] What, then, has become of the discontinuity of the object-concept? In particular, what's become of the *incommensurability* of the infant's object-concept with grown-up Gopnik's? It turns out that Gopnik can, after all, say *exactly* what (according to her theory) the infant's earliest concept of an object is: it's the concept of *a theoretical entity which explains sequences of . . . etc. . . . and which ceases to cause appearances in you when you turn your back on it . . .* etc.

I suppose what Gopnik really ought to say, if she wants to be true to the implicit definition picture, is that the concept of an object is that of 'AN *X* WHICH . . .', and that cognitive development consists in adding more and more relative clauses. But it's hard to see why such a thesis would count as construing concept development as discontinuous. And, anyhow, it's hard to see how it could be swallowed by a meaning holist. Isn't meaning holism, by definition, committed to there *not* being a notion of content identity that tolerates the addition of *new* information to the same *old* concept?

The local moral, to repeat, is that maybe you can make sense of concept introduction as implicit theoretical definition, and maybe you can make sense of meaning holism. But it's very unclear that you can make sense of both at the same time. The general moral is that, if the theory theory has a distinctive and coherent answer to the 'What's a concept?' question on offer, it's a well-kept secret.

I should add, in minimal fairness, that it's not clear that theory theorists are really all that interested in what concepts are. Certainly it's often hard to tell whether they are from what they say. For example, Medin and Wattenmaker (1987; see also Murphy and Medin 1985) undertake to "review evidence that suggests concepts should be viewed as embedded in theories" (34–5), a thesis which they clearly regard as tendentious, but which, as it is stated, it's hard to imagine that anyone could disagree with. What I suppose they must have in mind is that concepts are somehow *constituted* (their identity is somehow determined) by the theories in which they are embedded. But that claim, though tendentious enough, doesn't amount to a new account of conceptual content; unless the 'somehows' are somehow cashed, it just reiterates IRS.

The situation in Medin and Wattenmaker is especially confusing because its so hard to figure out what they think that the theory theory is a theory of; they are explicit that it's supposed to provide an account of the

---

[25] If "object" means *thing that causes appearances* then, of course, the rule isn't that objects *disappear* when you turn your back on them; it's just that they cease, for the nonce, to cause you to experience them.

"coherence" of concepts, but it's far from clear what they think conceptual coherence is. At one point, having suggested that the theory theory should provide "guidelines concerning which combinations of features form possible concepts and which form coherent ones" (1987: 30), they offer, as an example of an incoherent concept, "bright red, flammable, eats mealworms, found in Lapland, and used for cleaning furniture". So it sounds as though the question about conceptual coherence that the theory theory answers is: What's wrong with this and other such concepts?

But it's hard to believe that *is* the question since the answer, though perfectly obvious and entirely banal, is one that Medin and Wattenmaker don't even consider. What's wrong with the concept BRIGHT RED, FLAMMABLE, EATS MEALWORMS, . . . etc. is that, as far as anybody knows, there's nothing that is, or would be, true of things in virtue of their falling under it (except what follows trivially from their falling under it; e.g. that they are, or would be, found in Lapland). In particular, there are no substantive, counterfactual-supporting generalizations about such things; so why on earth would anybody want to waste his time thinking about them? Compare such unsatisfied (but coherent) concepts as UNICORN. At least there's a *story* about unicorns. That is, there are interesting things that are *supposed to be* true about them: that their ground-up horns are antidotes to many poisons; that if there were unicorns, virgins could catch them if there were virgins, and so on. In short, such examples as Medin and Wattenmaker offer suggest that being 'coherent' isn't even a *psychological* property: the incoherence of BRIGHT RED, FLAM-MABLE, . . . etc. is a defect not of the concept but of the world. It's therefore hard to see why a psychologist should care about it (though perhaps a zoologist might).

Or perhaps Medin and Wattenmaker have some other construal of conceptual coherence in mind; but search me what it is.[26]

To return to the main theme: many of the typical preoccupations of theory theorists seem to be largely neutral on the issue of concept

---

[26] See also Keil: "Prototypes merely represent correlated properties, they offer no explanation of the reasons for those correlations (e.g. why the prototypical features of birds, such as beaks, feathers, and eggs tend to co-occur)" (1987: 195). The suggestion seems to be that the difference between prototype theories and theory theories is that the latter entail that having a concept involves knowing the explanation of such correlations (or knowing that there is an explanation? or knowing that some expert knows the explanation?). But, if so, it seems that theory theories set the conditions for concept possession impossibly high. I'm pretty confident that being liquid and transparent at room temperature are correlated properties of water. But I have no idea *why* they are correlated. Notice, in particular, that learning that *being water* is *being H_2O* didn't advance my epistemic situation in this respect since *I don't know why being liquid and transparent at room temperature are correlated properties of H_2O*. Do you?

individuation—Is conceptual change discontinuous? What makes a concept coherent? Are children metaphysical essentialists?—and the like. There is, to be sure, much that's of interest to be said on these topics. But, thank Heaven, not here. From our point of view, the crucial question is whether, when a theory theorist says that concepts are typically embedded in theoretical inferences, he means to claim that knowing (some or all) of the theory is a necessary condition for having the concept. If yes, then the 'which inferences' question has to be faced. If no, then some positive account of concept possession/individuation is owing. The definition story and the prototype story are bona fide competing theories of concepts because they do have answers to such questions on offer. As far as I can make out, the theory theory doesn't, so it isn't.

6

Innateness and Ontology, Part I:
The Standard Argument[1]

I find only myself, every time, in everything I create.
                                        —Wotan in *Die Walküre*, Act II

Are you also puzzled, Socrates, about cases that might be thought absurd, such as hair or mud or dirt or any other trivial and undignified objects. Are you doubtful whether or not to assert that each of these has a separate form? . . . Not at all, said Socrates. In these cases, the things are just the things we see; it would surely be too absurd to suppose that they have a form.

                                        —Plato, *Parmenides*

Virginia Woolf has summed up this state of things with perfect vividness and conciseness in the words, 'Tuesday follows Monday'.
                                        —E. M. W. Tillyard, *Shakespeare's Last Plays*

Introduction

RTM requires there to be infinitely many concepts that are complex and finitely many that are primitive. RTM also requires concepts to have their contents essentially. The versions of RTM that are currently standard in philosophy and in cognitive science, however, want still more: most lexical concepts should *not* be primitive, and the content of concepts should be determined, at least *inter alia*, by their inferential-cum-causal relations to one another. I think, however, that the evidence is getting pretty solid that the last two conditions can't be met; lexical concepts typically don't act as though they were internally structured by either psychological or linguistic

---

[1] This chapter reconsiders some issues about the nativistic commitments of RTMs that I first raised in Fodor 1975 and then discussed extensively in 1981*a*. Casual familiarity with the latter paper is recommended as a prolegomenon to this discussion.

I'm especially indebted to Andrew Milne and to Peter Grim for having raised (essentially the same) cogent objections to a previous version.

test. And the question *which* aspects of a concept's inferential role are the ones that determine its meaning appears to be hopeless. Thus far has the World Spirit progressed.

I propose, therefore, that we scrap the standard versions of RTM and consider, in their place, a doctrine that I'll call Informational Atomism. (IA for short.) IA has an informational part and it has an atomistic part. To wit:

— *Informational semantics*: content is constituted by some sort of nomic, mind–world relation. Correspondingly, having a concept (concept possession) is constituted, at least in part, by *being in* some sort of nomic, mind–world relation.

— *Conceptual atomism*: most lexical concepts have no internal structure.

As far as I can tell, nobody but me thinks that IA has a prayer of being true; not even people who are quite sympathetic to RTM. Now, why is that, do you suppose?

I can imagine three objections to IA (however, see Appendix 7A). The first of these I'm prepared not to take very seriously, but the second two need some discussion. Most of this chapter and the next one are devoted to them. I should say at the outset that I regard what follows as very tentative indeed. Though the standard versions of RTM have been explored practically to death, IA is virgin territory. The best I hope for is a rough sketch of the geography.

First objection: If atomism is true and most lexical concepts have no internal structure, then there is no such thing as the analysis of most of the concepts that philosophers care about. That BROWN COW has a philosophical analysis (into BROWN and COW) isn't much consolation.

Reply: Strictly speaking, you can have conceptual analysis without structured concepts since, strictly speaking, you can have analyticity without structured concepts (see Appendix 5A). You do, however, have to live with the failure of attempts to reduce analyticity to conceptual containment. And you have to live with the general lack of empirical sanction for claims that satisfying the possession conditions for some concept *A* requires satisfying the possession conditions for some other concept *B*. As far as I can tell, there is little or no evidence for such claims except brute appeals to intuition; and, as we saw in Chapter 4, a case can be made that the intuitions thus appealed to are corrupt.

On the other hand, who cares about conceptual analysis? It's a commonplace that its successes have been, to put it mildly, very sparse. Indeed, viewed from the cognitive psychologist's perspective, the main point about conceptual analysis is that it's *supposed* to fail. For all sorts of quotidian concepts, its answers to 'What is their content?' and to 'How do you acquire them?' are, respectively, 'It has none' and 'You don't'. It's worth bearing in mind that analytic philosophy, from Hume to Carnap inclusive, was a *critical* programme. For the Empiricists, the idea was to constrain the conditions for concept possession a priori, by constraining the acceptable relations between concepts and percepts. It would then turn out that you really don't have many of the concepts that you think you have; you don't have GOD, CAUSE, or TRIANGLE at all, and though perhaps you do have DOG, it's not the sort of concept that you had supposed it to be. "When we run over the libraries, persuaded of these principles, what havoc must we make?" (Hume 1955: 3.) Post-Positivist philosophical analysis has wavered between reconstruction and deconstruction, succeeding in neither. Most practitioners now hold that we do have DOG, CAUSE, and TRIANGLE after all; maybe even GOD. But they none the less insist that there are substantive, a priori, epistemological constraints on concept possession. These, in the fullness of time, analysis will reveal; to the confusion of Sceptics, Metaphysical Realists, Mentalists, Cartesians, and the like. Probably of Cognitive Scientists too.

But, between friends: nothing of the sort is going to happen. In which case, what's left to a notion of conceptual analysis that's detached from its traditional polemical context? And what on earth are conceptual analyses *for*?

Second objection: The informational part of IA says that content is constituted by nomic symbol-world connections. If that is true, then there must be laws about everything that we have concepts of. Now, it may be there are laws about *some* of the things that we have concepts of (fish, stars, grandmothers(?!)). But how could there be laws about, as it might be, *doorknobs*?[2] Notice that it's only in conjunction with conceptual atomism that informational semantics incurs this objection. Suppose the concept DOORKNOB is definitionally equivalent to the complex concept . . . *ABC* . . . Then we can think the former concept if there are laws about each of the constituents of the latter. In effect, all informational semantics per se requires for its account of conceptual content is that there be laws about the properties expressed by our *primitive* concepts. However, IA says that practically every (lexical) concept is primitive. So, presumably, it says that DOORKNOB is primitive.[3] So there must be laws about doorknobs

---

[2] For discussions that turn on this issue, see Fodor 1986; Antony and Levine 1991; Fodor 1991.

[3] Actually, of course, DOORKNOB isn't a very good example, since it's plausibly a compound composed of the constituent concepts DOOR and KNOB. But let's ignore that for the sake of the discussion.

qua doorknobs, as it were, not qua *ABC*s. But how could there be laws about doorknobs? Doorknobs, of all things!

Third objection: If most lexical concepts have no internal structure, then most lexical concepts must be primitive. But primitive concepts are, *ipso facto*, unlearned; and if a concept is unlearned, then it must be innate. But how could DOORKNOB be innate? *DOORKNOB*, of all things!! Prima facie, this objection holds against (not just IA but) any version of RTM that is not heavily into conceptual reduction; that is, against any theory that says that the primitive conceptual basis is large. In particular, it holds prima facie against any atomistic version of RTM, whether or not it is informational.

Objections two and three both turn on the peculiarly central roles that primitive concepts play in RTMs. Primitive concepts are supposed to be the special cases that problems about conceptual content and concept acquisition reduce to. But if not just RTM but also conceptual atomism is assumed, then the special case becomes alarmingly general. If, for example, DOORKNOB is primitive, then whatever metaphysical story we tell about the *content* of primitive concepts has to work for DOORKNOB. And so must whatever psychological story we tell about the *acquisition* of primitive concepts. And the metaphysical story has to work in light of the acquisition story, and the acquisition story has to work in light of the metaphysical story. Hume wouldn't have liked this at all; he wanted the primitives to be just the sensory concepts, and he wanted them to be acquired by the stimulation of an innate sensorium. Pretty clearly, he gets neither if DOORKNOB is among the primitives.

I propose, in this chapter, to explore some of the ways that these issues play out in IA versions of RTM. We'll consider how, because of the way it construes conceptual content, IA is maybe able to avoid some extremes of conceptual nativism to which other atomistic versions of RTM are prone. (Though at a price, to be sure. No free lunches here either.) In Chapter 7, I'll take up the question about laws.

The Standard Argument

There is a plausible argument which says that informational atomism implies radical conceptual nativism; I'll call it the 'Standard Argument' (SA). Here, in very rough form, is how the Standard Argument is supposed to go.

SA begins by assuming that learning a concept is an *inductive* process; specifically, that it requires devising and testing hypotheses about what the property is in virtue of which things fall under the concept. This is relatively unproblematic when the concept to be acquired is a definition. If the concept BACHELOR is the concept UNMARRIED MALE, you can learn BACHELOR by learning that things fall under it in virtue of *being male* and *being unmarried*. But, on pain of circularity, the (absolutely) primitive concepts can't themselves be learned this way. Suppose the concept RED is primitive. Then to learn RED inductively you'd have to devise and confirm the hypothesis that things fall under RED *in virtue of being red*. But you couldn't devise or confirm that hypothesis unless you already had the concept RED, *since the concept RED is invoked in the formulation of the hypothesis*. So you can't have learned the concept RED (or, *mutatis mutandis*, any other primitive concept) inductively, by hypothesis testing and confirmation. But SA assumes that induction is the only sort of concept learning that there is. So it follows that you can't have learned your primitive concepts at all. But if you have a concept that you can't have learned, then you must have it innately. So the Standard Argument says. What, if anything, is wrong with this?

To begin with, it might be replied that the inductive account of concept *acquisition* is plausible only assuming a cognitivist account of concept *possession*; an account of concept possession according to which having a concept is *knowing something*. This assumption is natural enough if you are thinking of concepts on the model of definitions (/stereotypes/ theories): having a concept is knowing what its definition (/stereo-type/theory) is. By contrast, IA is explicitly *non*-cognitivist about concept possession; it says that having a concept is (not knowing something but) being in a certain nomic mind–world relation; specifically, it's being in that mind–world relation in virtue of which the concept has the content that it does. This changes the geography in ways that may be germane to the present issues. Because it is non-cognitivist about concept possession, IA invites a correspondingly non-cognitivist account of how concepts are acquired. That might be just what you're looking for if you're looking for a way out of SA.

Avoiding nativism by endorsing a non-cognitivist view of concept possession is, of course, hardly a new idea. At least since Ryle (1949), a lot of philosophical ink has been invested in the thought that having a concept is knowing how, not knowing that. Correspondingly, concept acquisition is arguably *learning how*, rather than *learning that*, and it isn't obvious that learning how needs to be inductive. Maybe construing concept possession as know-how is all that avoiding SA requires. I think philosophers quite generally find this plausible.

But it isn't. For one thing, if it's not obvious that learning how requires hypothesis testing, it's also not obvious that it doesn't: in lots of cases, it appears that how-learning itself depends on that-learning.[4] For example, my linguist friends tell me that learning how to talk a first language requires quite a lot of learning that the language has the grammar that it does. I tell my linguist friends that my philosophy friends tell me that it is a priori and necessary that this cannot be so. Then my linguist friends laugh at me. What am I to do?

And, for another thing, whatever the *general* story about knowing how and knowing that may be, the particular skills that concept possession is usually supposed to implicate are *perceptual* and *inferential*, and these look to be just saturated with knowing that. Surely, you can't identify a dog by its barking unless you know(/believe) that dogs bark. Surely, you won't infer from *dog* to *animal* unless you know(/believe) that dogs are animals. Indeed, in the second case, opposing knowing how to knowing that looks like insisting on a distinction without a difference.[5]

Where we've got to is: even if it's supposed that concepts are skills,[6] very little follows that helps with avoiding SA. That's because to avoid SA you need a non-cognitivist view of concept possession. And supposing concepts to be skills doesn't guarantee a non-cognitivist view of concept possession, because it is perfectly possible to be a cognitivist *about the possession of skills*, if not in every case, then at least in the case of the skills that concept possession requires. The moral: *it's unclear that Ryle can deny SA the premiss that it centrally requires, viz. that concept acquisition is mediated by hypothesis formation and testing.*

But IA can. Let's see where this leads.

Following Loewer and Rey (1991*a*) (who are themselves following the usage of ethologists) I'll say that acquiring a concept is getting *nomologically locked* to the property that the concept expresses. So, then, consider a supplemented version of IA (I'll call it SIA) which says everything that IA does and also that concept possession is some kind of locking. The question before us is whether SIA requires radical nativism.

---

[4] That learning how can't depend on learning that in *every* case is, I suppose, the moral of Lewis Carroll's story about Achilles and the tortoise: Carroll 1895/1995.

[5] CogSci footnote: the present issue isn't whether inferential capacities are 'declarative' rather than 'procedural'; it's whether they are interestingly analogous to skills. A cognitive architecture (like SOAR, for example) that is heavily committed to procedural representations is not thereby required to suppose that drawing inferences has much in common with playing basketball or the piano. Say, if you like, that someone who accepts the inference from *P* to *Q* has the habit of accepting *Q* if he accepts *P*. But this sort of 'habit' involves a relation among one's propositional attitudes and, prima facie, being able to play the piano doesn't.

[6] Concepts *aren't* skills, of course; concepts are mental particulars. In particular, they are the constituents of beliefs, whereas skills can't be the constituents of anything except other skills. But though all this is so, the argument in the text doesn't presuppose it.

Notice that the question before us is *not* whether SIA *permits* radical nativism; it's patent that it does. According to SIA, having a concept is being locked to a property. Well, being locked to a property is having a disposition, and though perhaps there are some dispositions that must be acquired, hence can't be innate, nothing I've heard of argues that being locked to a property is one of them. If, in short, you require your metaphysical theory of concept possession to *entail* the denial of radical nativism, SIA won't fill your bill. (I don't see how any metaphysics could, short of question begging, since the status of radical nativism is surely an empirical issue. Radical nativism may be false, but I doubt that it is, in any essential way, *confused*.) But if, you're prepared to settle for a theory of concepts that is plausibly *compatible* with the denial of radical nativism, maybe we can do some business.

If you assume SIA, and hence the locking model of concept possession, you thereby deny that learning concepts necessarily involves acquiring beliefs. And if you deny that learning concepts necessarily involves acquiring beliefs, then you can't assume that hypothesis testing is an ingredient in concept acquisition. It is, as I keep pointing out, primarily cognitivism about the metaphysics of concept possession that motivates inductivism about the psychology of concept acquisition: hypothesis testing is the natural assumption about how *beliefs* are acquired from experience. But if it can't be assumed that concept acquisition is *ipso facto* belief acquisition, then it can't be assumed that locking DOORKNOB to *doorknobhood* requires a mediating hypothesis. And if it can't be assumed that locking DOORKNOB to *doorknobhood* requires a mediating hypothesis, then, a fortiori, it can't be assumed that it requires a mediating hypothesis in which the concept DOORKNOB is itself deployed. In which case, for all that the Standard Argument shows, DOORKNOB could be *both* primitive *and* not innate.

This maybe starts to sound a little hopeful; but not, I'm afraid, for very long. The discussion so far has underestimated the polemical resources that SA has available. In particular, there is an independent argument that seems to show that *concept acquisition has to be inductive, whether or not the metaphysics of concept possession is cognitivist*; so SA gets its inductivist premiss even if SIA is right that having a concept doesn't require having beliefs. The moral would then be that, though a non-cognitivist account of concept possession may be necessary for RTM to avoid radical nativism, it's a long way from being sufficient.

In short, Patient Reader, the Standard Argument's way of getting radical nativism goes like this:

(1) cognitivism about concept *possession* → (2) inductivist (i.e.

hypothesis-testing) model of concept *learning* → (3) primitive concepts can't be learned.

SIA denies (1), thereby promising to block the standard argument. If, however, there's some *other* source for (2)—some plausible premiss to derive it from that doesn't assume a cognitivist metaphysics of concept possession—then the standard argument is back in business.

And there is. Here's a narrowly based argument for the hypothesis-testing model of concept acquisition; one that presupposes neither a cognitivist account of concept possession nor even any general inductivist thesis about the role of hypothesis testing in the acquisition of empirical beliefs.

Nobody, radical nativists included, doubts that what leads to acquiring a concept is typically *having the right kinds of experiences*. That experience is *somehow* essentially implicated in concept acquisition is common ground to both Nativists and Empiricists; their argument is over whether concepts are abstracted from, or merely occasioned by, the experiences that acquiring them requires. That this is indeed the polemical situation has been clear to everybody concerned (except the Empiricists) at least since Descartes. In short, SIA, like everybody else, has to live with the fact that it's typically acquaintance with doorknobs that leads to getting locked to *doorknobhood*. So, like everybody else, SIA has to explain why it's those experiences, and not others, that eventuate in locking to that property. *But that's enough, all by itself, to make the search for a non-inductivist account of concept acquisition look pretty hopeless.* For, even if a cognitivist model of concept possession is *not* assumed, the hypothesis-testing story has the virtue of solving what I'll call the doorknob/DOORKNOB problem:[7] why is it so often experiences of doorknobs, and so rarely experience with whipped cream or giraffes, that leads one to lock to *doorknobhood*?

According to the hypothesis-testing model, the relation between the content of the concepts one acquires and the content of the experiences that eventuate in one's acquiring them is *evidential*; in particular, it's mediated by content relations between a hypothesis and the experiences that serve to confirm it. You acquire DOORKNOB from experience with doorknobs because you use the experiences to confirm a hypothesis about the nature of *doorknobhood*; and doorknobs, unlike giraffes or whipped cream, are *ceteris paribus* a good source of *evidence* about the nature of doorknobs. Come to think of it, one typically gets DOORKNOB from

---

[7] I had thought at first that I would call this the fire hydrant/FIRE HYDRANT problem, as a sort of *hommage* to the Fido/Fido fallacy. But perhaps the joke isn't worth the extra syllables.

experience with *good* or *typical* examples of doorknobs, and good or typical doorknobs are a *very good* source of evidence about doorknobs. I'll return to this presently.

If, by contrast, you assume that, in the course of concept acquisition, the relation between the eliciting experience and the concept acquired is *not* typically evidential—if, for example, it's just 'brute causal' (for this terminology, see Fodor 1981*a*)—then why *shouldn't* it be experience with giraffes that typically eventuates in locking to doorknobhood? Or vice versa? Or both? It appears there's more to be said for the hypothesis-testing model of concept acquisition than even SA had supposed.[8] Compare a proposal that Jerry Samet once made for avoiding the assumption that hypothesis testing mediates concept acquisition (and hence for avoiding the Standard Argument): perhaps concepts are not learned but 'caught', sort of like the flu (Samet 1986). No doubt this suggestion is a bit underspecified; the 'sort of' does all the work. But there's also a deeper complaint: it's left wide open why you generally catch DOORKNOB from doorknobs and not, as it might be, from using public telephones (again sort of like the flu).

UnDarwinian Digression

At this point in the dialectic, there's a strong temptation to dump the load on Darwin; a standard tactic, these days, when a philosopher gets in over his head. Suppose that the mechanism of concept acquisition is indeed non-cognitivist; suppose, for example, that it's some sort of triggering. Still, wouldn't a mechanism that triggers the concept X consequent upon experience with Xs be more of a help with surviving (or getting reproduced, or whatever) than, say, a mechanism that triggers the concept X consequent upon encounters with things that aren't Xs? If so, then maybe SIA together with not-more-than-the-usual-amount of handwaving about Darwin might after all explain why the relation between the content of experiences and the content of the concepts they eventuate in locking to is so rarely arbitrary.

[8] *Linguistic footnote*: as far as I can tell, linguists just take it for granted that the data that set a parameter in the course of language learning should generally bear some natural, unarbitrary relation to the value of the parameter that they set. It's hearing *sentences without subjects* that sets the null subject parameter (maybe); what could be more reasonable? But, on second thought, the notion of triggering as such, unlike the notion of hypothesis testing as such, requires no particular relation between the state that's acquired and the experience that occasions its acquisition. In principle *any* trigger could set *any* parameter. So, prima facie, *it is an embarrassment for the triggering theory if the grammar that the child acquires is reasonable in light of his data*. It may be that here too the polemical resources of the hypothesis-testing model have been less than fully appreciated.

Well, maybe. But, of course, that's cold comfort if what you want is a *non*-nativist version of SIA. You can only trigger a concept that's there, genetically specified, waiting to be triggered. So the Darwinian/ethological story about concept acquisition does no better than the old-fashioned hypothesis-testing story at making DOORKNOB not be innate. Out of one frying pan but into another; ethologists are nativists by definition.

And, anyhow, even if the doorknob/DOORKNOB relation is selected for by evolution, what, if not inductive learning, could be the mechanism by which it is implemented? If concept acquisition isn't inductive, then *how* does Mother Nature contrive to insure that it *is* instances of *F-ness* (and not of *G-ness*) that trigger the concept *F* in the course of ontogeny? After all, if Mother N wants to select for the doorknob/DOORKNOB type of relation between concepts and their experiential causes, she has to do so by selecting *a mechanism that produces* that relation between one's concepts and their causes. This is a special case of the entirely general truth that whenever Mother N wants to select for *any* phenotypic property she has to do so by selecting a proximal mechanism that produces it. The obvious candidate to select if one wants to ensure that concept acquisition exhibits the d/D relation is inductive learning. But we have it on independent grounds that primitive concepts can't be learned inductively. There may be a way for a conceptual atomist to get out of this dilemma, but waving his hands about Darwin certainly isn't it.

The preliminary moral, anyhow, is that radical nativism is very hard for a conceptual atomist to avoid. If he starts out thinking about concept acquisition the way Empiricists do—as a kind of hypothesis testing— radical concept nativism follows; and if he starts out thinking about concept acquisition the way that ethologists do—as a kind of triggering— radical concept nativism still follows. It looks like a conceptual atomist ends up being a radical concept nativist pretty much however he starts out thinking about concept acquisition. So maybe conceptual atomism is just false.

Or maybe radical concept nativism is true, despite its wide unpopularity in the philosophical community. Speaking just as a private citizen, I've always sort of thought it wouldn't be all that surprising if radical concept nativism did turn out to be true. So it didn't much embarrass me that all the roads from concept atomism seemed to lead there. It is, after all, God and not philosophers who gets to decide what creatures have genotypically built in. That is surely *much* the best arrangement from the creature's point of view.

So, in any case, it seemed to me in 1975 or so. But maybe this relaxed stance won't do after all. The problem with the theory that the primitive concepts are learned inductively was that it's *circular*. But now we seem to have an apparently respectable argument that they *must* be learned inductively: nothing else appears likely to account for the content relation between the concept that's acquired and the experience that mediates its acquisition. But look, it can't be that inductivism about the acquisition of primitive concepts is *both* circular *and* mandatory.

Please note that, though this is an embarrassment for those of us who are inclined towards atomism, it is also an embarrassment for those of you who aren't. For, whatever you may think about the *size* of the primitive conceptual basis—and, in particular, about whether DOORKNOB is in it—on any version of RTM *some* concepts are going to have to be primitive. And, on the one hand, SA does seem to show that primitive concepts can't be acquired inductively. And, on the other hand, whatever the primitive concepts are, their acquisition is pretty sure to exhibit the familiar d/D relation between the content of the concept and the content of the experience that occasions it. Of what concept does the acquisition not?[9]

In fact, it's the concepts that have traditionally been practically everybody's favourite candidates for being primitive that exhibit the doorknob/DOORKNOB effect most clearly. Like RED, for example. To be sure, philosophers of both the Cartesian and the Empiricist persuasion have often stressed the *arbitrariness* of the relation between the content of sensory concepts and the character of their causes. It's bumping into photons (or whatever) that causes RED; but RED and PHOTON couldn't be less alike in content. (According to Descartes, this shows that not even sensory concepts can come from experience. According to Locke, it shows that secondary qualities are mind-dependent.) Well, if the relation between sensory concepts and their causes really is arbitrary, then there can be no d/D problem about sensory concepts. In which case, if Empiricists are right and *only* sensory concepts are primitive, everything turns out OK. Sensory concepts don't have to be learned inductively, so they can be innate; just as the Standard Argument requires, and just as Empiricists and Rationalists have both always supposed them to be. Empiricism would be cheap at the price if it shows the way out of a foundational paradox about RTM.

But, on second thought, no such luck. The thing to keep your eye on, *pace* Locke and Descartes both, is that the relation between the content of

---

[9] Well, maybe the acquisition of PROTON doesn't; it's plausible that PROTON is *not* typically acquired from its instances. So, as far as this part of the discussion is concerned, you are therefore free to take PROTON as a primitive concept if you want to. But I imagine you don't want to.

Perhaps, in any case, it goes without saying that the fact that the d/D effect is widespread in concept acquisition is itself contingent and a posteriori.

a sensory concept and the character of its cause is *not* arbitrary *when the cause is intentionally described*. The thing to keep your eye on is that we typically get the concept RED from (or, anyhow, on the occasion of) experiencing things *as red*.

There is, I think, more than a hint of a muddle about this in Fodor 1981*a*, where the following is a favourite line of argument: 'Look, *everybody*—Empiricists and Rationalists—agrees that there is at least one psychological mechanism which effects a *non*-rational, arbitrary relation between at least *some* primitive concepts and their distal causes. In particular, everybody agrees that the sensorium works that way.' "[E]ven the Empiricists hold that primitive concepts are merely triggered by [rather than learned from] experience . . . It is . . . just a fact about the way that we are put together than the sensory concepts we have are dependent in the ways they are upon the particular stimulations which occasion them" (ibid.: 275). On this account, Rationalism is simply the generalization of the Empiricist picture of the sensorium to cover whatever primitive concepts there turn out to be, sensory or otherwise: some kinds of arbitrary stimuli trigger (sensory) concepts like RED; other kinds of arbitrary stimuli trigger (non-sensory) concepts like DOORKNOB. What's the big sweat?

That I still like using the sensorium as a model of concept innateness at large will presently become clear. But, to repeat, prima facie it has a problem that needs to be taken seriously. The problem is that the triggering stimuli for RED *aren't* arbitrary when you take them under *intentional* (rather than psychophysical) description. If you take them under intentional description, the doorknob/DOORKNOB problem instantly emerges for sensory concepts too. It is encounters with doorknobs that typically occasion the acquisition of what Empiricists (and practically everybody else) have taken to be a *complex* concept like DOORKNOB; likewise it is typically encounters with red things (and not with green things, and not with square things, and not with elephants (unless they are red squares or red elephants)) that typically occasion the acquisition of what practically everybody takes to be a *primitive* concept like RED. Surely that's no accident in either case? And if it's not an accident, what else but an inductive model of concept acquisition could explain it?

This begins to seem a little worrying. It is perhaps tolerable that representational theories of mind should lead by plausible arguments to quite a radical nativism. But it is surely not tolerable that they should lead by plausible arguments to a contradiction. If the d/D effect shows that primitive concepts *must be* learned inductively, and SA shows that primitive concepts *can't be* learned inductively, then the conclusion has to be that there aren't any primitive concepts. But if there aren't any primitive concepts, then there aren't any concepts at all. And if there aren't any concepts all, RTM has gone West. Isn't it a bit late in the day (and late in the book) for me to take back RTM?

Help!

Ontology

This all started because we were in the market for some account of how DOORKNOB is acquired. The story couldn't be hypothesis testing because Conceptual Atomism was being assumed, so DOORKNOB was supposed to be primitive; and it's common ground that the mechanism for acquiring primitive concepts can't be any kind of induction. But, as it turned out, there is a further constraint that whatever theory of concepts we settle on should satisfy: it must explain why there is so generally a content relation between the experience that eventuates in concept attainment and the concept that the experience eventuates in attaining. At this point, the problem about DOORKNOB metastasized: assuming that primitive concepts are triggered, or that they're 'caught', won't account for their content relation to their causes; apparently only induction will. But primitive concepts can't be induced; to suppose that they are is circular. What started as a problem about DOORKNOB now looks like undermining all of RTM. This is not good. I was relying on RTM to support me in my old age.

But, on second thought, just *why* must one suppose that only a hypothesis-testing acquisition model can explain the doorknob/ DOORKNOB relation? The argument for this is, I'm pleased to report, non-demonstrative. Let's go over it once more: the hypothesis-testing model takes the *content* relation between a concept and the experience it's acquired from to be a special case of the *evidential* relation between a generalization and its confirming instances (between, for example, the generalization that Fs are Gs and instances of things that are both F and G). You generally get DOG from (typical) dogs and not, as it might be, from ketchup. That's supposed to be because having DOG requires believing (as it might be) that typical dogs bark. (Note, once again, how cognitivism about *concept possession* and inductivism about *concept acquisition* take in one another's wash.) And, whereas encounters with typical dogs constitute evidence that dogs bark, encounters with ketchup do not (*ceteris paribus*). If the relation between concepts and experiences is typically evidential, that would explain why it's so often a relation of content: and what other explanation have we got?

That is what is called in the trade a 'what-else' argument. I have nothing against what-else arguments in philosophy; still less in cognitive science. Rational persuasion often invokes considerations that are convincing but not demonstrative, and what else but a what-else argument could a convincing but non-demonstrative argument be? On the other hand, it is in the nature of what-else arguments that '*Q* if not *P*' trumps 'What else, if not *P*?'; and, in the present case, I think there is a prima facie plausible *ontological* candidate for *Q*; that is, an explanation which makes the d/D effect the consequence of a *metaphysical* truth about how concepts are constituted, rather than an empirical truth about how concepts are acquired. In fact, I know of two such candidates, one of which might even work.

First Try at a Metaphysical Solution to the d/D Problem

If you assume a causal/historical (as opposed to a dispositional/counterfactual) construal of the locking relation, it might well turn out that there is a metaphysical connection between acquiring DOORKNOB and causally interacting with doorknobs. (Cf. the familiar story according to which it's because I have causally interacted with water and my Twin hasn't that I can think *water*-thoughts and he can't.) Actually, I don't much like causal/historical accounts of locking (see Fodor 1994: App. B), but we needn't argue about that here. For, even if causally interacting with doorknobs is metaphysically *necessary* for DOORKNOB-acquisition, it couldn't conceivably be metaphysically *sufficient*; *just* causally interacting with doorknobs doesn't guarantee you any concepts at all. That being so, explaining the doorknob/DOORKNOB effect requires postulating some (contingent, psychological) mechanism that reliably leads from having *F*-experiences to acquiring the concept of *being F*. It understates the case to say that no alternative to hypothesis testing suggests itself. So I don't think that a causal/historical account of the locking relation can explain why there is a d/D effect without invoking the very premiss which, according to SA, it can't have: viz. that primitive concepts are learned inductively.

Note the similarity of this objection to the one that rejected a Darwinian solution of the d/D problem: just as you can't satisfy the conditions for having the concept *F just* in virtue of having interacted with *F*s, so too you can't satisfy the conditions for having the concept *F* just in virtue of your grandmother's having interacted with *F*s. In both cases, *concept acquisition requires something to have gone on in your head in consequence of the interactions*. Given the ubiquity of the d/D phenomenon, the natural candidate for what's gone on in your head is inductive learning.

Second Try at a Metaphysical Solution to the d/D Problem

Maybe what it is to be a doorknob isn't *evidenced* by the kind of experience that leads to acquiring the concept DOORKNOB; maybe what it is to be a doorknob is *constituted* by the kind of experience that leads to acquiring the concept DOORKNOB. A Very Deep Thought, that; but one that requires some unpacking. I want to take a few steps back so as to get a running start.

Chapter 3 remarked that it's pretty clear that if we can't define "doorknob", that can't be because of some accidental limitation of the available metalinguistic apparatus; such a deficit could always be remedied by switching metalanguages. The claim, in short, was not that we can't define "doorknob" *in English*, but that we can't define it *at all*. The implied moral is interesting: if "doorknob" can't be defined, the reason that it can't is plausibly not *methodological* but *ontological*; it has something to do with what kind of property *being a doorknob* is. If you're inclined to doubt this, so be it; but I think that you should have your intuitions looked at.

Well, but *what* could it be about *being a doorknob* that makes 'doorknob' not definable? Could it be that doorknobs have a "hidden essence" (as water, for example, is supposed to do); one that has eluded our scrutiny so far? Perhaps some science, not yet in place, will do for doorknobs what molecular chemistry did for water and geometrical optics did for mirrors: make it clear to us what they *really* are? But *what* science, for heaven's sake? And what could there be for it to make clear? Mirrors are puzzling (it seems that they double things); and water is puzzling too (what could it be made of, there's so much of it around?). But doorknobs aren't *puzzling*; doorknobs are *boring*. Here, for once, "further research" appears not to be required.

It's sometimes said that doorknobs (and the like) have *functional* essences: what makes a thing a doorknob is what it is (or is intended to be) used for. So maybe the science of doorknobs is psychology? Or sociology? Or anthropology? Once again, believe it if you can. In fact, the intentional aetiology of doorknobs is utterly transparent: they're intended to be used as doorknobs. I don't at all doubt that's what makes them what they are, but that it is gets us nowhere. For, if DOORKNOB plausibly lacks a conceptual analysis, INTENDED TO BE USED *AS A DOORKNOB* does too, and for the same reasons. And surely, *surely*, that can't, in either case, be because there's something secret about *doorknobhood* that depth psychology is needed to reveal? No doubt, there is a lot that we don't know about intentions towards doorknobs *qua intentions*; but I can't believe there's much that's obscure about them qua intentions towards *doorknobs*.

Look, there is presumably something about doorknobs that makes them doorknobs, and either it's something complex or it's something simple. If it's something complex, then 'doorknob' must have a definition, and its definition must be either "real" or "nominal" (or both). If 'doorknob' has a nominal definition, then it ought to be possible for a competent linguist or analytical philosopher to figure out what its nominal definition is. If 'doorknob' has a real definition, then it ought to be possible for a science of doorknobs to uncover it. But linguists and philosophers have had no luck defining 'doorknob' (or, as we've seen, anything much else). And there is nothing for a science of doorknobs to find out. The direction this is leading in is that if 'doorknob' is undefinable, that must be because *being a doorknob* is a *primitive property*. But, of course, that's crazy. If a thing has *doorknobhood*, it does so entirely in virtue of others of the properties it has. If doorknobs don't have hidden essences or real definitions, that can't possibly be because *being a doorknob* is one of those properties that things have simply because they have them; ultimates like *spin, charm, charge,* or the like, at which explanation ends.

So, here's the riddle. How could 'doorknob' be undefinable (contrast 'bachelor' $=_{df}$ 'unmarried man') and lack a hidden essence (contrast water $= H_2O$) without being metaphysically primitive (contrast spin, charm, and charge)?

The answer (I think) is that 'doorknob' works like 'red'.

Now I suppose you want to know how 'red' works.

Well, 'red' hasn't got a nominal definition, and *redness* doesn't have a real essence (ask any psychophysicist), and, of course, *redness* isn't metaphysically ultimate. This is all OK because *redness* is an *appearance property*, and the point about appearance properties is that they don't raise the question that definitions, real and nominal, propose to answer: viz. 'What is it that the things we take to be *X*s have in common, *over and above our taking them to be X*s?' This is, to put it mildly, not a particularly original thing to say about red. All that's new is the proposal to extend this sort of analysis to doorknobs and the like; *the proposal is that there are lots of appearance concepts that aren't sensory concepts.*[10] That this should be so is, perhaps, unsurprising on reflection. There is no obvious reason why

---

[10] So, then, which appearance properties *are* sensory properties? Here's a line that one might consider: *S* is a sensory property only if it is possible to have an experience of which *S*-ness is the intentional object (e.g. an experience (as) of red) *even though one hasn't got the concept S*. Here the test of having the concept *S* would be something like being able to think thoughts whose truth conditions include . . . *S* . . . (e.g. thoughts like *that's red*). I think this must be the notion of 'sensory property' that underlies the Empiricist idea that RED and the like are learned 'by abstraction' from experience, a doctrine which presupposes that a mind that lacks RED can none the less have experiences (as) of redness. By this test, DOORKNOB is presumably *not* a sensory concept since, though it is perfectly possible to

a property that is constituted by the *mental* states that things that have it evoke in us must *ipso facto* be constituted by the *sensory* states that things that have it evoke in us.

All right, all right; you can't believe that something's being a doorknob is "about us" in anything like the way that maybe something's being red is. Surely 'doorknob' expresses a property that a thing either has or doesn't, regardless of our views; as it were, a property of things in themselves? So be it, but *which* property? Consider the alternatives (here we go again): is it that 'doorknob' is definable? If so, what's the definition? (And, even if 'doorknob' is definable, some concepts have to be primitive, so the present sorts of issues will eventually have to be faced about *them*.) Is it that doorknobs qua doorknobs have a hidden essence? Hidden where, do you suppose? And who is in charge of finding it? Is it that being a doorknob is ontologically ultimate? You've got to be kidding.[11]

If you take it seriously that DOORKNOB hasn't got a conceptual analysis, and that doorknobs don't have hidden essences, all that's left to make something a doorknob (anyhow, all that's left that I can think of) is *how it strikes us*. But if being a *doorknob* is a property that's *constituted* by how things strike us, then the intrinsic connection between the content of DOORKNOB and the content of our doorknob-experiences is metaphysically necessary, hence not a fact that a cognitivist theory of concept acquisition is required in order to explain.

To be sure, there remains something about the acquisition of DOORKNOB that does want explaining: viz. why it is the property that these guys (several doorknobs) share, and not the property that those guys (several cows) share, that we lock to from experience of good (e.g. stereotypic) examples of doorknobs. And, equally certainly, it's got to be something about our kinds of minds that this explanation adverts to. But, I'm supposing, such an explanation is *cognitivist* only if it turns on the *evidential* relation between *having the stereotypic doorknob properties* and *being a doorknob*. (So, for example, triggering explanations aren't

have an experience (as) of doorknobs, I suppose only a mind that has the concept DOORKNOB can do so.

'But *how* could one have an experience (as) of red if one hasn't got the concept RED?' It's easy: in the case of *redness*, but not of *doorknobhood*, one is equipped with sensory organs which produce such experiences when they are appropriately stimulated. *Redness* can be *sensed*, whereas the perceptual detection of *doorknobhood* is always *inferential*. Just as sensible psychologists have always supposed.

[11] The present discussion parallels what I regard as a very deep passage in Schiffer 1987 about *being a dog*. Schiffer takes for granted that 'dog' doesn't name a species, and (hence?) that dogs as such don't have a hidden essence. His conclusion is that there just isn't (except pleonastically) any such property as *being a dog*. My diagnosis is that there is too, but it's mind-dependent.

cognitivist according to this criterion, *and wouldn't be even if (by accident) the concept DOORKNOB happened to be triggered by doorknobs*.) Well, by this criterion, my story isn't cognitivist either. My story says that what doorknobs have in common qua doorknobs *is being the kind of thing that our kind of minds (do or would) lock to from experience with instances of the doorknob stereotype*. (Cf. to be red *just is* to have that property that minds like ours (do or would) lock to in virtue of experiences of typical instances of redness.) Why isn't that OK?[12]

If you put that account of the metaphysics of *doorknobhood* together with the metaphysical account of concept possession that informational semantics proposes—having a concept is something like "resonating to" the property that the concept expresses—then you get: *being a doorknob* is having that property that minds like ours come to resonate to in consequence of relevant experience with stereotypic doorknobs. That, and *not* being learned inductively, is what explains the content relation between DOORKNOB and the kinds of experience that typically mediates its acquisition. It also explains how *doorknobhood* could seem to be undefinable and unanalysable without being metaphysically ultimate. And it is also explains how DOORKNOB could be both psychologically primitive and not innate, the Standard Argument to the contrary not withstanding.

Several points in a spirit of expatiation:

The basic idea is that what makes something a doorknob is just: being the kind of thing from experience with which our kind of mind readily acquires the concept DOORKNOB. And, conversely, what makes something the concept DOORKNOB is just: expressing the property that our kinds of minds lock to from experience with good examples of instantiated *doorknobhood*. But this way of putting the suggestion is too weak since experience with stereotypic doorknobs might cause one to lock to any of a whole lot of properties (or to none), depending on what else is going on at the time. (In some contexts it might cause one to lock to the property *belongs to Jones*.) Whereas, what I want to say is that *doorknobhood* is the property that one gets locked to when experience with typical doorknobs causes the locking and does so *in virtue of the properties they have qua typical doorknobs*. We have the kinds of minds that often

---

[12] Modal footnote (NB): Here as elsewhere through the present discussion, 'minds like ours' and 'the (stereo)typical properties of doorknobs' are to be read *rigidly*, viz. as denoting the properties that instances of *stereotypic doorknobs* and typical minds have in *this* world. That the typical properties of minds and doorknobs are what they are is meant to be contingent.

acquire *the concept X from experiences whose intentional objects are properties belonging to the X-stereotype.*[13]

Notice that this is not a truism, and that it's not circular; it's contingently true if it's true at all. What makes it contingent is that being a doorknob is neither necessary nor sufficient for something to have the stereotypic doorknob properties (not even in 'normal circumstances' in any sense of "normal circumstances" I can think of that doesn't beg the question). *Stereotype* is a *statistical* notion. The only theoretically interesting connection between *being a doorknob* and *satisfying the doorknob stereotype* is that, contingently, things that do either often do both.

In fact, since the relation between instantiating the doorknob stereotype and being a doorknob is patently contingent, you might want to buy into the present account of DOORKNOB even if you don't like the Lockean story about RED. The classical problem with the latter is that it takes for granted an unexplicated notion of 'looks red' ('red experience', 'red sense datum', or whatever) and is thus in some danger of circularity since "the expression 'looks red' is not semantically unstructured. Its sense is determined by that of its constituents. If one does not understand those constituents, one does not fully understand the compound" (Peacocke 1992: 408). Well, maybe this kind of objection shows that an account of *being red* mustn't presuppose the property of *looking red* (though Peacocke doubts that it shows that, and so do I). In any event, no parallel argument could show that an account of *being a doorknob* mustn't presuppose the property of *satisfying the doorknob stereotype*. The conditions for satisfying the latter are patently specifiable without reference to the former, viz. by enumerating the shapes, colours, functions, and the like that doorknobs typically have.

It's actually sort of remarkable that all of this is so. *Pace* Chapter 5, concepts really *ought* to be stereotypes. Not only because there's so much evidence that having a concept and having its stereotype are reliably closely correlated (and what better explanation of reliable close correlation could there be than identity?) but also because it is, as previously noted, generally *stereotypic* examples of *X-ness* that one learns *X* from. Whereas, what you'd *expect* people reliably to learn from stereotypic examples of *X isn't*

---

[13] How much such experience? And under what conditions of acquisition? I assume that there are (lots of) empirical parameters that a formulation of the laws of concept acquisition would have to fill in. Doing so would be the proprietary goal of a serious psychology of cognitive development. Which, to quote a poet, "in our case we have not got".

the concept X but the X stereotype.[14] A stereotypic *X* is *always* a better instance of the *X* stereotype than it is of *X*; that *is* a truism.[15]

Interesting Digression

The classic example of this sort of worry is the puzzle in psycholinguistics about 'Motherese'. It appears that mothers go out of their way to talk to children in stereotypic sentences of their native language; in the case of English, relatively short sentences with NVN structure (and/or Agent Action Object structure; see Chapter 3). The child is thereby provided with a good sample of stereotypic English sentences, from which, however, he extracts not (anyhow, not only) the concept STEREOTYPIC ENGLISH SENTENCE, but the concept ENGLISH SENTENCE *TOUT COURT*. But why on Earth does he do that? Why doesn't he instead come to believe that the grammar of English is $S \rightarrow$ NVN, or some fairly simple elaboration thereof, taking such apparent counter-examples as he may encounter as not well-formed? Remember, on the one hand, that Mother is following a strategy of screening him from utterances of unstereotypic sentences; and, on the other hand, that he'll hear lots of counter-examples to *whatever* grammar he tries out, since people say lots of ungrammatical things. I think the answer *must* be that it's *a law about our kinds of minds* that they are set up to make inductions from samples consisting largely of stereotypic English sentences to the concept ENGLISH SENTENCE (viz. the concept sentences satisfy in virtue of being well-formed relative to the grammar of English) and not from samples consisting largely of stereotypic English sentences to the concept STEREOTYPIC ENGLISH SENTENCE (viz. the concept sentences satisfy in virtue of being NVN).

In short, I do think there's good reason for cognitive scientists to be unhappy about the current status of theorizing about stereotypes. The kinds of worries about compositionality that Chapter 5 reviewed show that the relation a stereotype bears to the corresponding concept *can't* be constitutive. The standard alternative proposal is that it is simply heuristic; e.g. that stereotypes are databases for fast recognition procedures. But this seems not to account for the ubiquity and robustness of stereotype phenomena; and, anyhow, it begs the sort of question that we just discussed: why is it the concept *X* rather than the concept STEREOTYPIC *X* that one normally gets from experience with stereotypic *X*s? (*Mutatis mutandis*, if the way perception works is that you subsume things under

---

[14] Reminder: 'the *X* stereotype' is rigid. See n. 12 above.
[15] Except in the (presumably never encountered) case where all the *X*s are stereotypic. In that case, there's a dead heat.

DOORKNOB by seeing that they are similar to stereotypic doorknobs, why is it that you generally see a doorknob as a doorknob, and not as *something that satisfies the doorknob stereotype*?) If our minds are, in effect, functions from stereotypes to concepts, that is a fact *about us*. Indeed, it is a *very deep* fact about us. My point in going on about this is to emphasize the *un*triviality of the consideration that we typically get a concept from instances that exemplify its stereotype.

That a concept has the stereotype that it does is never truistic; and that a stereotype belongs to the concept that it does is never truistic either. In particular, since the relation between a concept and its stereotype is always contingent, no circularity arises from defining 'the concept *X*' by reference to 'the stereotype of the concept *X*'. But, according to the present proposal, the relation between being a doorknob and instantiating the doorknob stereotype is, as it were, *almost* constitutive. Instantiating *doorknobhood* and instantiating the corresponding stereotype are logically, conceptually, and metaphysically independent in both directions.[16] But the following is *metaphysically necessary*, according to the line I'm selling: being a doorknob is having the property to which minds like ours generalize from experiences (as of) the properties by which the doorknob stereotype is constituted. *That's what the mind-dependence of doorknob-hood consists in.*

By way of a sort of summary, I want to rub in something that I said before: there is a sense, quite different from the one I've been discussing, in which it's pretty untendentious that *being a doorknob* is a mind-dependent property. Perhaps it's in the nature of doorknobs that they are artefacts. Perhaps, for example, nothing that *just grew* on a door could be a doorknob. Since it's in the nature of artefacts that have a certain kind of intentional history, it follows that there would be no doorknobs but that there are intentions with respect to doorknobs. A fortiori, there would be no doorknobs if there were no minds. Have this however you will; I raise the issue only to distinguish it from the one that I care about.

My line is that whether a thing is a doorknob is a matter of how it strikes us. By contrast, if being a doorknob is having the right sort of intentional history, then it's straightforwardly a matter of fact whether a

---

[16] In principle, they are also *epistemically* independent in both directions. As things are now, we find out about the stereotype by doing tests on subjects who are independently identified as having the corresponding concept. But I assume that if we knew enough about the mind/brain, we could *predict* a concept from its stereotype and vice versa. In effect, given the infinite set of actual and possible doorknobs, we could predict the stereotype from which our sorts of minds would generalize to it; and given the doorknob stereotype, we could predict the set of actual and possible objects which our kinds of minds would take to instantiate *doorknobhood*.

thing *is* a doorknob. That's because what intentional history a thing has is metaphysically independent of what intentional history it strikes anyone as having.[17] *Being married* is a matter of intentional history; one has to have said certain things, under certain conditions, with certain intentions, . . . etc. But whether Napoleon was married isn't up to us; nor, for that matter, is whether you are married up to you. Whether you are married is metaphysically independent of whether you wish or take yourself to be. It's too late to change your mind, and 'I forgot' does not defend against a charge of bigamy.

And, anyhow, I think the metaphysics of lots of concepts that do *not* subsume artefacts, and are patently not constituted by their intentional histories, works in much the same way that the metaphysics of DOORKNOB does. In fact, I rather think that is true of *all* concepts that aren't logico-mathematical and don't express natural kinds. More of this in Chapter 7.

I've been suggesting that whether a thing is a doorknob is maybe constituted by facts about whether we (do or would) take it to be a doorknob; just as whether something is red is maybe constituted by facts about whether it looks red to us. The metaphysical camel I'm trying to get you to swallow is, to repeat, an analogy between DOORKNOB and *appearance* concepts: with *doorknob* as with *red*, all there is to being it is how things tend to strike us. This account of the metaphysics of doorknobs would seem to explain why DOORKNOB exhibits the d/D effect without having to assume that DOORKNOB is learned inductively. So far, then, the present picture is compatible with the idea that DOORKNOB is primitive. So it's compatible with Semantic Atomism.

Suppose, if only for the sake of the discussion, that you're prepared to consider the ontology I've been trying to sell you. Then: *what's the bottom line about Innate Ideas?*

Innateness and Ontology

The natural, appalled, reaction to radical concept nativism is: 'But how *could* you have a concept like DOORKNOB innately?' To which the proper answer is: 'That depends a lot on what the concept DOORKNOB is and it depends a lot on what it is to have a concept.' According to the present proposal, to have a concept is to be locked to the corresponding property. But also, according to the present proposal, DOORKNOB is

---

[17] If you were an "interpretivist" about the ontology of the mental, you would, of course, have to deny this. So much the worse for interpretivists, as usual.

an appearance concept; the property it expresses is constituted by the way that things that have it (do or would) strike us (if we have had or were to have appropriate experiences with stereotypic doorknobs). Well, if a property is *constituted* by the way that things that have it strike us (under certain circumstances), then being locked to the property requires only that things that have it do reliably strike us that way (under those circumstances).

The model, to repeat, is *being red*: all that's required for us to get locked to *redness* is that red things should reliably seem to us as they do, in fact, reliably seem to the visually unimpaired. Correspondingly, all that needs to be innate for RED to be acquired is whatever the mechanisms are that determine that red things strike us as they do; which is to say that all that needs to be innate is the sensorium. Ditto, *mutatis mutandis*, for DOORKNOB if *being a doorknob* is like *being red*: what has to be innately given to get us locked to *doorknobhood* is whatever mechanisms are required for doorknobs to come to strike us as such. Put slightly differently: if the locking story about concept possession and the mind-dependence story about the metaphysics of *doorknobhood* are both true, then the kind of nativism about DOORKNOB that an informational atomist has to put up with is perhaps not one of *concepts* but of *mechanisms*. That consequence may be some consolation to otherwise disconsolate Empiricists.

I suppose the philosophically interesting question about whether there are innate ideas is whether there are innate *ideas*. It is, after all, the thought that the 'initial state' from which concept acquisition proceeds must be specified in intentional terms (terms like 'content', 'belief', etc.) that connects the issues about concept innateness with the epistemological issues about a prioricity and the like. (By contrast, I suppose the *ethologically* interesting question is not whether what's innate is strictly speaking intentional, but whether it is domain specific and/or species specific. Perhaps you find the ethologically interesting question more interesting than the philosophically interesting question. And perhaps you're right to do so. Still, they are *different* questions.) Correspondingly, the 'innate sensorium' model suggests that the question how much is innate in concept acquisition can be quite generally dissociated from the question whether any *concepts* are innate. The sensorium is innate by assumption, and there would quite likely be no acquiring sensory concepts but that this is so. But, to repeat, the innateness of the sensorium isn't the innateness of anything that has intentional content. Since the sensorium isn't an idea, it is a fortiori not an *innate* idea. So, strictly speaking, the innate sensorium model of the acquisition of RED doesn't require that it, or any other concept, be innate.

To be sure, RED and DOORKNOB *could* both be innate for all I've said so far. But the main motivation for saying that they are is either that one finds inductivist theories of concept acquisition intrinsically attractive, or that noticing the d/D effect has convinced one that some such theory must be true whether or not it's attractive. Well, SA blocks the first motivation. And, as we've been seeing, it may be that the explanation of the d/D effect is metaphysical rather than psychological. In which case, unless I've missed something, there isn't *any* obvious reason why the initial state for DOORKNOB acquisition needs to be intentionally specified. A fortiori, there isn't any obvious reason why DOORKNOB needs to be innate. *NOT EVEN IF IT'S PRIMITIVE.* The moral of all this may be that though there has to be a story to tell about the structural requirements for acquiring DOORKNOB, intentional vocabulary isn't required to tell it. In which case, it isn't part of cognitive psychology.

Not even of "cognitive neuropsychology", if there is such a thing (which I doubt). Suppose we were able to specify, in neurological vocabulary, the initial state from which DOORKNOB acquisition proceeds. The question would then arise whether the neurological state so specified is intentional—whether it has conditions of semantic evaluation (and, if so, what they are). So far, we haven't found a reason for supposing that it does. To be sure, it is an innate, possibly quite complicated, state from which DOORKNOB may be acquired, given experience of e.g. doorknobs. But this is all neutral as to whether the initial state is an intentional state; it's all true *whether or not* the initial state is an intentional state. So it's all true whether or not the initial state for DOORKNOB acquisition is in the domain of *cognitive* neuropsychology (as opposed, as it were, to neuropsychology *tout court*).

None of this could be *much* comfort to a disconsolate Empiricist, since none of it is supposed to deny, even for a moment, that a lot of stuff that's domain specific or species specific or both has to be innate in order that we should come to have the concept DOORKNOB (or for that matter, the concept RED). But the issue isn't whether acquiring DOORKNOB requires a lot of innate stuff; anybody with any sense can see that it does. The issue is whether it requires a lot of innate *intentional* stuff, a lot of innate stuff that has content. All the arguments I know that say that innate intentional stuff has to mediate concept acquisition depend on assuming either that concept acquisition is inductive or that the explanation of the d/D effect is psychological or both. Well, where a primitive concept expresses a mind-dependent property, it is very unclear that either of these kinds of argument will work.

Maybe there aren't any innate *ideas* after all.

APPENDIX 6A
Similarity

'Hey, aren't you just saying that all that has to be innate in a DOORKNOB-acquisition device is the capacity to learn to respond selectively to things that are relevantly similar to doorknobs? And didn't Quine say that years ago?'

No, I'm not and no, he didn't. Not quite.

There are two ways to understand the claim that the process of acquiring DOORKNOB recruits an innate 'similarity metric'. One is platitudinous, the other is committed to innate ideas—in effect, to the innateness of the concept SIMILAR TO A DOORKNOB. The geography around here is pretty familiar, so we can settle for a quick tour.

On the first way of running it, the similarity story is just the remark that, given appropriate experience of doorknobs, creatures like us converge on a capacity to respond selectively to things that are like doorknobs *in respect of their doorknobhood*. This is perfectly self-evidently true; nobody reasonable could wish to deny it. It doesn't, however, *explain* the fact that we learn DOORKNOB from doorknobs; it just repeats the fact that we do. So construed, the similarity story is completely neutral on the issues this chapter is concerned with, viz. whether the structures in virtue of which we are able to converge on selective sensitivity to *doorknobhood* need to be innate, and whether they need to be intentional.

On the other, unplatitudinous, way of running the similarity theory, it is itself a version of concept nativism: it's the thesis that what's innate is the concept SIMILAR TO A DOORKNOB. There seems, to put it mildly, to be no reason to prefer that view to one that has DOORKNOB itself be innate. (Indeed, the first would seem to imply the second; since the concept SIMILAR TO A DOORKNOB is, on the face of it, a construct out of the concept DOORKNOB, it's hard to imagine how anyone could think the one concept unless he could also think the other.) None of this bothers Quine much, of course, because he pretty explicitly assumes the Empiricist principle that the innate dimensions of similarity, along which experience generalizes, are sensory. But Empiricism isn't true, and it is time to put away childish things.

Quine's story is that learning DOORKNOB is learning to respond selectivity to things that are *similar to doorknobs*. What the story amounts to depends, in short, on how *being similar to doorknobs* is construed. Well, there's a dilemma: if *being similar to doorknobs* is elucidated by appeal to *doorknobhood*, then the story is patently empty; 'How is the concept that expresses *doorknobhood* acquired?' is the very question that it was supposed to be the answer to. If, on the other hand, *being similar to doorknobs* is spelled out by reference to properties other than *doorknobhood*, Quine has to say which properties these are, where the concepts of these properties come from, and how radical nativism with respect to them is to be avoided.

Like Quine, I've opted for the second horn of the dilemma. But, unlike Quine, I'm no Empiricist. Accordingly, I can appeal to the doorknob stereotype to say what 'similarity to doorknobs' comes to, and—since 'the doorknob stereotype' is independently defined—I can do so without invoking the concept DOORKNOB and thereby courting platitude.

So I'm not saying what Quine said; though it may well be what he should have said, and would have said but for his Empiricism. I often have the feeling that I'm just saying what Quine would have said but for his Empiricism.[18]

---

[18] I am also, unlike Quine, not committed to construing locking in terms of a capacity for discriminated responding (or, indeed, of anything epistemological). Locking reduces to nomic connectedness. (I hope.) See Fodor 1990; Fodor forthcoming *b*.

Innateness and Ontology, Part II: Natural Kind Concepts

[It is] a matter quite independent of . . . wishing it or not wishing it. There happens to be a definite intrinsic propriety in it which determines the thing and which would take me long to explain.

—Henry James, *The Tragic Muse*

HERE'S how we set things up in Chapter 6: suppose that radical conceptual atomism is inevitable and that, atomism being once assumed, radical conceptual nativism is inevitable too. On what, if any, ontological story would radical conceptual nativism be tolerable?

However, given the preconceptions that have structured this book, we might just as well have approached the ontological issues from a different angle. I've assumed throughout that informational semantics is, if not self-evidently the truth about mental content, at least not known to be out of the running. It's been my fallback metaphysics whenever I needed an alternative to Inferential Role theories of meaning. But now, according to informational semantics, content is constituted by some sort of nomic, mind–world relation. Correspondingly, *having* a concept (concept possession) is constituted by *being in* some sort of nomic, mind–world relation. It follows that, if informational semantics is true, then there must be *laws about* everything that we have concepts of. But how could there be laws about *doorknobs*?

The answer, according to the present story, is that there is really only one law about doorknobs (qua doorknobs); viz. that we lock to them in consequence of certain sorts of experience.[1] And this law isn't really about doorknobs because, of course, it's really about us. This is quite a serious point. I assume that the intuition that there aren't laws about doorknobs (equivalently, for present purposes, the intuition that doorknobs aren't a 'natural kind') comes down to the thought that there's nothing in the world

---

[1] There are, of course, lots of (intentional psychological) laws about the concept DOORKNOB; but that's quite a different matter.

whose states are reliably connected to doorknobs qua doorknobs *except our minds*. No doubt, some engineer might construct a counter-example— a mindless doorknob detector; and we might even come to rely on such a thing when groping for a doorknob in the dark. Still, *the gadget would have to be calibrated to us* since there is nothing else in nature that responds selectively to doorknobs; and, according to the present account, it's *constitutive of doorknobhood* that this is so. The point is: it's OK for there to be laws about doorknobs that are really laws about us. Doorknobs aren't a natural kind, but *we are*.

What with one thing and another, I've been pushing pretty hard the notion that properties like *being a doorknob* are mind-dependent. I needed to in Chapter 6 because, if doorknobs aren't mind-dependent, there is only one way I can think of to explain why it's typically *doorknob*-experiences from which the concept DOORKNOB is acquired: viz. that DOORKNOB is learned inductively. And I didn't want that because the Standard Argument shows that only *non*-primitive concepts can be learned inductively. And it's been the main burden of this whole book that all the evidence—philosophical, psychological, and linguistic—suggests that DOORKNOB is primitive (unstructured); and, for that matter, that so too is practically everything else. Likewise, in this chapter, I need *being a doorknob* to be mind-dependent because there is only one way I can think of to reconcile informational semantics, which wants there to be laws about doorknobs, with the truism that doorknobs aren't a natural kind; viz. to construe what appear to be laws about doorknobs as really laws about "our kinds of minds".

But all this stuff about the mind-dependence of *doorknobhood* invites a certain Auntie-esque complaint. Viz.:

> *I get it; the good news is that DOORKNOB isn't innate; the bad news is that there aren't any doorknobs. Aren't you ashamed of yourself?*

I am definitely sensitive to this criticism. For I'm a Realist about doorknobs, I am. I think there are *lots* of doorknobs, and I wouldn't consider for a moment holding a metaphysical view which denies that there are. So, one of the main questions I want to consider in this chapter is: what, if any, consequences would the (putative) mind-dependence of *doorknobhood* have for issues about Metaphysical Realism? My answer will be 'none', and this for two reasons: first, because being mind-dependent is perfectly compatible with being real; and second, and more important, because DOORKNOB isn't the general case. If there are lots of our concepts that express mind-dependent properties, *there are also lots of them that don't*. Something needs to be said about the metaphysics of that kind of concept too.

Doorknobs are Real because Minds are Real

The first of these considerations is entirely banal. Suppose, per hypothesis, that DOORKNOB expresses a property that things have in virtue of their effects on us. Suppose, in particular, that *being a doorknob* is just *having the property that minds like ours reliably lock to in consequence of experience with typical doorknobs*. Well, then, there *are* doorknobs iff the property that minds like ours reliably lock to in consequence of experience with typical doorknobs is instantiated. Which, of course, it is; every doorknob has it, and there are, as previously remarked, lots of doorknobs.

Look, there is simply *nothing wrong* with, or ontologically second-rate about, being a property that things have in virtue of their reliable effects on our minds. For we really do have minds, and there really are things whose effects on our minds are reliable. If you doubt that we do, or that there are, then whatever is the source of your scepticism, it can't be metaphysical considerations of the sort that I've been claiming bear on the nature of *doorknobhood*. Perhaps it's that you're worried about evil demons?

Fingers, I suppose, are, hand-dependent: if there were no hands, there could be no fingers; if you had your fingers on your feet they'd be your toes. This is all entirely compatible with the rigorous Metaphysical Realism about fingers which, surely, common sense demands. For, since there really are hands, such metaphysical conditions for the instantiation of *fingerhood* as its hand-dependence imposes are *ipso facto* satisfied. *Since there are hands, the metaphysical dependence of fingers on hands is not an argument for there not being fingers.* Similarly, *mutatis mutandis*, for the case of doorknobs. Since there are minds, the ontological conditions which the mind-dependence of *doorknobhood* imposes on there being doorknobs are *ipso facto* satisfied. The mind-dependence of *doorknobhood* is not an argument for there not being doorknobs.

I wouldn't be going on about this so, except that it appears to have occasioned much confusion, and some inadvertent comedy, in the cognitive science community. (And in ever so many Departments of English Literature. And in France.) Here, for one example among multitudes, is George Lakoff getting himself into a thorough muddle about Tuesdays:

If . . . symbols get their meaning only by being associated with things in the world, then weeks must be things in the world. But weeks do not exist in nature . . . Does 'Tuesday' refer to an aspect of 'external reality'—reality external to human beings? Obviously not. That reality is constituted by the minds of human beings collectively—it is not an 'external' reality. [The word] 'Tuesday' cannot get its meaning by reference to a reality external to and independent of human minds . . . These realities reside in human minds, not in anything 'external'. (1988: 135)

I'm unclear exactly what work Lakoff thinks "external" is doing in this passage, and his persistently putting it into shudder-quotes suggests that he is too. But notice the repeated contrast of "constituted by human minds" and the like with (externally) "real" and the like. The inference that we're being offered is apparently: constituted by minds and so *not* (externally) real.

Now, it's true, of course, that Tuesdays are mind-dependent in at least the following pretty straightforward sense: whether today is Tuesday depends on what conventions people adhere to; and that people adhere to the conventions that they do, or to any conventions at all, depends on their having minds. So: no minds, no Tuesdays. But *it does not follow that there are no Tuesdays*; the minor premiss is missing. Nor does it follow that there is no fact of the matter about whether today is Tuesday (or about whether it is true that today is Tuesday). Nor does it follow that Tuesdays aren't real. Nor does it follow that 'Tuesday' doesn't really refer to Tuesday. As for whether it follows that Tuesdays aren't "'externally'" real, or that 'Tuesday' doesn't refer to an "'external'" reality, that depends a lot on what "'external'" means. Search me. I would have thought that minds don't have outsides for much the same sorts of reasons that they don't have insides. If that's right, then the question doesn't arise.

Likewise, there are many properties that are untendentiously mind-dependent though plausibly *not* conventional; *being red* or *being audible* for one kind of example; or *being a convincing argument*, for another kind; or *being an aspirated consonant*, for a third kind; or *being a doorknob*, if I am right about what doorknobs are. It does not follow that there are no doorknobs, or that no arguments are convincing, or that nothing is audible, or that the initial consonant in 'Patrick' is anything other than aspirated.[2] All that follows is that whether something is audible, convincing, aspirated, or a doorknob depends, *inter alia*, on how it affects minds like ours. Nor does it follow that doorknobs aren't "in the world". Doorknobs are constituted by their effects on our minds, and *our minds are in the world*. Where on earth else could they be?

---

[2] Compare Jackendoff: "Look at the representations of, say, generative phonology . . . It is strange to say that English speakers know the proposition, *true in the world independent of speakers* [*sic*], that syllable-initial voiceless consonants aspirate before stress . . . In generative phonology . . . this rule of aspiration is regarded as a principle of internal computation, not a fact about the world. Such semantical concepts as implication, confirmation, and logical consequence seem curiously irrelevant" (1992: 29). Note that, though they are confounded in his text, the contrast that Jackendoff is insisting on isn't between *propositions* and *rules/principles* of computation; it's between *phenomena of the kind that generative phonology studies* and *facts about the world*. But that 'p' is aspirated in 'Patrick' is a fact about the world. That is to say: it's a fact. And of course the usual logico-semantical concepts apply. That 'p' is aspirated in 'Patrick' is what makes the claim that 'p' is aspirated in 'Patrick' true; since 'p' is aspirated in 'Patrick', something in 'Patrick' is aspirated . . . and so forth.

I'm considering (and endorsing) reasons why no sort of Idealism is implied by the view that the relation between *being a doorknob* and *falling under a concept that minds like ours typically acquire from stereotypic doorknob-experiences* is metaphysical and constitutive. I've been arguing that *not even Idealism about doorknobs* follows; doorknobs are real but mind-dependent, according to the story I've been telling.

But I think there's another, and considerably deeper, point to make along these lines: I haven't suggested, and I don't for a moment suppose, that *all* our concepts express properties that are mind-dependent. For example, we have the concept WATER, which expresses the property of *being water*, viz. the property of *being H_2O*. We also have the concept H_2O, which expresses the property of *being H_2O*, viz. the property of *being water*. (What distinguishes these concepts, according to me, is that the possession conditions for H_2O, but not for WATER, include the possession conditions for H, 2, and O. See Chapters 1 and 2.) Assuming informational semantics, having these concepts is being locked to the property of *being water*; and being water is a property which is, of course, *not* mind-dependent. It is not a property things have in virtue of their relations to minds, ours or any others.

I suppose that natural kind predicates *just are* the ones that figure in laws; a fortiori, since water is a natural kind, there isn't a problem about how there could be laws about the property that the concept WATER expresses. But if water isn't mind-dependent, where do concepts like WATER come from? How do you lock a mental representation to a property which, presumably, things have in virtue of their hidden essences? And what, beside hypothesis testing, could explain why you generally get WATER from experience with water and not, as it might be, from experience with giraffes? What, in short, should an enthusiast for informational theories of content say about concepts that express natural kinds?

All in due time. For now, I propose to tell you a fairy tale. It's a fairy tale about how things were back in the Garden, before the Fall; and about what the Snake in the Garden said; and about how, having started out by being Innocents, we've ended up by being scientists.

Concepts of Natural Kinds

How Things Were, Back in the Garden

Once upon a time, back in the Garden, all our concepts expressed (viz. were locked to) properties that things have in virtue of their striking us as being of a certain kind. So, we had the concept DOORKNOB, which expresses the property that things have when they seem to us to be of the same kind as instances of the doorknob stereotype; and we had the concept HOLE, which expresses the property that things have when they seem to us to be of the same kind as instances of the hole stereotype; and we had the concept A NICE DAY, which expresses the property that things have when they seem to us to be of the same kind as instances of the nice day stereotype . . . etc. (Also, I suppose we had logico-mathematical concepts; about which, however, the present work has nothing to say.)

Because the concepts we had back in the Garden were all concepts of mind-dependent properties, there was, back then, a kind of appearance/reality distinction that we never had to draw. We never had to worry about whether there might be kinds of things which, though they satisfy the DOORKNOB stereotype, nevertheless are not doorknobs. We never had to worry that there might be something which, as it might be, had all the attributes of a doorknob but was, in its essence, a Twin-doorknob. Or, who knows, a giraffe.[3]

But also, because we were Innocent, we didn't have the concept WATER, or the concept CONSONANT, or the concept LEVER, or the concept STAR. Perhaps we had concepts that were (extensionally) sort of like these; perhaps we used to wonder who waters the plants. But, if so, these concepts were importantly different from the homophonic counterparts that we have now. For it's compatible with the real concept WATER that there should be stuff that strikes us as being of the very same kind as instances of the water stereotype but that isn't water because it has the wrong kind of hidden essence (XYZ, perhaps). And it's compatible with the real concept STAR that there should be things that strike us as very different from paradigm stars, but which do have the right kind of hidden essences and are therefore stars after all (a black dwarf, perhaps; or the Sun). And it's compatible with the concept CONSONANT that we have now that there should be sorts of things that strike us as neither clearly consonants nor clearly not consonants but which, because they have the right kinds of hidden essences, really are consonants whether or not we think they are (ls and rs, perhaps).

I'll presently have much more to say about what concept of water we could have had in the Garden; and about how it would have been different

---

[3] There were, to be sure, *faux* doorknobs, fake doorknobs, *trompe l'œil* doorknobs, and the like; these were particulars which looked, at first glance, to satisfy the doorknob stereotype but, on closer examination, turned out not to do so. *Doorknob* vs. *trompe l'œil doorknob* is a distinction *within* mind-dependent properties; hence quite different from the difference between *doorknob* and, as it might be, *water*. (In consequence, drawing an appearance/reality distinction is not all there is to being a metaphysical essentialist. See n. 5.)

from the concept of water that we have now. And about how to square that difference with what an atomistic and informational semantics says about the individuation of concepts. But this will do to be getting on with: back in the Garden, when we were Innocent, we never thought about kinds of things which, though they are much the same in their effects on us, are *not* much the same in their effects on one another. Or about kinds of things which, though they are much the same in their effects on one another, are strikingly different in their effects on us. Back in the Garden, when we were Innocent, we took it for granted that there isn't any difference between similarity *for us* and similarity *sans phrase*; between the way we carve the world up and the way that God does.

Then came the Snake.

What the Snake Said

'I have here,' the Snake said, 'some stuff that will no doubt strike you, in your Innocence, as a sample of bona fide, original, straight off the shelf, X-ness. But come a little closer—come close enough to see how the stuff is put together—and you'll see that it isn't X after all. In fact, it's some kind of Y.'

—'Sucks to how it's put together,' we replied, in our Innocence. 'For a thing to strike us as of a kind with paradigm Xs *just is* for that thing to be an X. X-ness *just is* the property of being the kind of thing to which we do (or would) extrapolate from appropriate experience with typical Xs. Man is the measure; *vide* doorknobs.'

—'That,' the Snake replied, 'depends. Since we're assuming from the start that Xs and Ys are, for practical purposes, indistinguishable in their effects on you, it follows that thinking of both Xs and Ys as Xs will do you no practical harm. For example, for purposes of longevity, reproductive efficiency, and the like, it's all one whether you ingest only Xs under the description 'X' or you ingest both Xs and Ys under that description. But that is ingest; I am in earnest. If you want to carve Nature at the joints, if you want to know *how the world seems to God*, you will have to learn sometimes to distinguish between Xs and Ys even though they taste (and feel, and look, and sound, and quite generally strike you as) much the same. It's entirely up to you of course. Far be it from me to twist your arm. (Sign here, please. In blood.)'

We fell for that, and it was, on balance, a fortunate Fall. The trouble with being Innocent is that, although how God made things *sometimes* shows up in broad similarities and differences in the way that they strike us (trees reliably strike us as quite different from rocks; and they are), sometimes it only shows up in similarities and differences in the way things strike us in very highly contrived, quite unnatural environments; experimental environments, as it might be. For it's sometimes only in terms of a taxonomy that classifies things by similarities and differences among the ways that they do (or would) behave in *those* sorts of environments, that we can specify the deep generalizations that the world obeys. We are, after all, peculiar and complicated sorts of objects. There is no obvious reason why similarity in respect of the way that things affect us should, in general, predict similarity in the way that they affect objects that are less peculiar than us, or less complicated than us, or that are peculiar and complicated in different ways than us.[4]

Unless, however, we contrive, with malice aforethought, that things should strike us as alike only if they are alike in respect of the deep sources of their causal powers: that they should strike us as alike only if they share their hidden essences. So, for example, we can set things up so that the chemicals in the bottles will both turn the paper red (and thereby strike us as similar) if, but only if, they are both acids. Or, we can set things up so that both meters will register the same (and thereby strike us as similar) if, but only if, there's the same amount of current in both the circuits; and so on. The moral is that whereas you lock to *doorknobhood* via a metaphysical necessity, if you want to lock to a natural kind property, you have actually to *do the science*.

So much for the fairy tale. It's intuitively plausible, phylogenetically, ontogenetically, and even just historically, to think of natural kind concepts as late sophistications that are somehow constructed on a prior cognitive capacity for concepts of mind-dependent properties. But intuitively plausible is one thing, true is another. So, *is* it true? And, what does "doing the science" amount to? How, having started out as Innocents with no concepts of natural kinds, could we have got to where we are, with natural kind concepts like WATER? I turn to these questions in, more or less, that order.

---

[4] In just this spirit, Keith Campbell remarks about colours that if they are "integrated reflectances across three overlapping segments clustered in the middle of the total electromagnetic spectrum, then they are, from the inanimate point of view, such highly arbitrary and idiosyncratic properties that it is no wonder the particular colors we are familiar with are manifest only in transactions with humans, rhesus monkeys, and machines especially built to replicate just their particular mode of sensitivity to photons" (1990: 572–3). (The force of this observation is all the greater if, as seems likely, even the reflectance theory underestimates the complexity of colour psychophysics.)

See also J. J. C. Smart who, it seems to me, got more of this right than he is these days given credit for: "This account of secondary qualities explains their unimportance in physics. For obviously the discriminations . . . made by a very complex neurophysiological mechanism are hardly likely to correspond to simple and nonarbitrary distinctions in nature" (1991: 172). My point is: this is true not just of colours, but of doorknobs too.

Natural Kinds Come Late

I think natural kind concepts have been getting more of a press than they deserve of late. It's past time to put them in their place; and their place is that of self-conscious and cultivated intellectual achievements. Much of what is currently being written about concepts—by philosophers, but also, increasingly, by psychologists—suggests that natural kind concepts are the paradigms on which we should model our accounts of concept acquisition and concept possession at large. This is, I think, hopeless on the face of it. For one thing, as Putnam in particular has argued, natural kind concepts thrive best—maybe only—in an environment where conventions of deference to experts are in place. But, patently, only creatures with an *antecedently* complex mental life could make a policy of adherence to such conventions. Adherence to conventions of deference couldn't be a precondition for conceptual content in general, if only because deference has to stop somewhere; if *my* ELM concept is deferential, that's because *the botanist's* isn't. Anyhow, it seems just obvious that concepts like STAR in, as one says, the 'technical sense'—the concept of stars that is prepared to defer about the Sun and black dwarfs on the one hand and meteors and comets on the other—come after, and sometimes come to replace, their colloquial counterparts.

As I say, this view flies in the face of the current fashions in developmental cognitive psychology, which stress how early, and how universally, natural kind concepts are available to children. But I find that I'm not much convinced. There is, to be sure, getting to be a lot of evidence (contra Piaget) that young children are deeply into appearance/reality distinctions: they're clear that you can't make a horse into a zebra just by painting on stripes (Keil 1989); and they're clear that, for some categories (animals but not vases, for example), what's on the inside matters to what kind a thing belongs to (Carey 1985). It's usual to summarize such findings as showing that young children are 'essentialists', and if you like to talk that way, so be it.[5] My point, however, is that being an essentialist in this sense clearly does *not* imply having natural kind concepts; not even if a cognitivist picture of concept possession is assumed for sake of the argument. What's further required, at a minimum, is the idea that what's 'inside' (or otherwise hidden) somehow is causally responsible for how

---

[5] I don't, myself, advise it. Grant that children think that properties that don't appear can matter to whether a thing is a horse. It isn't implied that they think what a bona fide essentialist should: that there are properties (other than being a horse) that *necessitate* a thing's being a horse. But, for present purposes, never mind.

things that belong to the kind appear; for their 'superficial signs'. It is, of course, an empirical issue, but I don't know of any evidence that children think that sort of thing.

If it's easy to miss the extent to which natural kind concepts are sophisticated achievements, that's perhaps because of a nasty ambiguity in the term. (One that we've already encountered, in fact; it's why I had to pussyfoot about whether they had WATER in the Garden). Consider this dialectic:

—*Did Homer have natural kind concepts?*
Sure, he had the concept WATER (and the like), and water is a natural kind.

But also:

—*Did Homer have natural kind concepts?*
Of course not. He had no disposition to defer to experts about water (and the like); I expect the notion of an expert about water would have struck him as bizarre. And, *of course* Homer had no notion that water has a hidden essence, or a characteristic microstructure (or that anything else does); a fortiori, he had no notion that the hidden essence of water is causally responsible for its phenomenal properties.

A 'natural kind concept' can be the concept of a natural kind; or it can be the concept of a natural kind *as such* (i.e. the concept of a natural kind *as* a natural kind). It's perfectly consistent to claim that Homer had plenty of the first but none of the second. In fact, I think that's pretty clearly true. So the suggestion is that, in the history of science, and in ontogeny, and, for all I know, in phylogeny too, concepts of natural kinds as such only come late. Homer, and children, and animals, have few of them or none. Somehow, concepts of natural kinds as such emerge from a background of concepts of mind-dependent properties, and of concepts of natural kinds that *aren't* concepts of natural kinds as such. Presumably it's because they do somehow emerge from a background of other kinds of concepts that concepts of natural kind as such don't have to be innate.

Fine. So now all I owe you is a story about what "emerging" comes to: and I have to tell this story in a way that an informational semantics can tolerate, viz. without assuming that there is more to concept possession than locking even in the case of bona fide, full-blown, natural kind concepts as such. *Then* I get to go sailing.

I'll start with natural kind concepts and informational semantic and just let the "emerging" emerge.

Natural Kinds and Informational Semantics

We've just distinguished between *merely* having a natural kind concept and having a natural kind concept *as such*. What I'm asking now is *whether an atomistic informational semantics* can honour that distinction. And I'm inviting you to share my concern that, prima facie, it cannot. Prima facie an informational semantics has to say that whether you have the concept WATER is a matter of whether you are locked to water; if you are then you do, and if you aren't then you don't. Whereas (still prima facie) having WATER as a full-blown natural kind concept requires also having, for example, concepts like MICROSTRUCTURE and HIDDEN ESSENCE and NATURAL KIND. Atomism and informational semantics are natural allies, and it's been my strategy throughout to enlist each in the other's service. But maybe we've come to where their joint resources run out. If the possession conditions for full-blown natural-kind-as-such concepts invoke the possession conditions of concepts like NATURAL KIND, then they aren't atomistic.

So, the issue is how an informational semantics should treat full-blown natural kind terms. That's a large topic, and I wish I didn't have to think about it. For what it's worth, however, here's a sketch of a story: whether Homer had the (our) concept WATER doesn't depend on what other concepts he had (on whether he had HIDDEN ESSENCE and MICROSTRUCTURE, for example). Rather, it depends on whether he was locked to water *as such*; or was merely locked to water *in any reasonably nearby world*.

Homer had (and children and animals have) a concept that is locked to water via its familiar phenomenological properties; via its 'superficial signs'. So the locking Homer had was reliable only in worlds where water *has* the familiar phenomenological properties; which is to say only in nomologically possible worlds near ours. That is, I suppose, the usual, pretheoretic way of having a natural kind concept. The kind-constituting property is a hidden essence and you get locked to it via phenomenological properties the having of which is (roughly) nomologically necessary and sufficient for something to instantiate the kind. This explains, by the way, why concepts like WATER exhibit the d/D effect. WATER, like DOORKNOB, is typically learned from its instances; but that's not, of course, because *being water* is mind-dependent. Rather, it's because you typically lock to *being water* via its superficial signs; and, in point of nomological necessity, water samples are the only things around in which those superficial signs inhere.

So much for the *pretheoretic* way of having natural kind concepts. By contrast, our official, full-blown, chemical concept of water is *post-*

theoretic. For us (but not for Homer), WATER is a concept whose locking to water is mediated by our adherence to a theory about what water is. Since, by assumption, this theory that we adhere to is true, the locking depends on a property that water has in every metaphysically possible world, not just in nomologically possible worlds that are near here. *We're locked to water via a theory that specifies its essence, so we're locked to water in every metaphysically possible world.* That, I'm suggesting, is what an informational semanticist should say that it *is* to have a concept of a natural kind *as* a natural kind: it's for the mechanism that effects the locking not to depend on the superficial signs of the kind, and hence to hold (*ceteris paribus* of course) even in possible worlds where members of the kind lacks those signs.

So, does this, or doesn't it, amount to Homer's having had the same concept of water that we do? Did they or didn't they have the concept WATER back in the Garden?

Actually, I don't much care which you say, so long as you like the general picture. Suffice it that it's quite in the spirit of informational semantics to decide to talk like this: Homer did have the concept WATER (he had a concept that is nomologically linked to *being water*) and, of course, *being water* isn't a mind-dependent property. So Homer had a concept of a natural kind. But WATER wasn't, for Homer, a concept of a natural kind *as such*; and for us it is. We're locked to *being water* via a chemical-cum-metaphysical theory, that specifies its essence, and that is quite a different mechanism of semantic access from the ones that Homer relied on. In particular, the two ways of locking to water support quite different counterfactuals. This shows up (*inter alia*) in the notorious thought experiments about Twin-Earth: we think that XYZ wouldn't be water; Homer wouldn't have understood the question.

But an entirely informational and atomistic semantics can also do justice to the intuition that Homer had the same WATER concept as ours. All the metaphysics of concept possession requires, of our concept WATER or Homer's, is being locked to water. If you are locked to water our way, you have the concept WATER as a natural kind concept; if you are locked to concept WATER Homer's way, you have the concept WATER, but not *as* a natural kind concept. But, on a perfectly natural way of counting, if you are locked to water either way, you have the concept WATER. (I suppose that God is locked to *being water* in still a third way; one that holds in every metaphysically possible world but *isn't* theory-mediated. That's OK with informational semantics; God can have the concept WATER too. He can't, however, have the *pretheoretic* concept WATER; the one that's locked to water *only* by its superficial signs. Nobody's Perfect.)

If you're lucky, you can have concepts of natural kinds on the cheap. Homer maybe didn't need much to get WATER locked to *water*; maybe all he needed was innate detectors for the phenomenological properties which, in point of nomological necessity, water has in all the worlds near to him (and us). But, of course, you only get what you pay for: Homer didn't have the concept of water *as* a natural kind concept. To have that, he would need to have been locked to the essence of water *via* the essence of water; that is, in a way that doesn't depend on water's superficial signs. Probably, de facto, all such lockings (except God's) are theory-mediated; indeed, they are perhaps all *meta*theory-mediated; they may well depend, de facto, on having not just concepts of natural kinds, but also the concepts NATURAL KIND and HIDDEN ESSENCE. Which *nobody* did until quite recently.

But I want to emphasize what I take to be a main moral of the discussion: the 'de facto' matters. Just as IA says there are *no* concepts the possession of which is metaphysically necessary for having WATER (except WATER), so I'd like it to say that there are no concepts the possession of which is metaphysically necessary for having WATER *as a natural kind concept* (except WATER); *all* that's required is being locked to water in a way that doesn't depend on its superficial signs. But, of course, metaphysically necessary is one thing, on the cards is quite another. I'm quite prepared to believe that, de facto, until we had (indeed, had more or less self-consciously), the concepts that cluster around NATURAL KIND, there was probably no way that we *could* link to WATER except the sort of way that Homer did and children and animals do; viz. via water's metaphysically accidental but nomologically necessary properties. But now we have a theory that tells us what water is, and we are linked to water via our acceptance of that theory. Science discovers essences, and doing science thereby links us to natural kinds *as such*.

I think, by the way, that the ethological analogies play out quite nicely on this sort of analysis. It's natural and handy and, for most purposes harmless, to say that ducklings have the concept MOTHER DUCK innately; that male sticklebacks have the concept CONSPECIFIC RIVAL innately, and so on. And it's quite true in such cases that, given normal experience, the creatures end up locked to the properties that these concepts express. So, as far as informational semantics is concerned, they therefore end up having concepts that have these properties as their contents. But, in fact, the innate endowment that they exploit in doing so is quite rudimentary. Male sticklebacks get locked to *conspecific rivalhood* via not much more than an innate ability to detect red spots. To do so, they exploit a certain (actually rather fragile) ecological regularity: there's normally nothing around that wears a red spot *except* conspecific rivals.

This is nomologically necessary (anyhow, it's counterfactual supporting) in the stickleback's ecology, and nomological necessity is transitive. So sticklebacks end up locked to *conspecific rivalhood* via *one of its reliable appearances.*

To repeat: informational semantics suggests that, so far as the requisite innate endowment is concerned, if the world co-operates you can get concepts of natural kinds very cheap. That's what the sticklebacks do; it's what Homer did; it's what children do; it's what all of us grown-ups do too, most of the time. By contrast, for you to have a natural kinds concept *as such* is for your link to the essence of the kind *not* to depend on its inessential properties. This is a late and sophisticated achievement, historically, ontogenetically, and phylogenetically, and there is no reason to take it as a paradigm for concept possession at large. I suppose you start to get natural kind concepts in this strong sense only when it occurs to you that, if generality and explanatory power are to be achieved, similarity and difference in respect of how things affect minds like ours has sometimes got to be ignored in deciding what kinds of things they are; perhaps, de facto, this happens only in the context of the scientific enterprise.

Well, what about the 'technical' concept WATER? Does that have to be innate if it's primitive?

Of course not. For one thing, on the present view, there really is no 'technical concept water'; there's just, as it were, the technical way of having the concept WATER. Once you've got a concept that's locked to water via its (locally reliable) phenomenological properties, you can, if you wish, make a project of getting locked to water in a way that doesn't depend on its superficial signs. The easy way to do this is to get some expert to teach you a theory that expresses the essence of the kind. To be sure, however, that will only work if the natural kind concept that you're wanting to acquire is one which somebody else has acquired already. Things get a deal more difficult if you're starting *ab initio*; i.e. without any concepts which express natural kinds as such. It's time for me to tell my story about how concepts of natural kinds might "emerge" in a mind that is antecedently well stocked with concepts of other kinds. Actually, it's a perfectly familiar story and not at all surprising.

'Emerging'

Suppose you have lots of concepts of mind-dependent properties, and lots of logico-mathematical concepts, and lots of concepts of natural kinds which, however, aren't concepts of natural kinds as such.[6] Then what you need to do to acquire a natural kind concept as a natural kind concept *ab initio* is: (i) construct a true theory of the hidden essence of the kind; and (ii) convince yourself of the truth of the theory. If the theory is true, then it will say of a thing that it is such-and-such when and only when the thing is such-and-such; and if you are convinced of the truth of the theory, then you will make it a policy to consider that a thing is such-and-such when and only when the theory says that it is. So your believing the theory locks you to such-and-suches via a property that they have in every metaphysically possibly world; namely, the property of being such-and-suches; the property that makes the theory true. The upshot is that, if the moon is blue, and everything goes as planned, you will end up with a full-blown natural kind concept; the concept of *such-and-suches as such*.

Aha, but how do you go about constructing a true theory of the essence of such-and-suches and convincing yourself that it is true? How do you do it in, say, the case of being water?

Oh, well, you know: you have to think up a theory of what water is that both explains why the superficial signs of *being water* are reliable and has the usual theoretical virtues: generality, systematicity, coherence with your other theories, and so forth. You undertake to revise the theory when what it says about water isn't independently plausible (e.g. independently plausible in light of experimental outcomes); and you undertake to revise your estimates of what's independently plausible (e.g. your estimates of the construct validity of your experimental paradigms) when they conflict with what the theory says about water. And so on, round and round the Duhemian circle.

In short, you do the science. I suppose the Duhemian process of scientific theory construction is possible only for a kind of creature that antecedently has a lot of concepts of properties that are mind-dependent, and a lot of natural kind concepts that aren't concepts of natural kinds as such. And it's also only possible for a kind of creature that is able to pursue policies with respect to the properties that it locks its concepts to. Probably, we're the only kind of creature there is that meets these conditions. Which explains, I suppose, why we're so lonely.

---

[6] As I remarked in Chapter 6, I rather suspect that these, together with the concepts of natural kinds as such, exhaust the sorts of concepts that there are; but I don't know how to argue that they do.

Notice, in any case, that this is a mixed taxonomy. The distinction between concepts of mind-dependent properties and the rest is ontological; mind-dependence is a property of the property that a concept expresses. By contrast, the distinction between natural-kind-as-such concepts and the rest is about how a concept is attached to a property, not what kind of property the concept is attached to.

A natural kind enters into lots of nomic connections to things other than our minds. We can validate a theory of the kind with respect to those connections because the theory is required to predict and explain them. You can't follow this Duhemian path in the case of DOORKNOB, of course, because there is nothing to validate a theory of doorknobs against except how things strike us. In effect, what strikes us as independently plausibly a doorknob *is* a doorknob; the mind-dependence of *doorknobhood* is tantamount to that. The more we learn about what water is, the more we learn about the world; the more we learn about what doorknobs are, the more we learn about ourselves. The present treatment implies this and, I think, intuition agrees with it. At least, Realist intuition does.

We do science when we want to lock our concepts to properties that *aren't* constituted by similarities in how things strike us. We do science when we want to reveal the ways that things would be similar *even if we weren't there*. Idealists to the contrary not withstanding, there's no paradox in this. We can, often enough, control for the effects of our presence on the scene in much the same ways that we control for the effects of other possibly confounding variables. To be sure, here as elsewhere, the design of well-confirmed theories is hard work and often expensive. And the only recompense is likely to be the cool pleasure of seeing things objectively; seeing them as they are when you're not looking. Objectivity is an educated taste, much like Cubism. Maybe it's worth what it costs and maybe it's not. It's entirely your choice, of course. Far be it from me to twist your arm.

So much, then, for how we got from the Garden to the laboratory. It is, as I say, quite a familiar story.

Short Summary

You aren't actually required to believe any of what's in this chapter or the last; I have mostly just been exploring the geography that reveals itself if conceptual atomism is taken seriously. Still, I do think our cognitive science is in crisis, and that we're long overdue to face the dilemma that confronts it. On one hand, everybody knows, deep down, that Inferential Role Semantics makes the problem of concept individuation intractable. And, on the other hand, everybody gags on Informational Atomism. (Well, *practically* everybody does.) And nobody seems to be able to think of any other alternatives. Probably that's because those are all the alternatives that there are.

It's my view that we're eventually going to have to swallow Informational Atomism whole. Accordingly, I've been doing what I can to sweeten the pill. It seemed to me, for a long while, that a cost of atomism would be failing to honour the distinction between theoretical concepts and the rest. For, surely, theoretical concepts are ones that you have to believe a theory in order to have? And, according to conceptual atomism, there are *no* concepts that you have to believe a theory in order to have. But it doesn't seem to me that way now. A theoretical concept isn't a concept that's *defined* by a theory; it's just a concept that is, de facto, locked to a property via a theory. Informational Atomism doesn't mind that *at all*, so long as you keep the "de facto" in mind.

Likewise, it used to seem to me that atomism about concepts means that DOORKNOB is innate. But now I think that you can trade a certain amount of innateness for a certain amount of mind-dependence. *Being a doorknob* is just: striking our kinds of minds the way that doorknobs do. So, what you need to acquire the concept DOORKNOB "from experience" is just: the kind of mind that experience causes to be struck that way by doorknobs. The price of making this trade of innateness for mind-dependence is, however, a touch of Wotan's problem. It turns out that much of what we find in the world is indeed "only ourselves". It turns out, in lots of cases, that we *make things be of a kind* by being disposed to *take them to be of a kind*.

But not in every case; not, in particular, in the case of kinds of things that are alike in respect of the hidden sources of their causal powers, regardless of their likeness in respect of their effects on us. To describe it in terms of *those* sorts of similarities is to describe the world the way that God takes it to be. Doing science is how we contrive to cause ourselves to have the concepts that such descriptions are couched in. Not philosophy but science is the way to get Wotan out of his fly-bottle. That story seems to me plausibly true; and it is, as we've seen, compatible with an informational and atomistic account of the individuation of concepts. But dear me, speaking of fly-bottles, how Wittgenstein would have loathed it; and Wagner and Virginia Woolf too, for that matter. Well, you can't please everyone; I'll bet it would have been all right with Plato.

Short Conclusion: A Consolation for Philosophers

That's really the end of my story; but a word about what I think of as the Luddite objection to conceptual atomism is perhaps in order.

It's natural, *pace* Appendix 5A, to suppose that conceptual atomism means that there are no conceptual truths, hence that there are no analytic truths. And, if there are no analytic truths, I suppose that there are no such things as conceptual analyses. And it would be worrying if 'no analyticity' entailed not just 'no analyses' but 'no analytic philosophy' as well. Technological unemployment would then begin to threaten.

But I guess I'm not inclined to take that prospect very seriously; certainly I'm not one of those end-of-philosophy philosophers. If, there aren't any conceptual analyses, the moral isn't that we should stop doing philosophy, or even that we should start doing philosophy in some quite different way. The moral is just that we should stop saying that conceptual analysis is what philosophers do. If analytic philosophers haven't been analysing concepts after all, at least that explains why there are so few concepts that analytic philosophers have analysed.

I guess what I really think is that philosophy is just: whatever strikes minds like ours as being of the same kind as the prototypical examples. But maybe that's wrong; and, if it is, then maybe if we were to stop saying that philosophy is conceptual analysis, that would leave philosophers without a defensible metatheory. Well, if so, so be it. We wouldn't be worse off in that respect than doctors, lawyers, dentists, artists, physicists, chicken sexers, psychologists, driving instructors, or the practitioners of any other respectable discipline that I can think of. Why should philosophers be exempt from this practically universal predicament? There are many classes of performances in which intelligence is displayed, but the rules or criteria of which are unformulated. Efficient practice precedes the theory of it; methodologies presuppose the application of the methods, of the critical investigation of which they are the products . . . It is therefore possible for people intelligently to perform some sorts of operations when they are not yet able to consider any propositions enjoining how they should be performed.

But, bless me, it seems that I am quoting from *The Concept of Mind*.[7] I'm sure that means that it's time for me to stop.

APPENDIX 7A
Round Squares

I want briefly to consider an ontological worry about IA that's relatively independent of the main issues that this chapter is concerned with.

It seems pretty clear that IA is going to have to say that it's *metaphysically* impossible for there to be a primitive concept of a self-contradictory property; e.g. a primitive concept ROUND SQUARE. (Remember that "ROUND SQUARE" is a name, not a structural description. The notation leaves it open whether the corresponding

---

[7] Ryle 1949.

concept is atomic.) How the argument goes will depend on the details of IA's formulation. But, roughly: IA says that concepts have to be locked to properties. Maybe it's OK for a concept to lock to a property that exists but happens not to be instantiated (like *being a gold mountain*), but presumably there isn't any property of *being a round square* for the *necessarily* uninstantiated concept ROUND SQUARE to lock to.

That's all right if ROUND SQUARE is assumed to be complex; it's pretty plausible that there really isn't anything to having ROUND SQUARE beyond the inferential dispositions that its compositional semantics bestows (viz. the disposition to infer ROUND and SQUARE). But the corresponding *primitive* concept would have *neither* content (there's no property for it to lock to) *nor* compositional structure (it has no constituents), so there could be nothing to having it at all. The objection is that it's not obvious that it's metaphysically necessary that ROUND SQUARE couldn't be primitive.

A possible reply is that it's also not obvious that it could, so all you get is a hung jury. But I think maybe we can do a little better. Consider a *non-self-contradictory* property like *being a red square*. It's common ground for any RTM that there is a *complex* concept of this property (constructed from the concepts RED and SQUARE). But it's built into *informational* versions of RTM that it also allows there to be a *simple* concept of this property; viz. a *primitive* mental representation REDSQUARE (*sic*; this *is* intended to be a structural description) that is locked to *being red and square*. Presumably, one could acquire REDSQUARE ostensively. That is, one could get locked to *being red and square* (not by first getting locked to *being red* and *being square*, but) by learning that redsquares (*sic*) are the things that look like *those*. So Informational Atomism acknowledges the metaphysical possibility of having the concept of a red square without having either the concept RED or the concept SQUARE. (You won't, of course, admit that RED SQUARE could be, in this sense, primitive if you boggle at concepts without conceptual roles. But if you boggle at concepts without conceptual roles you can't accept a pure informational semantics *at all*, so why should you care what a pure informational semantics says about concepts of self-contradictory properties?)

If, on the other hand, you find it intuitively plausible that there *are* two ways of having a concept of a red square (viz. RED SQUARE, which you can't have unless you've got RED and SQUARE, and REDSQUARE, which you can because it's primitive) then everything is OK about IA's treatment of the concept ROUND SQUARE. For the (anyhow, my) intuition is very strong that there is only *one* way to have *that* concept. In particular, that there is no concept of a round square that one could have without also having ROUND and SQUARE. If you share the intuition that there is this asymmetry, between RED SQUARE and ROUND SQUARE, then you should be very happy with IA. IA *explains* the asymmetry because it entails that there can be no *primitive* concept without a corresponding property for it to lock to.

BIBLIOGRAPHY

ANTONY, L. (1995). "Law and order in psychology." *Philosophical Perspectives*, **9**, 429–46.

ANTONY, L. and LEVINE, J. (1991). "The nomic and the robust". In Loewer and Rey (1991*b*).

ARMSTRONG, S., GLEITMAN, L., and GLEITMAN, H. (1983). "What some concepts might not be." *Cognition*, **13**, 293–308.

BAKER, C. L. (1979). "Syntactic theory and the projection problem." *Linguistic Inquiry*, **10**, 533–81.

BARSOLOU, L. (1987). "The instability of graded structure: implications for the nature of concepts." In U. Neisser (ed.), *Concepts and Conceptual Development*, Emory Symposia in Cognition, 1. New York: Cambridge University Press.

BLOCK, N. (1993). "Holism, hyper-analyticity and hyper-compositionality." *Mind and Language*, **8**, 1–26

CAMPBELL, K. (1990). "The implications of Land's theory of colour vision." In W. Lycan (ed.), *Mind and Cognition*. Oxford: Blackwell.

CAREY, S. (1982). "Semantic development: the state of the art." In L. Gleitman and E. Wanner (eds.), *Language Acquisition: The State of the Art*. New York: Cambridge University Press.

—— (1985). *Conceptual Change in Childhood*. Cambridge, Mass.: MIT Press.

—— (1988). "Conceptual differences between children and adults." *Mind and Language*, **3**, 167–81.

—— (1991). "Knowledge, acquisition: enrichment or conceptual change?" In S. Carey and R. Gelman (eds.), *The Epigenesis of Mind*. Hillsdale, NJ: Lawrence Erlbaum.

CARROLL, L. "What the tortoise said to Achilles." *Mind*, **4**, 278–80; repr. in *Mind*, **104**, 691–3.

CARRUTHERS, P. (1996). *Language, Thought and Consciousness*. Cambridge: Cambridge University Press.

CHOMSKY, N. (1965). *Aspects of the Theory of Syntax*. Cambridge, Mass.: MIT Press.

CHURCHLAND, P. M. (1991). "Some reductive strategies in cognitive neurobiology." In P. M. Churchland, *A Neurocomputational Perspective: The Nature of Mind and the Structure of Science*, 77–110. Cambridge, Mass.: MIT Press.

—— (1995). *The Engine of Reason and the Seat of the Soul*. Cambridge, Mass.: MIT Press.

CLARK, A. (1991). *Microcognition: Philosophy, Cognitive Science and Parallel Distributed Processing*. Cambridge, Mass.: MIT Press.

—— (1993). *Associative Engines*. Cambridge, Mass.: MIT Press.

COLLINS, ALAN and LOFTUS, E. (1988). "A spreading activation theory of semantic processing." In A. Collins and E. Smith (eds.), *Readings in Cognitive Science: A Perspective from Psychology and Artificial Intelligence*. San Mateo, Calif.: Morgan Kaufmann.

—— and QUILLIAN, M. (1969). "Retrieval time from semantic memory." *Journal of Verbal Learning and Verbal Behavior*, **8**, 240–7.

COLLINS, ARTHUR (1987). *The Nature of Mental Things*. Notre Dame, Ind.: University of Notre Dame Press.

CUMMINS, R. (1996). "Systematicity." *Journal of Philosophy*, **93**, 591–614.

DAVIDSON, D. (1967). "Truth and meaning." *Synthese*, **17**, 304–23.

DENNETT, D. (1993). "Learning and labeling." *Mind and Language*, **8**, 540–93.

DEVITT, M. (1996). *Coming to our Senses*. Cambridge: Cambridge University Press.

DRETSKE, F. (1981). *Knowledge and the Flow of Information*. Cambridge, Mass.: MIT Press.

DUMMETT, M. (1993*a*). "What is a theory of meaning (1)?" In Dummett (1993*c*).

—— (1993*b*). "What is a theory of meaning (2)?" In Dummett (1993*c*).

—— (1993*c*). *The Seas of Language*. Oxford: Clarendon Press.

ECO, U., SANTAMBRIOGIO, M., and VIOLI, P. (eds.) (1988). *Meaning and Mental Representation*. Bloomington, Ind.: University of Indiana Press.

FODOR, J. A. (1970). "Three reasons for not deriving "kill" from "cause to die"." *Linguistic Inquiry*, **1**, 429–38.

—— (1975). *The Language of Thought*. New York: Crowell.

—— (1981*a*). "The present status of the innateness controversy." In Fodor (1981*c*): 257–316.

—— (1981*b*). "Tom Swift and his procedural grandmother." In Fodor (1981*c*): 204–24.

—— (1981*c*). *Representations*. Cambridge, Mass.: MIT Press.

—— (1986). "Why paramecia don't have mental representations." In P. A. French, T. E. Uehling, and H. K. Wettstein (eds.), *Midwest Studies in Philosophy*, **10**. Minneapolis, Minn.: University of Minnesota Press.

—— (1987). *Psychosemantics*. Cambridge, Mass.: MIT Press.

—— (1990). "A theory of content." In J. A. Fodor, *A Theory of Content and Other Essays*, 51–136. Cambridge, Mass.: MIT Press.

—— (1991). "Replies." In Loewer and Rey (1991*b*).

—— (1994). *The Elm and the Expert*. Cambridge Mass.: MIT Press.

—— (1995*a*). Review of *The Engine of Reason and the Seat of the Soul*, by P. M. Churchland. *Times Literary Supplement* (25 August), 5–6.

—— (1995*b*). Review of *Mind and Language*, by John McDowell. *London Review of Books* **17** (20 April), 8.

—— (forthcoming *a*). "There are no recognitional concepts: not even RED." In Fodor (forthcoming *b*).

—— (forthcoming *b*). *In Critical Condition*. Cambridge, Mass.: MIT Press.

—— and LEPORE, E. (1992). *Holism: A Shopper's Guide*. Oxford: Blackwell.

—— —— (1994). "The red herring and the pet fish: why concepts still can't be prototypes." *Cognition*, **58**, 253–70.

—— —— (forthcoming *a*). "The emptiness of the lexicon."

—— —— (forthcoming *b*). "Morphemes matter."

—— and McLaughlin, B. (1990). "Connectionism and the problem of systematicity: why Smolensky's solution doesn't work." *Cognition*, **35**, 183–204.

—— and Pylyshyn, Z. (1988). "Connectionism and cognitive architecture: a critical analysis." *Cognition*, **28**, 3–71.

Gibson, J. J. (1966). *The Senses Considered as Perceptual Systems*. Boston, Mass.: Houghton Mifflin.

Gleitman, L. (1990). "Structural sources of verb learning." *Language Acquisition*, **11**, 1–54.

Gopnik, A. (1988). "Conceptual and semantic development as theory change." *Mind and Language*, **3**, 197–216.

Gordon, R. (1986). "Folk psychology as simulation." *Mind and Language*, **4**, 158–71.

Grandy, R. (1990). "Understanding and the principle of compositionality." In J. Tomberlin (ed.), *Philosophical Perspectives*, 4: *Action Theory and Philosophy of Mind*. Atascadero, Calif.: Ridgeview.

Grice, H. P. and Strawson, P. F. (1956). "In defense of a dogma." *Philosophical Review*, **65**, 141–58.

Harman, G. (1993). "Meaning holism defended." In J. A. Fodor and E. Lepore (eds.), *Holism: A Consumer Update*. Amsterdam: Rodopi.

Higginbotham, J. (1994). "Priorities of thought." *Proceedings of the Aristotelian Society*, supp. vol. **20**.

Hume, D. (1955). *Enquiry Concerning Human Understanding*. Indianapolis, Ind.: Bobbs-Merrill.

Jackendoff, R. (1992). *Languages of the Mind: Essays on Mental Representation*. Cambridge, Mass.: MIT Press.

Kamp, H. and Partee, B. (1995). "Prototype theory and compositionality." *Cognition*, **57**, 129–91.

Keil, F. (1987). "Conceptual development and category structure." In Neisser (1987).

—— (1989). *Concepts, Kinds and Cognitive Development*. Cambridge, Mass.: MIT Press.

—— (1991). "The emergence of theoretical beliefs as constraints on concepts." In S. Carey and R. Gelman (eds.), *The Epigenesis of Mind*. Hillsdale, NJ: Lawrence Erlbaum.

Konrfilt, R. and Correra, N. (1993). "Conceptual structure and its relation to the structure of lexical entries." In Reuland and Werner (eds.), *Language and Knowledge*, 2: *Lexical and Conceptual Structure*. Dordrecht: Kluwer.

Lakoff, G. (1988). "Cognitive semantics." in Eco, Santambrogio, and Violi (1988).

Lepore, E. (1997). "Conditions on understanding language." *Proceedings of the Aristotelian Society*, **98**, Pt. 1, 41–60.

LOEWER, B. and REY, G. (1991*a*). Editors' introduction to Loewer and Rey (1991*b*).
—— —— (eds.) (1991*b*). *Meaning in Mind: Fodor and his Critics*. Cambridge, Mass.: MIT Press.

LYCAN, W. (ed.) (1990). *Mind and Cognition*. Oxford: Blackwell.

MARCUS, G., ULLMAN, M., PINKER, S., HOLLANDER, M., ROSEN, T. J., and XU, F. (1992). "Overgeneralization in language acquisition." *Monographs of the Society for Research in Child Development*, 57.

MARGOLIS, E. (1994). "A reassment of the shift from classical theories of concepts to prototype theory." *Cognition*, **51**, 73–89.

MATES, B. (1962). "Synonymity." In L. Linsky (ed.), *Semantics and the Philosophy of Language*. Urbana, Ill.: University of Illinois Press.

MATTHEWS, R. (1993). Review of *Learnability and Cognition* by Steven Pinker. *Philosophical Psychology*, 100–4.

MEDIN, D. and Wattenmaker, W. (1987). "Category cohesiveness, theories and cognitive archaeology." In Neisser (1987).

MILLER, G. and JOHNSON-LAIRD, P. (1978). *Language and Perception*. Cambridge, Mass.: Harvard University Press.

MURPHY, G. and MEDIN, D. (1985). "The role of theories in conceptual coherence." *Psychological Review*, **92**, 289–316.

NEISSER, U. (ed.) (1987). *Concepts and Conceptual Development*. Cambridge: Cambridge University Press.

OSHERSON, D. and SMITH, E. (1996). "On typicality and vagueness." Unpublished ms.

PAIVIO, A. (1971). *Imagery and Verbal Processes*. New York: Holt.

PARTEE, B. (1995). "Lexical semantics and compositionality." In *Invitation to Cognitive Science*, 2nd edn., vol. i, ed. L. Gleitman and M. Liberman. Cambridge, Mass.: MIT Press.

PEACOCKE, C. (1992). *A Study of Concepts*. Cambridge, Mass.: MIT Press.

PINKER, S. (1984). *Language Learnability and Language Development*. Cambridge, Mass.: MIT Press.

—— (1989). *Learnability and Cognition: The Acquisition of Argument Structure*. Cambridge, Mass.: MIT Press.

PRETI, C. (1992). "Opacity, belief and analyticity." *Philosophical Studies*, **66**, 297–306.

PUTNAM, H. (1962). "The analytic and the synthetic." In H. Feigl and G. Maxwell (eds.), *Scientific Explanation: Space and Time*. Minnesota Studies in the Philosophy of Science, 3. Minneapolis, Minn.: University of Minnesota Press.

—— (1983). "'Two dogmas' revisited." In H. Putnam, *Realism and Reason: Philosophical Papers*, vol. iii. Cambridge: Cambridge University Press.

—— (1995). *Pragmatism*. Oxford: Blackwell.

PYLYSYHN, Z. (1984). *Computation and Cognition: Toward a Foundation for Cognitive Science*. Cambridge, Mass.: MIT Press.

QUILLIAN, M. R. (1988). "Semantic memory." In A. Collins and E. Smith (eds.), *Readings in Cognitive Science: A Perspective from Psychology and Artificial Intelligence*. San Mateo, Calif.: Morgan Kaufman.

RYLE, G. (1949). *The Concept of Mind*. New York: Barnes & Noble.

SAMET, J. (1986). "Troubles with Fodor's nativism." In P. A. French, T. E. Uehling, and H. K. Wettstein (eds.), *Midwest Studies in Philosophy*, **10**. Minneapolis, Minn.: University of Minnesota Press.

SCHIFFER, S. (1987). *Remnants of Meaning*. Cambridge, Mass.: MIT Press.

SMART, J. J. C. (1991). "Sensations and brain processes." In D. Rosenthal (ed.), *The Nature of Mind*. New York: Oxford University Press.

SMITH, E. and MEDIN, D. (1981). *Categories and Concepts*. Cambridge, Mass.: Harvard University Press.

—— and RIPS, L. (1984). "A psychological approach to concepts: comment's on Rey's "Concepts and stereotypes"." *Cognition*, **17**, 265–74.

—— and OSHERSON, D. (1984). "Conceptual combination with prototype concepts." *Cognitive Science*, **11**, 337–61.

SMOLENSKY, P. (1995). "Connectionism, constituency and the language of thought." In C. Macdonald and G. Macdonald (eds.), *Connectionism*. Oxford: Blackwell.

SOBER, E. (1984). *The Nature of Selection*. Cambridge, Mass.: MIT Press.

VAN GELDER, T. and NIKLASSON, L. (1994). "Classical and connectionist cognitive architecture." *Proceedings of the Sixteenth Annual Conference of the Cognitive Science Society*. Hillsdale, NJ: Lawrence Erlbaum.

WOODS, W. A. (1975). "What's in a link?" Repr. in D. Bobrow and A. Collins (eds.), *Representations and Understanding: Studies in Cognitive Science*. New York: Academic Press, 1988.

ZADROZNY, W. (1994). "From compositional to systematic semantics." *Linguistics and Philosophy*, **17**, 329–42.

AUTHOR INDEX